WITHDRAWN

BLOOD RED SUNSET

MA BO

TRANSLATED FROM THE CHINESE BY
HOWARD GOLDBLATT

VIKING

BLOOD

RED

SUNSET

A MEMOIR OF THE
CHINESE CULTURAL REVOLUTION

VIKING
Published by the Penguin Group
Penguin Books USA Inc., 375 Hudson Street, New York, New York 10014, U.S.A.
Penguin Books Ltd, 27 Wrights Lane, London W8 5TZ, England
Penguin Books Australia Ltd, Ringwood, Victoria, Australia
Penguin Books Canada Ltd, 10 Alcorn Avenue, Toronto, Ontario, Canada M4V 3B2
Penguin Books (N.Z.) Ltd, 182–190 Wairau Road, Auckland 10, New Zealand

Penguin Books Ltd, Registered Offices: Harmondsworth, Middlesex, England

First published in 1995 by Viking Penguin,
a division of Penguin Books USA Inc.

10   9   8   7   6   5   4   3   2   1

Copyright © Ma Bo, 1995
All rights reserved

This work was originally published in China
by the Workers Publishing House in 1988.

ISBN 0-670-84181-1

CIP data available

This book is printed on acid-free paper. ∞

Printed in the United States of America
Set in Electra
Designed by Katy Riegel

To the victims
of the Cultural Revolution

BLOOD

RED

SUNSET

1

TO INNER

MONGOLIA

In 1968 a raging tide of youth, a raging tide of hot blood, a raging tide of innocence surged toward the countryside, the mountains, and the vast wildernesses. Not an eastward crusade, yet history was about to be written; not a mass migration, yet tens of thousands of households would taste the bitter fruit of parting; not a battlefield incursion, yet a volunteer arm, solemn and purposeful, was on the march.

Lei Xia insisted on accompanying me to the train station to see our classmates off, even though the "Red Red Red" faction had made no secret of what they planned to do when they caught him. "I don't care," he said. "They can beat the shit out of me if they want, but I'm going to see my buddies off."

We arrived at Beijing Station with chains looped around our wrists and knives stuck in our belts. The group heading north to Heilongjiang had already assembled, and the platform was black with crowds of people milling around the excited departees.

Students who had stayed in the shadows during the early days of the Cultural Revolution now came out of hiding, and even sworn enemies of the "Red Red Red" faction risked life and limb to see their schoolmates off. Easy to spot, they were the ones looking over their shoulders from time to time.

How could the hearts of Red Guards steeled in the furnace of the Cultural Revolution swell with such tender emotions? They were stuffing photo albums, diaries, and snacks into schoolmates' pockets and backpacks. Everywhere I looked I saw puffy red eyes, and wherever I turned, I heard advice being given. Even people who normally shunned each other were reluctant to say good-bye.

Impossible to forget, those three frenzied years of the Cultural Revolution. Friendships that would stand the test of time were forged during those tense, feverish days, so no wonder it was such an emotional departure.

"You'll write, won't you?"

"Don't worry, sweetie, I won't forget you."

"Remember, you don't know who to trust out there."

"I'm no damned idiot. Don't worry."

"Take the fight to them. We'll meet on the battlefield of antirevisionism!"

"Who knows, maybe our chance will come, after all."

"Be careful what you say around others and try not to be a showoff."

"Sure, okay."

The platform buzzed with whispered conversations. Young couples afraid to hold hands under the scrutiny of so many people tried to keep their composure as they exchanged muted vows. Teary-eyed mothers pulled their daughters close to brief them for the umpteenth time. Armed, sweaty-faced members of "Red Red Red" were uncharacteristically civil as they helped schoolmates with their luggage.

When the departure bell sounded, a musical rendition of *Quotations from Chairman Mao* blared from the loudspeakers:

"The world is yours, and it is ours as well. But in the end it is truly yours . . ." Loud, zippy music, its lofty strains sending heated blood racing through the veins of energized youth.

The locomotive sounded a low whistle when the wheels began to turn, sending the crowd swarming up to the windows, and as the train picked up speed, sobs emerged from the clusters of girls. It even got to me, and I'd always thought I was too hardened to cry.

Every window of the passing train had an escort. Lei Xia ran down the platform, waving tearfully. "Mongrel!" he shouted. "Mongrel!" Someone's mother was knocked down, sending the oranges in her arms rolling all over the platform. But she scrambled to her feet, ignoring the oranges, and waddled after the train. The idea that we were standing shoulder to shoulder with the workers and peasants hardly lessened the agony of parting, and rousing revolutionary songs could not still the sobs. Beijing Station was awash with tears.

The train chugged out of the station amid a cacophony of farewells that swallowed up the rumble of the tracks. It took scarcely a moment for it to disappear from view, carrying the shouts and sobs along with it. A now-subdued mass of humanity surged toward the exits, past scowling members of "Red Red Red" who were looking right and left, suddenly itching for a fight.

I raised my thumb in the direction of the train.

"Here's to all you young heroes!"

LEI XIA AND I walked back to school in silence, lost in our thoughts: Some high-school sophomores on a trek to Tibet had been robbed by militiamen in a Shanxi village (two of them had made their way back, leaving the rest to continue the journey); a middle-school student had shaved her head, dressed in boy's clothes, and traveled alone to the Inner Mongolian frontier; a high-school freshman from a blacklisted family had written to the Central Committee and Chairman Mao begging to be sent to the most remote, least hospitable place possible, so he could reform his thoughts. Failing in that attempt, he tried the Municipal Revolutionary Committee several times, pleading to be allowed to go. But subsequent news of his mother's death left him dry-eyed.

That's how it was: People fought and scrambled to go somewhere, anywhere. There were no faint hearts, no internal conflicts, no

3

petty dodges. Nothing but raw self-determination and hot-blooded enthusiasm.

Back at school I stripped to the waist and began working out with Lei Xia. He was my human punching bag; no matter how many times I hit him, or how hard, he never uttered a sound. I wiped my mind clean and concentrated on my fists.

There wasn't a moment to lose, and I trained religiously during the little time I had left in Beijing, wanting to emulate the fighting spirit of the legendary Wu Song. That way, when I got where I was going I could fight for the people's welfare with courage and confidence.

TALL, handsome Lei Xia had thick black hair, a face as fair as magnolias, and rosy cheeks. No pimple ever marred his delicate skin. His well-shaped eyes had the liquid clarity of a child's, and his small, square nose was just right. More important, he was blessed with two essential virtues: First, he never fooled around with girls. They had been writing him since elementary school — still were, as a matter of fact — but he ignored them all. Second, he would stand up to anyone. Boys always picked fights with him, since his family background was so bad, but they never scared him off. When members of "Red Red Red" bragged about how they were going to rearrange his face, he asked me to teach him how to defend himself. Serving as my punching bag was a price he paid willingly.

Then there was Xu Zuo, whose father, a Red Army veteran, had once served as vice minister of public health, only to die a broken man after being cashiered in 1959. Xu himself was a frail young man with pencil-thin eyebrows and lips, soft, lustreless hair, and a tiny nose set on a small face. He had a terrible temper for someone so effeminate-looking. In April 1967 the three of us went to Vietnam as part of a "Mao Zedong Anti-American Blood and Steel Troupe," and when we were discovered by a border patrol in the woods, Xu Zuo fought like a wild man to keep from being trussed up; he even kicked one of the militiamen in the groin. But after his return from exchanging revolutionary experiences all over the country in the "linking-up" movement (a euphemism for free, unrestricted travel), he stopped participating in political campaigns, preferring to stay home and pore over the Marxist "scriptures." Before long, no one dared argue politics with him, since he could reel off hundreds of Chairman Mao's quotations.

After debating where to go, we settled on Genghis Khan's birthplace, spellbound by images of grassy steppes, virgin land, wind and snow, and powerful horses. Plus, of course, if war broke out with the Soviet Revisionists, that would be the front line.

Our other friends from school, the cream of the youthful crop, had already set out for the countryside and the frontiers, and we were burning with impatience. The only ones left on campus were some homesick crybabies, the sons and daughters of blacklisted families, those who'd gotten into trouble themselves, and a few sick and crippled kids.

So Lei Xia drafted a letter to the campus Mao Zedong Thought Workers Propaganda Team to inform them that we had decided to leave for Inner Mongolia, in line with the policy of going up to the mountains and down to the countryside.

Then we went to work. Xu Zuo borrowed some books on animal husbandry from the agricultural college, and a middle-school student named Jin Gang, one of Lei Xia's friends, carved a campus revolutionary committee seal from the sole of a plastic sandal so we could forge travel papers that would secure us lodging along the way. Jin Gang was skinnier even than Xu Zuo, and his pointy features—nose, mouth, and chin—gave him the look of a billy goat. He was clever and handy by nature; his greatest talents were carving seals, forging bus tickets, playing the accordion, and telling outrageous lies.

We assembled at Tiananmen Square for the obligatory photo in front of the Monument to the People's Heroes, little red books in hand, heads held high, chests thrown out proudly. Xu Zuo, a notorious slouch, stood straight for a change, and Jin Gang removed his glasses to keep from looking so frail and bookish. Four young men with shining eyes stood before the granite edifice that had served as the embarkation point for tens of thousands of Beijing urban students since early '68.

Knowing we were part of this flood tide filled us with pride. Then, after standing silently for a moment—no blustery vows or false bravado—we walked off.

EVERYTHING WAS READY: money, ration books, clothes, back-packs, compasses, Chairman Mao badges, knives, chilblain ointment, antidiarrhea medicine.

But somehow word of our imminent departure leaked out. The Workers Propaganda Team held me for two days, letting me go only af-ter I'd convinced them we weren't running *from* anything and that we wouldn't try again. Fat chance of that! We didn't waste a minute before making new preparations, just waiting for an opportunity to leave. This time we were so tight-lipped, we didn't even tell our families until the day of our departure.

"Mother, I'm leaving for Inner Mongolia tonight."

"Tonight?" She looked at me wide-eyed.

"The eleven-fifty train."

Silence, except for the moans of a cold wind outside. "Of course you should answer Chairman Mao's call to go to the frontiers," she said weakly. "But don't you need permission?"

"No sweat. Lots of kids go on their own, and people welcome them with open arms."

"What about the paperwork? Your dossier. Your residence card."

"I'll come back and take care of all that after I'm settled in."

Mother was silent for a moment.

"I won't stand in your way if you're sure this is what you want. What can I get you?"

"I don't need anything. I'm taking only one bag."

I went out and didn't return until seven o'clock that evening. Mother had cooked dinner for Father and herself, but he had been summoned to the office to confess something or other, and she wasn't around, so I sat down to eat alone. I'm sure the food must have been de-licious, but my taste buds were so numb that even the roast chicken seemed bland.

"Here, take this." She held out a bundle of clothes.

I didn't take it. We were traveling light, knowing we might have to do a lot of walking.

She saw me out the gate on that pitch-black winter night. "Bo," she said, "try to get along with people. No fighting . . ."

I watched wisps of gray hair blown loose by the cold wind flutter in the pale light of the streetlamp. Mother had aged a lot over the past couple of years, and about all I could see was thinning hair, a deeply wrinkled face, and drooping eyelids.

Her advice fell like gentle snowflakes on my feverish head.

"Don't worry, I'll be fine."

Instinctively I grasped her warm hand. I knew how bad things were. There were posters up now, labeling her patriotic novel *Song of Youth* a monstrous poisonous weed. Work units were clamoring to denounce her with such stridency that she was afraid to show her face in public. Even I had "rebelled" against her once, cursing her roundly. I felt sorry for her and ashamed of myself.

She reached out to fasten my collar button, then smoothed the wrinkles in my pocket. "Go on," she said softly, "don't miss your train."

I walked off without a backward glance. There were none of the tearful, wrenching good-byes I was used to seeing in the movies.

Mill Bridge Street was cold, cheerless, and deserted under the pale bluish light of streetlamps that shone weakly through the cold air; dead, twisted branches of roadside trees split the black night like demonic claws. The darkness and cold swallowed me up. Shrouded in stillness, I joined my friends, not knowing if good times or bad awaited me. A foreboding raced through my tangled mind, but I drove it out, cheering myself by thinking of my comrades-in-arms.

During the "August 21" battle at school, Lei Xia had come to my rescue when I was hurt, for which he was rewarded with a split head. Bleeding like a stuck pig, yet undaunted, he had impressed even our attackers with his loyalty. With friends like that I had nothing to fear. Besides, I could do ninety pull-ups on the parallel bars and kick-box with either leg. Flipping Lei Xia was as easy as tossing a head of bok choy, and the twenty boxing techniques were second nature to me. I could clean and jerk 240, more than anyone else in school. They'd have been crazy to take me on. The fire blazing in my heart transformed feelings of desolation and loneliness into puffs of smoke.

AFTER TAKING a train to Zhang Family Pass, we set out on foot on the northern highway, wearing those padded blue caps that were so popular in the fifties. Having gotten used to traveling for free, we balked at wasting our money on train tickets. If we could ride for nothing, fine; if not, we'd walk. As night fell and the temperature plummeted, we watched our noses turn red. The frozen majesty of the great northland made us sigh in awe, but we didn't dare stop, and whenever we spotted a vehicle, we stood in the middle of the road jumping and waving and shouting. Dignity be damned! We cajoled and we begged, but nine times out of ten we succeeded only in making asses of ourselves.

In Baochang we spent the night huddled fully dressed on a brick kang in a dark, squalid wagoners' inn, quietly listening to a wagon master boast and bitch about women. We finally drifted off to sleep with the motley stench of cheap tobacco, sheepskin coats, and oat flour filling our nostrils. The place had the smell of Inner Mongolia: Even in the winter the toilet reeked of mutton, and that is a smell I'll never forget.

Our first stop was the Urban Student Office of the Prefectural Revolutionary Committee in Xilinhot City, where we pestered and wheedled the clerk day in and day out. But the stone-faced little bureaucrat was unmoved by our fine-sounding words. Why? Because every banner region in the area was filled to overflowing, and he wasn't authorized to assign another soul.

A week went by, and our money was running out. Xilinhot restaurants were perversely expensive: The cheapest thing on the menu cost far more than we wanted to pay. Then Xu Zuo had an idea: "Let's write letters in blood to Commandant Zhao of the military subdistrict. The only way to get things done is to go straight to the top."

It was a terrific idea. We'd blaze a trail with our own blood.

Punch holes in a few fingers? No big deal. What do young people care about a little blood, anyway? But when we realized that we'd actually be gouging our own flesh, we sat in silence for a long while to muster the courage. Then Lei Xia and I used a razor blade on our left forefingers, spilling enough fresh red blood to write a short story. But Xu Zuo's blunt paring knife wouldn't draw blood, even after several tries, so finally, in exasperation, he bore down and damn near amputated his finger. Blood gushed and splattered all over his pants. As for Jin Gang, who refused to use a knife no matter how much we teased and cajoled, he insisted on pricking his finger with a needle. So he dug and he squeezed but managed only a few drops. In the end, however, intrepid or timid, large cut or small, dark blood or light, each of us wrote a letter by dipping a pen in blood that had coursed through his own veins. In the squalor of a Xilinhot middle-school dormitory four Beijing students vowed that, having left home of their own free will, they would never return, dead or alive. Then, letters in hand, we went straight to the commandant's home and told him what we wanted. This veteran of the revolutionary Eighth Route Army, a pleasant and unpretentious man, disapproved of blood vows but still wrote at the top of each letter: "Request granted."

It took some doing, but we had accomplished our goal, for the placement office assigned us to the Injgan Sum pasture area in Mongolia's Western Ujimqin Banner region. We had not spilled our blood in vain and were spared the humiliation of returning to Beijing with our tails between our legs.

Being hot-blooded beats anything!

THE INJGAN SUM pasture area occupies a hundred square miles in the northeast section of Western Ujimqin Banner. Nothing could have prepared us for the desolation that greeted us. It was far worse than any production brigade in the interior. We saw only a couple of rows of adobe huts that housed the county and regiment offices, and some dugouts in the ground called Dictatorship of the Proletariat Square, which housed at least forty "ox demons and snake spirits"—enemies of the people—of every type and description: Mongolian People's Revolutionary Party members, traitors, counterrevolutionaries, whores, and horse thieves. They emerged each day to work silently with bowed heads.

A few days later a wagon from Company Seven came for us.

In the winter the gray bleakness of the Mongolian steppes is broken only by an occasional yellow tuft of stiff wild grass partially buried in the snow and here and there the chilling white bones of dead livestock. There was nothing to the west but sky, snow, and a twisting wagon path all the way to the horizon.

The unimaginable vastness of the steppe drains your heart and rocks your very being. In this landscape even the most arrogant, the most self-involved person in the world feels as insignificant as a grain of sand. White, bare, flat, boundless: That is the steppe. Instead of the chiseled elegance we had expected, we found a primitive and deafeningly silent landscape—natural beauty, untouched by artifice, that radiated a harsh, icy glare one never saw in the city.

Horse-drawn wagons moved across the steppe like so many ants. A wagon master called Old Gigolo mumbled through chattering teeth, "You can't live out here without sheepskin pants and coat. On a cold day your piss turns to ice before it hits the ground. It's so cold, the poor herdsmen have to be careful their noses and ears don't fall off. But they're used to it. When a wind comes up, the sky turns so dark, you can't see the whip in your hand. Here in Inner Mongolia you can freeze to death in June. We don't need any heroes, so forget about going out on windy days."

The immense Huolin Gol, was it really as unfeeling, as churlish, as wild as all that?

2

A STEPPE SHROUDED
IN BITTER COLD

I'LL NEVER FORGET my first night in a yurt, or *ger*, as the Mongols call their tents.

Before turning in I dumped a basketful of cowchips into the stove, which quickly filled the yurt with a cloud of thick, stifling smoke. Then *whoosh*, the chips caught fire and turned the chimney bright red. A freezing wind beat against the felt outer skin of the yurt, yet I was sweaty dressed only in an undershirt and underpants.

As soon as the fire died out the yurt turned into an icebox. Sometime during the night my sheepskin cover slipped to the floor, and I awoke shivering and curled up like a shrimp. Yurts have large ventilation holes at the top called *toonos*, and I could see the stars through ours. The cold was unbearable, so I slipped under Lei Xia's covers. He yelped when my icy limbs touched him.

As I gazed at the sky I thought back to our meeting with the herdsmen earlier that day at a spot called East River. They had received us with indifferent gapes, their unsmiling, leathery faces displaying all the emotion of men appraising horses. They talked among themselves in Mongol for a moment, then mounted up and rode off. All those newspaper reports we'd read about student workers being greeted as heroes were a real crock.

A kindhearted middle-aged woman made a fire for us in the yurt, but as we were thanking her we noticed a piece of white cloth sewn onto the back of her sheepskin coat, on which the word *herdowner* was written in Chinese and Mongol.

Lesson number one: Class struggle.

That night we attended a denunciation meeting called by the herdsmen of our team. The dim light of a kerosene lantern fell on the weathered faces of men whose sheepskin coats made them look taller and beefier than usual. As the meeting was called to order, everyone rose, faced Chairman Mao's portrait, and sang, "We Wish Chairman Mao a Long Long Life."

Chairman Mao is a blazing sun in our hearts . . .

They sang softly, slowly, and slightly out of sync. In Mongol the song sounded heavy, the singers seemed weary.

The three people being denounced, all members of the Inner Mongolian People's Revolutionary Party, stood with their heads bowed, looking very glum.

A pall of smoke hung over the meeting. Herdsmen are heavy smokers—chain-smokers, in fact—and most of them were looking on inattentively, or chewing the fat, or gawking at us, or heating horse mane for insoles. The women were bent over their sewing, and one old man was sound asleep, making queer, loud grunting noises that had the people around him laughing. One of the Mongols, a man by the name of Daoerji, had an astonishing ability to spit. He barely cracked his lips, and a line of spit arched straight to a pile of burning sheep manure. He never missed.

This first lesson in class struggle took us by surprise, for the minute the meeting was called to order, the poor and lower-middle-class herdsmen began to giggle, goof off, brag, hold spitting contests, or stretch out to catch up on their sleep, clutching the grimiest "Little Red Books" I'd ever seen. Once again the newspapers had fed us a crock.

———

A CAMPAIGN TO expose the pernicious Ulanfu Black Line had paralyzed leadership at all levels, and Company Seven was no exception. Cadres refused to take a position and no one came to inspect our work. So we did little but loaf, our only job being to take care of the horses— water them three times a day, groom them, exercise them, massage their legs, feed them straw, and generally treat them like family. We learned from the herdsmen that if horses sweat in the winter, they shed a layer of fat. So we took ours out for only a brief run when the itch was overpowering. My roan was a real beauty, a dream of a ride, and the envy of Lei Xia and Jin Gang. Once, when its back was rubbed raw, I threw the saddle over my shoulder and walked the fifteen miles back to camp, which the herdsmen thought was pretty funny. A man's horse was his first love, and you stood a better chance of borrowing money from someone than of using his horse.

It was a carefree life: out for a ride when we felt like it; tea when we were thirsty and good food when we were hungry; the choice to work or not; and the freedom to go where we wanted when we wanted to. Liu Yinghong, a student who'd come on her own from Beijing, once rode to headquarters for some shopping and got caught in a windstorm. The search team didn't get her back to her yurt until ten that night. Somehow she'd spooked her camel, and it had sent her flying, one of its hooves tearing a two-foot gash in her sheepskin coat. She was lying in the snow laughing her head off when we found her. That night she wrote to one of her classmates back home, telling how she'd gotten lost, and what a terrific experience it had been. What other girl in Beijing could boast of being thrown by a camel?

ON NEW YEAR'S EVE, 1968, after a meal of dumplings, we sat around the radio listening to the New Year's editorial, "Mao Zedong Thought Is in Total Command." That was followed by a rendition of "The Internationale," its electrifying melody echoing in our ears long after it was over.

The editorial had quickened Lei Xia's pulse. "Class lines didn't appear here until long after the Cultural Revolution," he said excitedly, "and nobody's ransacked the herdowners' homes yet! The Mongols still haven't drawn a line between friend and foe. Since students in other companies have ransacked their herdowners' homes, I say it's time for us to do the same!"

His cheeks were flushed and his eyes shone. That always happened when he was excited. The hot blood of youth.

"I'm against it," Xu Zuo said bluntly. "The situation in the pasture areas is very complex, and we're new here. Let's get the lay of the land first."

Rightist! Rightist! The place buzzed with talk of his rightist tendencies. The rest of us sided with Lei Xia, which brought a pained look to Xu Zuo's pretty face. Leafing through his Mongol-Chinese phrase book, he ignored our criticism.

Finally we agreed to put our plan into action early the next morning: We would ransack the home of every herdowning family in our company. The Beijing students of Company Seven wouldn't take a backseat to anybody. We'd usher in the new year by forging our way boldly to the front lines of class struggle.

New Year's Day, 1969, was hazy and overcast. We saddled up and split into action groups—all but Xu Zuo, the sole holdout, who went to make the rounds of the other yurts.

Lei Xia and I burst into the home of herdowner Gonggele.

There was hardly any light inside the squalid yurt, which served as cramped living quarters for a family of nine. An old-timer lay under two sheepskin blankets at the foot of a filthy cupboard next to the door flap, breathing weakly, like a man at death's door. A little old woman with matted hair crouched in the corner watching our every move like a hoary witch. The lady of the house was the same woman who had made a fire for us, but now she knew something bad was about to happen, and a look of impending doom showed in her tear-filled eyes. Three children in grimy clothes eyed us with curiosity.

"Class struggle is infallible," Lei Xia announced somberly. "We're here to confiscate the property of Gonggele the herdowner."

Gonggele, a skinny man in his fifties who always seemed to be smiling, nodded vigorously as a sign of welcome and cooperation. We ordered the family outside, all but his wife and two children, and told them not to leave the area. They picked up the sick old man and carried him outside, where a girl of eighteen or nineteen started to mount her horse. Lei Xia stopped her and ordered them to sit bunched together on a felt rug in the back of their wagon.

Inside the yurt all we saw were piles of junk. Where were the riches we'd heard so much about? Maybe it was all a show, maybe the good stuff was hidden. So we began the search, turning the place upside down until the floor was covered with tattered clothes, broken toys, and scraps of paper. I found a horn-handled knife; with a menacing grin, I pointed it at the woman, sending her children scurrying behind her in fright. Lei Xia, who was clearly up to the task, ransacked the place like a pro, having gained plenty of experience from his raids on the "Red Red Red" stronghold back in Beijing.

We had hoped to find weapons or hidden loan records, or at least some jewelry and stuff like that. We overlooked no possible hiding place—vats, grain sacks, cardboard boxes, the wagon, even the insides of their boots.

Meanwhile, the family members were behaving themselves outside, not even walking around to get their blood circulating in the freezing air. Knowing how dangerous sympathetic thoughts could be, I forced them out of my mind.

When we finished, the yurt looked like a disaster zone. We had trampled on the girls' formal robes and thrown goatchips all over the rug. No loan records, no weapons, no reactionary books or letters, no gold or silver, no jewelry. Nothing! How could a herdowner be that poor? We, the victors, surveyed our spoils: a sheepskin blanket, two sheepskin coats, and a sack of dried yoghurt. The housewife had watched us the whole time, her eyes filled with sadness instead of the loathing we deserved. That did not make our job any easier.

As we were carrying our spoils outside, a snarling brown dog charged us. His mistress couldn't hold him back. I had never seen such raw fury. The only way to take this family down a peg or two was to kill their reactionary dog. So we dumped our loot onto the ground and ordered the woman to tie the animal to a wagon wheel. Then I picked up a hoe and raised it over my head.

Gonggele rushed over and wrapped his arms around the dog, begging piteously for me to spare his life. When I shoved him away, he fell to his knees, wrapped his arms tightly around the dog, and buried his face in the fur to shield him with his own body. So it's trouble you want! Grabbing him by the scruff of his neck, I jerked him off his knees like a baby chick, then drop-kicked him headfirst to the ground. His wife rushed to his side.

That really set the dog snarling and growling. His fur stood on end, and a murderous gleam flashed in his bloodshot eyes. He leapt at me, jerking the leash so taut that it sang.

Gonggele's face had turned ashen, and snot dribbled onto his filthy beard. He bellowed at the dog to shut up, even kicked it a couple of times, but then he wrapped his arms around it again and implored lovingly, "Don't, please don't!"

Who did he think he was, defying me like that? I grabbed him just as the dog broke free and sank his teeth into my wrist. The searing pain made me break out in a cold sweat. Instinctively I slapped the old man, launching snot and tears from his wizened old face. But he just smiled and mumbled meekly, "Please don't."

"Get him out of here," Lei Xia demanded. "I'll take care of the dog."

Child's play. As soon as I grabbed the old guy, he wilted like a dough stick, and I dragged him off a few paces, leaving gouges in the snow. When his sad-faced old wife tried to pull me away, I drove my fist into her chest and sent her reeling backwards. But when I turned to force her husband to the ground, something whacked me on the head, and everything went black. As the world spun, I slumped to the ground.

I wasn't out for more than a few seconds, and when I opened my eyes I saw Lei Xia charging one of the onlookers, the one called Old Gigolo. He kicked him to the ground. "What do you think you're doing?" he bellowed.

Now I saw what had happened. Old Gigolo had tried to crack my skull with an ax handle. It was the first time I'd ever been knocked out in a fight, the very first time! I picked up the hoe and took out after Old Gigolo. We'll see what *his* head's made of! Lei Xia wrapped his arms around me. I flipped him like a rag doll. Then Jin Gang, who had heard all the commotion, ran up with some of the others and tried to restrain me. With a roar I sent him flying. He landed like a stone. No one was going to stop me now. Howling like a wounded boar, I charged again. But before I reached Old Gigolo, Xu Zuo blocked my way and grabbed the raised hoe with both hands. "Drop it, Ma Bo!" he screamed. "Drop it!" Where the hell had he come from?

Rage, hostility, and a hot rush of adrenaline took over. No longer rational, I fought as if my life depended on it. After knocking Xu Zuo to the ground, I started kicking him, but he held on for dear life. I inched closer to Old Gigolo, straining with all my might and dragging Xu Zuo along with me. Old Gigolo stood his ground defiantly, his broken ax handle raised and ready for action. Just a few more steps, closer, closer. Suddenly Xu Zuo bent over and sank his teeth into my finger. Ouch! Shit! I loosened my grip just enough for him to wrench the hoe out of my hand. And before I knew it, the enemy was gone. I twisted and turned to see where he was.

All this had taken place in front of a mob of herdsmen and students. By then Lei Xia had already killed the dog, so I ran over to the old herdowner and began whipping him with a bridle; when I realized he couldn't feel a thing through his sheepskin coat, I grabbed a stick and really laid into him. He wrapped his arms around his head, curled up on the ground, and screamed in pain.

"Shut up!" I kept hitting him.

More screams.

"I said, shut up!" I hit him harder.

Still more screams.

Good old Gonggele, you unrepentant reactionary.

"I'll give you something to scream about!" I must have hit him a dozen times. He writhed on the ground, curled into a ball to escape the blows raining down on him; but the stick found him as if it had eyes. More futile screams. Lei Xia watched my back to make sure the other herdsmen stayed where they were.

"You fucking, no-good herdowner, the more you scream the harder I'll beat you!" The stick whistled down on his ass and thighs five or six more times. Finally he stopped screaming.

As Xu Zuo dragged me away, I kicked the old man one last time. He lay mute in the dirt, all but unconscious.

His blubbering wife rushed to him as he gazed up at me and forced an apologetic smile on his face.

"The old guy's okay, Lei Xia. He can take a beating."

Lei Xia patted me on the shoulder. "That noggin of yours isn't bad either. The fucking ax handle broke in two, but you don't look any the worse for wear."

A DEJECTED Old Gigolo, his own face by then a mass of welts and bruises, hitched up his horse to take Gonggele to the Geritu Brigade in Eastern Ujimqin (our infirmary wouldn't treat landlords, herdowners, rich peasants, counterrevolutionaries, or bad elements).

After the crowd dispersed, Xu Zuo spat on the ground and glared at me. "What if you'd killed Old Gigolo? He's a poor peasant, you know."

"No way! If you know what you're doing, you can kick the shit out of someone without doing any serious damage."

"Bullshit," Xu Zuo muttered.

It was, as I said, the first time in my life anyone had knocked me down, and I was pissed. After discussing the day's events that night, we concluded that the bloodshed had reaffirmed Company Seven's stand on class struggle and that the malcontent who had sicced his dog on us because we'd searched his home was an enemy of the people. Xu Zuo cast the only dissenting vote. "I don't approve of your raids," he said, "and I strongly disapprove of beatings. Not even a herdowner deserves that sort of treatment. You know party policy as well as I do. I can't believe you'd resort to violence and get us all involved—over a dog."

What does he mean, over a dog? He must be stupider than I thought. Has he really missed the significance of all this? Why can't he go along with us once in a while? What happened to his class consciousness? After eating at the Marxist-Leninist trough all those years, he was still a rightist. A strange, stubborn guy. No one said he couldn't break up a fight, but why did he have to bite me, and why did everybody have to do things his way?

The revolutionary committee announced its ruling the next day. First, Company Seven's raid on the herdowner's home was a justified revolutionary act. Second, Old Gigolo was to be remanded into custody of the masses, who would determine his fate for hitting me with an ax handle. Third, owing to his bad attitude, Gonggele was to be turned over to the masses for criticism.

That, in a nutshell, was our introduction to the steppe.

My skull had been cracked, not by a herdowner's whip, but by an ax handle wielded by a poor herdsman. Who'd have believed it?

Society is too complex for me.

THE HERDSMEN, upset with us for keeping our plans to ransack their homes secret, kept us at arm's length after that. They knew who I was now and stayed out of my way.

When we ran out of cowchips, we decided to split up and live in the Mongols' yurts. I volunteered to stay behind to guard the loot so I could be alone.

The worst part of living alone is cooking. I'd never had to do that before, and all I could manage was some barely palatable porridge. I made do. If I burned the millet, I ate it anyway. When the wok still had left-over rice in it, I cooked in the teapot; if I couldn't find a chopping board, I used the wok lid.

One day I was making noodle cakes (the herdsmen fry noodles in little squares they call cakes), and the oil was hot before the dough was ready. My hands flew, but I was still rolling the dough out when the oil began to smoke. Bathed in sweat, I spurred myself on with a quote from Chairman Mao: "When the enemy is at his strongest and you are in trouble, that is when his problems begin and the situation turns in your favor. A favorable situation and a return of initiative comes from perseverance and hard work."

Stick it out, just stick it out, and everything will be okay, I consoled myself as I sliced the noodles. Then all of a sudden, *whoosh*, the oil ignited and flames shot to the top of the yurt. I was too scared to move. Finally getting a grip on myself, I carried the pot of boiling oil outside. By then my eyebrows were singed, my hands were scalded, and the sliced noodles on the cutting board were stamped with black footprints.

The Mongols have a saying: "A smart cook watches the fire, a stupid one watches the pot." How was I supposed to know?

OUR NEW HOME was perfectly suited to people with no concept of hygiene: It was sparsely populated, and there were hardly any women. You could have dirt on your face an inch thick and hands as black as coal, and no one would laugh at you.

My rice bowl was coated with dust, goatchips floated on the water in the vat, scraps of meat were strewn all over the rug, and my hands were grimy. I didn't care—I ate, I drank tea, and I slept the same as I would anywhere. But taking a shit, that was sheer torture. In midwinter, with the wind blowing and the snow swirling, the steppe is flat as a piece of paper. The minute I squatted down and lowered my pants, I felt like someone was jabbing my ass with a knife.

Lei Xia came over one day and greeted me like a long-lost brother. Without taking off his sheepskin coat, he launched into an account of the lives of Mongol herdsmen.

First of all, they sleep in their clothing the year round and wear it out before it's ever washed. They never bathe. They eat with their hands and lick their bowls clean. One meal a day—dinner—is all they get; in the morning and at noon they settle for tea. Ideologically, they're nothing like their revolutionary image, for they get along fine with herd-owners, and some even intermarry. They are wonderful hosts: Anyone (including herdowners, even traitors) is treated to a glass of milky tea the minute he steps inside someone's yurt, whose door flaps are normally kept open just in case a passerby needs lodging for the night. The people are blissfully unaffected by Confucian concepts of relations between the sexes, but while they're relatively liberal, they're not incestuous, as so often described, and that bit about Mongol girls being little more than whores for houseguests is hogwash. They'll pay off a debt of pennies with a cow, if necessary, and are ready to fight to the death over a trifling matter.

SPRING FESTIVAL, 1969, was just around the corner, and I was surprised to see how seriously the herdsmen treated the old holiday. They were always out shopping for something, and it was not unusual for them to begin stocking up months ahead of time. Their stores often included as much as forty or fifty containers of strong white liquor.

An arctic wind ushered in the last day of the lunar year, sending the thermometer plummeting as the sun hid behind dark clouds. The bone-chilling wind whipped eddies of snow into the air, and dogs shivered as they curled up in piles of cowchips. No one ventured outside. No one except an old Mongol with a piece of white cloth pinned to his back, who went out in his grimy cap to kill a cow for us. As freezing winds whistled around him he bared his arm, reached into the slaughtered animal's chest, and ripped out its heart, then skinned the steamy corpse, sliced off a few chunks of meat, and walked inside, his hands dripping with blood. Sitting cross-legged on the floor, totally exhausted, he sighed, having completed his task in the bitter cold without a murmur. The man was Gonggele.

I'd be lying if I said I didn't feel sorry for him at that moment, and I couldn't forget the smile on his face after that horrible beating I'd given him earlier.

Lei Xia, who was staying with the herdsman Daoerji, invited me over for drinks that night. Herdsmen never eat when they drink—they just drink. We couldn't keep up with Daoerji, who gulped down the liquor as if it were water. The more he drank the redder his scarred puffy face became, until it looked like pork liver. Soon drunk, he bragged about how his chestnut colt could run two hundred miles in a single day and how his wife had presented him with four sons. Before long he was singing:

Chairman Mao is a blazing sun in our hearts . . .

What should have been a moving song sounded like croaks squeezed from a constricted chest, stifled and heavy. But even though he ruined the song, when he finished, a self-conscious smile creased his face and two lines of tears slid down his leathery face. Mongols are said to be highly emotional, and I can attest to that. "The Cultural Revolution is great," he blurted out, "just great. But we can't afford a pack of decent cigarettes for the holiday, and that's not right. Bright Light cigarettes, the ones that sell for seventeen fen a pack, leave your throat all scratchy." His chin crinkled like a squashed toad and his mouth twitched unhappily.

As I surveyed the seedy yurt, I took mental inventory of the man's possessions: a couple of wooden chests whose paint was peeling; a piece of red cloth on which thirty or more Mao badges had been pinned; an assortment of cooking utensils in a smoky cupboard; some patched, dirty flour sacks; and a rug covered with goat hairs, scraps of paper, cigarette butts, cinders, and slivers of goatchips—all, of course, pervaded by the stench of his children's urine.

They—his children—were sitting in the corner shoveling mutton stew into their mouths and sneaking an occasional look at their Chinese visitors. *Ssst*. A line of spit arched from Daoerji's mouth and landed unerringly on a tiny pile of goat manure. He staggered outside, mounted his horse, and galloped off to the other yurts. Strange, meandering, eerie wails cut through the deepening darkness of the steppe. They say Mongol herdsmen always wail like that when they're drunk, sometimes until their noses run and their eyes tear up.

Daoerji's three-year-old son, whose arms were wrapped around the family dog, was gnawing on a bone covered with goat hairs, swallowing his own snot along with the meat. The dog lay there obediently, occasionally licking the bone in the boy's hand.

I didn't get home till late that night.

A few head of cattle had gathered at the spot where Gonggele had slaughtered one of their number that day. Lowing sadly, they pawed the frozen ground and licked the dried traces of their fallen companion's blood. I had never heard cattle cry before, and it frightened me. All I could think was, Watch out they don't stampede and trample us to death. But I could see that grief had not clouded their reason, since I was able to drive them off with a few well-placed hits with a stick. Yet they closed up ranks each time and drifted back. Things reached a climax in the middle of the night, when the bellowing cows were so choked with sobs, they nearly broke down. Who could sleep with that racket going on?

I thought back to the gloomy targets of mass criticism in Dictatorship of the Proletariat Square, to the old woman with the white cloth sewn on her back, to the ragged boy and his dog sharing a bone in Daoerji's yurt.

The wailing cattle girded me with a curtain of desolation. Huolin Gol, for all its romanticism, was shrouded in bitter cold.

3

I BREAK WITH XU ZUO
OVER ANOTHER DOG

MY FIRST CHORE each morning was to feed the horses. Then I made a fire and cooked breakfast. I didn't have to worry about thieves, since the Mongols all stayed clear of me.

Loneliness, on the other hand, was a constant problem. I seldom saw any flies or rats, let alone people. Oh, once in a while a cow would stray over and bring a little life to the area around my yurt, even if it only stood motionless next to the wall with tears crusted in the corners of its eyes.

Thus liberated from distractions and outside pressures, my thoughts began to roam the mental landscape. Mostly I thought about girls, which I admit with no pride. Once, in the fourth grade, I had a crush on a girl, but she spurned me, and girls have mystified me ever since. I was curious, sure, especially as I grew older, but remained aloof in my dealings with girls so the kids in school wouldn't call me a "sex fiend." I even closed my eyes during the mushy scenes in movies.

There was something dirty about having girls on my mind all the time, and I hated myself for it. In 1964, when the campaign for self-revolution was gaining steam, I dredged up all the scruffy, vile thoughts I'd ever had and wrote a self-criticism, which I turned in to the authorities; I was so nervous, I was covered with goosebumps. But the same old thoughts quickly skulked back into my head, forcing me to transform my infatuation with girls into a love for my comrades-in-arms. Lei Xia and I actually vowed to remain eternally loyal to one another and never let any girl come between us.

Then I came to the steppes. Solitude forced me to rely on wild dreams to capture the sweet essence of youth. At night my mind was a welter of thoughts as I lay in my yurt and drooled over sexual fantasies. They nearly drove me crazy, and masturbation was the only answer. Then I'd get up the next morning feeling guilty and unspeakably dirty. Had I written a letter in my own blood and endured the hardships of a trip to Inner Mongolia just to huddle under the covers and obsess over girls?

A battle raged in me between a view that always thinking about girls was shameful and sordid and the opposite view that it was all perfectly natural and justified. A revolutionary youth walking shoulder to shoulder with the peasants and workers ought not to concern himself with things like that. But I was incorrigible; it was all I thought about.

I sometimes vented my frustrations by wrestling with the locals, whose clumsy brute force was no match for my superior skills. I always felt better following one of those bouts.

One morning after a major snowstorm I got up, dressed with an eerie premonition, and forced the yurt door open. The snow was at least two feet deep. But there, off to the left, a snow-covered puppy lay curled with his nose tucked under his tail. I picked him up, took him inside, and brushed the snow off. His clay-colored ears pointed straight up (the other local dogs all had droopy ears), and we hit it off right away: After I fed him, he began nibbling my toes, tossing my cap around, and playfully attacking me with fangs, claws, and what passed for a growl.

I named him Ingush, after the famous Russian breed.

Ingush could run like the wind and fight like the devil. After a few well-placed, lightning-quick nips, he'd hightail it out of harm's way, leaving his opponent—no matter how big or how mean—yelping in pain. Once I was attacked by a pack of dogs on my way to visit a nearby herdsman, and Ingush launched a vicious counterattack, refusing to retreat although he was badly mauled; he even ran over to the wagon to protect the horses.

I got a kick out of stroking Ingush's head as he sat propped up proudly on his forelegs, staring at me with his innocent black eyes. He never whimpered or caused trouble (which is more than you can say about a child), and he was housebroken: If he needed to go outside, he scratched at the flap and whined softly. In fact, his only shortcoming was a distaste for human flesh. To cure him of this defect, I made a dummy out of wood, dressed it in an old army coat, padded trousers, and army boots, and stuffed a piece of meat in the waistband. It was a waste of time. He wouldn't attack even after I hadn't fed him for two days. That was the only flaw in an otherwise perfect companion.

Ingush often lay at my feet and licked my dirty toes until they were spotless, and paternal feelings welled up inside me when I buried my face in his fur. Normally he ate what I ate, but I supplemented his diet with condensed milk and, once in a while, a bit of glutinous rice. He slept next to me under the covers, frequently waking me up by tickling my ear with his wet tongue.

One day, as the weather was turning warm, I rode over to see Lei Xia, Ingush following along, running and jumping friskily on the steppe. But before we reached Lei Xia's yurt, a herdsman caught up with us on his horse. It was Daoerji.

"Is that your dog?" he asked.

"Yes."

"It has to be killed," he said somberly.

"Why?"

"It slaughtered a dozen lambs and must pay with its life." He seemed to have forgotten how we'd drunk together in his yurt, and how I'd watched him sing as hot tears streamed down his face. Now he was all business, and I marveled over how quickly and easily the herdsmen could change. "Slow down," I said unhappily. "Let's talk this over."

"There's nothing to talk over. He has to die." He curled his lip and sent a stream of spit arching into a rathole.

Controlling the anger building inside me, I asked, "Whose lambs is he supposed to have killed?"

"Mine. The dog has to be killed!"

There was a mean look on his leathery face, with unfriendly wrinkles on his shriveled, crooked nose. No wonder people called him a cowardly back-stabber.

My anger took hold. "You plan to do the killing yourself?" I asked in a sinister tone.

"The dog has to be killed," he repeated angrily.

Not wanting to argue any longer, I dug my heels into the colt's sides, and we galloped off. Ingush led the way, blissfully unaware of what was happening.

Daoerji launched a line of spit at my retreating back and shouted, "It has to be killed, and that's all there is to it!"

I turned and waved my fist. "Your fucking old lady has to be killed!"

"Killed! Killed! It has to be killed!"

I COULDN'T KEEP WATCH over the confiscated loot without a dog, and when I told Lei Xia what had happened, he swore that Ingush would never die at the hands of Daoerji. According to him, the herdsman was so cheap, he had never once fed Lei Xia meat in all the time he'd shared his yurt; he wouldn't even give him fried rice kernels for his tea. Eventually Lei Xia had moved into another yurt just to get a decent meal now and again. Daoerji, who would fight at the drop of a hat but knew how to play the role of poor-but-honest shepherd to perfection, was not a popular man.

Ingush, who seemed to know he'd done something wrong, stuck to me like glue. I couldn't picture him as a lamb killer. But the next morning Xu Zuo came to inform me that the dog had killed fourteen lambs and that the law of the steppes demanded that sheep-killing dogs forfeit their lives.

"But I have to have a dog. I live alone."

"As soon as the production corps organization is completed, they'll put all students together again."

"The lambs are already dead, so what good will come of killing the dog? Why not let me pay for them?"

"A dog that's tasted blood is like a wolf. If it's killed once, it'll kill again. You must respect the law of the steppes."

I promised to think it over, but I wasn't happy about it.

Daoerji, the mean son of a bitch, strutted like a cock, now that Ingush was on everyone's hit list. But what about me, how could I let them kill a dog that had turned up on my doorstep cold and hungry, then later had become my protector?

I went to enlist the sympathy of my friends.

When Jin Gang, the youngest among us, wasn't forging bus tickets or carving phony official seals, he was quietly listening to music. Not long after arriving in the steppes he had witnessed the tragic sight of cattle mourning the death of one of their own and was so devastated that he wouldn't eat beef afterward. I counted on his support.

"I like Ingush as much as you do," he said awkwardly after hearing me out, "but it's the law of the steppes, and there are no exceptions, no matter whose dog it is."

Chickenshit bastard! I stormed off. "Hear me out . . ." I ignored him. I should have known I couldn't count on anyone who rode only nags that wouldn't run if you whipped them till your arm dropped off. He even avoided cows, afraid they'd gore him.

Next I went to enlist the support of Liu Yinghong, the girl who had made the trip from Beijing on her own. She seemed okay to me. When I entered her yurt she greeted me with a smile. Her face was deeply tanned, her hair carelessly combed. I detected the unmistakable odor of sheepskin.

"The shepherds have learned to keep themselves clean," she commented curiously when she saw how dark and grungy I was. "How come you're lagging behind?"

I smiled proudly.

"They're always commenting on your strength," she said somewhat doubtfully. "They say you can lift a wagon axle with one hand, and that you outwrestled the Western Ujimqin Banner Champion."

It was music to my ears. "What else do they say?"

"They say deep down you're a coward."

"Not as cowardly as some people I could mention!" I told her about the dead lambs and how Daoerji insisted on having my dog killed. Given all the time she spent taking care of old and sick animals, I assumed she'd have a little compassion for Ingush. You can imagine my shock when she said, "That's the law of the steppes."

If even an innocent young thing like Liu Yinghong wouldn't let my Ingush live, he was in big trouble.

IT WAS DARK by the time I got home. After tying up the colt, I walked toward the yurt but was hit from behind. I spun and swung—a reflex action—and heard a yelp. Ingush circled me in the blowing snow, leaping and jumping, then came up to paw me and lick my icy coat.

Good boy! I patted his head, which threw him into animated ecstasy. Lei Xia was waiting inside the yurt.

"You're late," he said.

"I went to see Liu Yinghong, and she kept me over for a bowl of noodles. Mongol style. Not bad."

"Don't you ever think about anything but your stomach? I was worried sick. They nearly got Ingush."

He told me how the stable had been surrounded by seven or eight shepherds when he'd come by that afternoon. Hearing some pitiful howls, he'd rushed up to find Ingush hanging upside down on a post, blood dripping from his mouth. Seething with a nameless fury, he'd pushed his way through the mob and cut the dog down.

Daoerji had tried to stop him. "What do you think you're doing?"

Lei Xia had shoved him away. "None of your damned business!" Holding a club in one hand and Ingush in the other, he'd defied the hostile shepherds to stop him.

Following an urgent conversation in Mongol, Daoerji and the others had decided to stay their hand. The campaign against the Inner Mongolian Party had them afraid of their own shadows.

I thumped Lei Xia on the shoulder. "Good for you, you old dog!"

He smiled. "I damned near starved in that cheapskate's yurt. I can't stand to look at him."

Ingush was asleep at my feet, traces of dried blood in the corners of his mouth. When I rubbed his cold nose, he opened his eyes and looked up at me, then licked my hand.

A FEW DAYS LATER a meeting was called to inform us that we were to "grasp revolution and promote production in line with the Party's sixteen-point revolutionary declaration of 1966." I glared at Daoerji, planning my revenge.

I met Xu Zuo when I went outside to take a leak. "Ma Bo," he said, "why not just kill the dog and be done with it?"

"Why should I?"

"Because he's not worth fighting the shepherds over. Those lambs are their life. Try to understand their feelings."

"But I can pay them for their loss, so why do they have to kill him?" Try to understand *my* feelings, I thought.

"Tradition. Attacking a person is one thing, but nobody can keep a dog that kills lambs."

I didn't say anything.

"They weren't happy about the way you killed Gonggele's dog when you ransacked his house. Our dealings with the Mongols are tense enough as it is, and if you're not careful, you won't be around much longer."

I didn't say anything.

Seeing how taciturn I'd grown, he paused before saying, "I might as well tell you that Ingush is already dead."

"What did you say?" I couldn't believe my ears. I'd just seen him on a pile of goat manure.

He tried to be nonchalant. "I finished him off myself."

"No shit?" I was shocked.

"Why should I lie? I tossed him in the ditch beside the stable."

I ran over there, but it was too dark to see much; I had to dig around for a while before I found Ingush alongside the frozen carcasses of some horses. Sticky blood from a gash in his chest stained my hand. I held him in my arms. What a shitty way to die, little friend. The blood soiling my jacket seemed to seep into my heart.

"Let it go, Ma Bo," Xu Zuo said. "It's not worth getting upset over."

I wept silently.

"Go on home, it's cold," he urged me, covering his ears with his hands.

Loyal little Ingush had passed every test. If I scalded his paws with hot cowchips or wrenched a tasty bone out of his mouth or whipped him, he not only endured it without a whimper but actually came up and licked my dirty feet.

I seethed with anger at Xu Zuo. Why would he want to murder my dog? I couldn't believe it.

He urged me to go home, but the blood had rushed to my head. *You don't treat me like a friend, so why should I treat you like one?* When he shoved me to get me going I nailed him right on the jaw. "Fuck you!"

Caught off guard, he stumbled backwards, then charged. "You bastard!"

He was no match for me, but since this was neither the time nor the place for a showdown, I toyed with him to teach him a lesson. Still he kept coming, fists flying, and we rolled around in the darkness in the snow for a while. Lei Xia, hearing the commotion, came out and pulled us apart.

"You bastard!" Xu Zuo spit out venomously.

"You're the bastard!"

"Bastard!"

Jin Gang, who had witnessed the whole episode, stood there looking petrified.

I buried Ingush on the mountain the next day.

My friendship with Xu Zuo was over. We'd been on the steppes for all of four months.

4

THE CORPS
TAKES CHARGE

THE CAMPAIGN AGAINST the indigenous, counterrevolutionary Ulanfu Black Line created tremendous tension between the students and the Mongol shepherds. We greeted enthusiastically the
news that the Inner Mongolian Production Corps was taking over our
farm, since we were looking forward to combat and a life of military
regimentation.

In March 1969, two hundred demobilized soldiers and a thousand
or more students from Tianjin, led by a hundred active-duty soldiers, arrived at the Injgan Sum pastureland, breathing life into the sleepy
steppes.

In June I was sent to Company Headquarters owing to my history of
fighting. This so-called "headquarters" was in reality three mud huts, a
stable, and a well. The Tianjin students inundated me with questions
upon my arrival. Their urban airs and passion hadn't worn off yet, and
compared to them, with their clean clothes and fresh, youthful faces, I
looked like a beggar. My jacket was torn and filthy, my hair was a mess,
and my face was covered with grime. But I didn't care—grime has its
own special beauty.

Jin Gang pumped my hand. "Our conquering hero!" he said excitedly. "I'd have been bored out of my skull alone out there day in and day out." A few months of living like Robinson Crusoe had sent my stock soaring.

I reported to Political Instructor Shen. "Are you Ma Bo?" he asked as I handed over my storeroom key.

I nodded tentatively.

"You shouldn't have fought."

"He tried to take advantage of me."

"That's no reason to fight."

"It wasn't my idea."

"Barbarian."

I just nodded. Shen was a tall soldier with a pot belly and deep wrinkles at the corners of his mouth. His average-sized eyes were clouded and bloodshot; the bridge of his nose had an awesome hook.

"They say you're a pretty good wrestler. Is that right?"

"I do okay. But don't believe everything you hear," I replied honestly.

"Tell me about the incident with the dog and the lambs."

I told him what had happened.

"You really are a barbarian, comrade. Xu Zuo did the right thing. The corps has set up strict disciplinary guidelines and will tolerate no nonsense."

I nodded.

"Now get out of here."

I turned to leave, but he called me to a halt. "And what's this I hear about you threatening Daoerji with a knife to keep him from killing your dog?"

"That's a lie."

"Do you have a knife?"

"Yes."

"Let me see it."

I handed over my horn-handled knife.

"Tell you what," he said after examining it. "Leave it with me. You'll get it back after we've checked out your story."

More of Daoerji's rumors. I had never threatened him.

———

Xu zuo was sent to the pastureland to implement new policy while Lei Xia, Jin Gang, and I were assigned to the (all-male) First Platoon. With the exception of the all-female Second Platoon, the company platoon leaders were demobilized soldiers. Altogether there were three active-duty soldiers: Political Instructor Shen, Company Commander Wang, and Medical Officer Wang.

Company Headquarters seemed to come alive. The newly created Inner Mongolian Production Corps, stretching for thousands of miles and embracing ten thousand students, expanded rapidly. Even in our remote little company headquarters we could sense the abundant power and vitality.

Combines, tractors, storage tanks, and seeders began arriving; goods and materials of all types were piling up. At first we spent our time weaving willow baskets, but the men were soon put to work making adobe blocks at a site that became a hotbed of activity, surrounded by the deathly stillness of the wilderness. About thirty of us were squeezed into a small area to dig and mix clay, carry baskets, and make blocks. We gave it our best, which wasn't much, since we managed fewer than a hundred blocks the first morning.

Our hands were a mass of blisters, our shoulders swelled up, and, of course, our trousers were covered with mud. But that didn't faze us — we'd have been embarrassed to slack off, even if given the opportunity. We went all out, taking pride in seeing who could raise the largest blisters, get the dirtiest, or have the most painful shoulders, for those were our badges of honor.

Someone complained that Jin Gang was loafing on the job, and he didn't smile all day. Then, after dinner, he went out to dig more clay, not returning until late that night. But the labels "softie" and "second-class laborer" stuck anyway.

Our illusions regarding the arid climate on the steppes were shattered by rains that fell suddenly and without warning. I don't know how many nights we were jolted out of our dreams by the shriek of a whistle and orders to go out into the rain to stack and protect the blocks. Grumbling and rubbing our sleepy eyes, we covered the block with raincoats, sheets of plastic, mats, and felt rugs, while we, on the other hand, were soaked to the skin. The sky crackled with lightning. Working shoulder to shoulder with women spurred us on to even more dramatic efforts.

Construction was men's work, which required strength, particularly on the walls. My favorite job was heaving the blocks, since it was such great exercise. Then Liu Yinghong came over and insisted on helping. Predictably, none of her blocks reached the top, and most shattered when they hit the ground. But she loved to compete with the men. A real exhibitionist, that girl. Her feet were rubbed raw from mixing the clay, but she could dig with the best of them. She worked like a demon, and that infuriated the weaker men, who hated being shown up by a woman.

Jin Gang mixed clay as if he were making wonton wrappings: smooth, soft, and perfect. His job required the most skill. He had to mix the right amount of straw and water into the clay, and though he lacked the strength for more physically demanding jobs, no one was better at work requiring finesse. The walls he finished were smooth as glass and the blocks he laid were straight as a die. Some of his co-workers were put off by his goatlike face, others called him effeminate, but whatever he did, he did it flawlessly. And when he was pissed off he could go weeks without changing or washing his clothes, until you couldn't see his trousers for all the mud.

Glory was hidden in the dirt.

The dignity of being a corps trooper was hidden in the dirt.

5

EIGHT-ZIP

WANG LIANFU, from Fenyang county in Shanxi province, had a
long face and bright little eyes. Standing well over six feet tall, he was
a robust man who seemed to be all bone and muscle. In the army he
had once carried nearly four hundred pounds of sorghum stalks on his
back for a quarter of a mile, the normal load for four men. Very impressive. And what an appetite: He could finish off a dozen and a half
stuffed buns at one sitting. His father, a martial-arts expert who had
served as a brigade party secretary during the War of Resistance
against Japan in the 1930s and '40s, had personally hacked three Jap
soldiers to death. He had passed his skills on to his son, who never
lost a fight.

In 1966, Wang joined the army; admitted into the party the following year, he promptly grew lazy and careless. In his three years as a soldier he had checked himself into the hospital six times. He had the
disposition of TNT. Afraid of no one, he'd as soon curse you as look at
you. "Who do you think you are? I'll lop your goddamned prick off!"
was one of his favorites. Rare was the person he could not intimidate.

Once he stood with his hands on his hips and watched Wei Xiaoli,
the daughter of a provincial first secretary, wrestle with a carrying pole

in the vegetable garden as she tried to lug baskets like everyone else. He was not pleased. "Damn it, Second Platoon Leader," he bellowed when he found Liu Yinghong. "The girl you assigned can't even lift two baskets. Send somebody else. I don't want any weak sisters in *my* garden!"

Everyone said he was one stubborn SOB.

One day, after boasting to the younger students about his martial-arts skills, his "swallow flight" technique in particular, he said, "I'll give a demonstration. Any volunteers?"

Glances all around, but no one willing to take him up.

"What are you scared of? I'll take it easy."

Curiosity got the better of me, so I plopped down on the ground to see what this "swallow flight" was all about.

After sitting on the small of my back, he wrenched my arms back and laid them on his legs. Then he grabbed my hair with one hand and my chin with the other and jerked my head back so hard, I thought my neck would snap. As he described the move, he twisted my head like a radish. The looks of pity and glee on the onlookers' faces embarrassed me. "Okay," I said, "that's enough." But he wouldn't get off, wanting to prolong the demonstration as long as possible.

When he learned that I knew how to wrestle he formally challenged me—twice—but I begged off in order not to call attention to myself so soon after the creation of the corps. We were supposed to meekly accept reeducation by the people, and it wouldn't look good to be wrestling all the time.

Naturally he assumed I was afraid. "Who does Ma Bo think he is? Every time I challenge him to a fight he chickens out. I'm not bragging when I say I can handle two Ma Bos!" "See these biceps?" "See these thighs?" "Don't make me fucking laugh. I can carry four hundred pounds of sorghum a quarter of a mile."

An indignant Lei Xia reported this to me, which immediately raised my hackles. Brag on, I thought. This time you're not dealing with one of the girls.

October 1, National Day. With the harvest completed, we were given three days off. That afternoon I encountered Wang Lianfu in the mess hall. "You want a fight? Okay, you got it," I said softly. He squinted, gave me a long look, then said without a second thought, "Okay, a fight to the finish."

"Fine with me." I didn't give a damn what we fought to.

"We'll start with a grapple."

"Okay."

"Don't blame if you get hurt."

"Don't worry."

I laid my rice bowl on the windowsill, and we assumed a fighting stance in the doorway. He spread his legs and wrapped his arms around my waist, giving him the opening advantage.

At first he tried to use his height to push me over backwards, straining his powerful arms and burying his chin in my temple. But by twisting sideways, I managed to keep my balance. So then he grabbed me in a bear hug. Even straining mightily and growling like a wild beast, he couldn't budge me. Finally I hooked my left leg around his right, and we hit the ground in a heap.

I was tense as a cat. The first round is always crucial, and I wanted to avoid losing at all costs. We were locked in a defensive stalemate; as long as I didn't make a move, he couldn't pin me. Not with my strong legs. But stalemate meant no winner. No, with this guy I had to take some risks. When we were back on our feet, I feinted right and left, twisted, then planted my feet and flipped him. He hit the ground like a sack of cement—*thunk*—and the first round was mine.

Stunned at being thrown and afraid I might run off, he jumped up and wrapped his arms around me again. As the second round began, more students gathered round to watch the drama unfold.

This time I broke his grip by bending his fingers backwards. Then I feinted, twisted, and caught him with a leg sweep, sending him crashing to the ground again.

Now that he'd been thrown twice, his eyes burned with rage. He tore off his shirt and pounced on me, grinding his teeth and snorting angrily. He assumed I'd be reluctant to go on, now that I'd thrown him twice.

The wide-eyed crowd nervously held its collective breath.

We wrapped our arms around each other again, and he quickly maneuvered himself into a vise grip over my right shoulder and under my left armpit. Then he squatted down cautiously, his rump sticking out, and squeezed my neck under his armpit, pinning my ear painfully against his chest. His sweaty skin gave off a strong masculine odor.

They said he could mount a tractor carrying two-hundred-pound sacks under each arm. But I weighed only one forty, and still he was red in the face from exhaustion. He strained, he squeezed, he tugged, but he couldn't lift me six inches, since my leg was wrapped around his. He straightened up to catch his breath, and that was my opening. I hopped on my left foot, kicked out with my right, and twisted free, then kneed him in the groin. His head banged me painfully in the ear on the way down.

When he stood up again, he was livid. Flames seemed to leap from his eyes. Perspiration beaded his forehead.

Less than two minutes later he was on the ground again. But he was no quitter. He climbed back to his feet, grabbed me without stopping to wipe his sweaty face, and was at it again. He must have felt that I was using tricks or was just plain lucky, and that sooner or later he'd get me. He had the power but lacked the skill; brute strength isn't much of a threat in martial arts.

By now my confidence had peaked. In the fifth round I whipped his leg out from under him; that one worked every time. By the eighth it was clear that I was too good for him and that keeping at it would only make me look better and him worse. His doggedness evaporated. As he wiped his forehead he said heavily. "No more for me. I'm no good at your kind of wrestling," then walked off with his head bowed, a look of disbelief and anguish in his eyes.

"You won!" a student who had bet on me shouted. "You won!"

Jin Gang couldn't contain his delight. It was the best free entertainment he and the others could have asked for. Except, maybe, Liu Yinghong. "You didn't have to rough him up so badly, did you?" she chided me.

No one was happier than I. Bruised and bloodied, nearly missing a left ear, I'd restored a bit of face to the students by showing we weren't the puny little weaklings the newspapers made us out to be.

6

BREAKING

A WILD HORSE

WHEN FOUR NEW wagons arrived, the branch committee formed a wagon team led by Wang Lianfu. Asked if I wanted to join the team, I jumped at the chance.

Wang, a cigarette dangling from his mouth, was sitting on the kang when I walked into the wagon shed on my first day. The place was a mess—lumber, grain sacks, and tires strewn all over the floor. "Get your wagon ready," he said coolly.

"How?"

"Hitch up a team." His tiny eyes settled on me with the blank expression of a billy goat.

I'd never so much as touched a big wagon before and didn't know where to start. I'd have to swallow my pride and ask him to teach me. A stony reaction. "Go look at my wagon and figure it out. Nobody taught me, and I've managed okay."

Apparently it would have to be trial and error, and it took two weeks, with Lei Xia and Jin Gang's help, to finally get a team hitched up. They urged me to ask for a transfer. "After what you did to Wang Lianfu," Lei Xia said urgently, "it'd be a miracle if he didn't get even. Working for him is a big mistake."

What was I supposed to do, avoid him? People would think I was afraid. No, since I had agreed to take on the job, I'd stick it out. I'm a man of my word, always have been. Besides, what was there to be afraid of? Wang Lianfu was good at carrying heavy sacks and little else, as our fight had proved.

It nearly wore me out, but I managed to hitch four skittish horses to the wagon on one cold December day. Dressed only in a ragged sweatshirt, I was all lathered. Now the time had come to take the wagon out on its first run. But I had no sooner raised my whip than the silver-gray on the outside reared up, brushing its hind leg against the traces and causing the roan in the middle to lower its head and lurch forward, which jerked the traces taut. The silver-maned horse on the other side backed up in panic until its traces went slack and scraped the ground. Three horses pulling in three separate directions. As for the black shaft horse, its legs got tangled in the traces and it nearly fell, snorting and whinnying in protest. The team dragged the wagon aimlessly, inching closer and closer to the wall, and I was smack in the middle. Big trouble! I leapt off just before it hit.

"Fucking coward!" Wang Lianfu screamed, a cigarette dangling from his mouth as usual. He snatched the whip out of my hand and laid into the silver-gray. Each time the whip sang out, the horse whinnied pitifully and reared up, its mane flying, its hooves barely missing the eaves.

City folk never witness such things, and the curious students crowded round to gape. Wang was really feeling his oats as the whip in his hand cracked and whistled. The three horses up front squeezed together, got tangled up in the traces, and lost their footing. Then as they struggled to their feet, *crack*, the whip snapped in two. Wang stormed off angrily. "Lousy fucking whip!"

So ended my maiden trip on the wagon.

The next time I hitched up the team, I forgot to set the brake, and they were off and running before I was ready. Dragging an empty wagon was like running free for four powerful horses. The silver-gray bucked; the black shaft horse kicked the air and bared its teeth. By running like hell, I managed to climb aboard and rein them in, finally bringing the wagon to a halt. But the uncooperative shaft horse kept straining forward. So after unhitching the three horses up front and straightening out the tangled traces, I set the brake and let "Blackie" pull by himself until he was puffing from exhaustion. The powerful animal, a gift from Company Commander Wang, stood as tall as a man, and it usually took three of us to get him in line; he balked every time I tried to position him on the shaft. When we were moving, I avoided touching his tail, since that made him buck. And one more thing: He was always trying to nip me, even caught me on the thigh once.

The blood red sun was sinking beneath the horizon; the pure white snowscape was perfectly silent. Blackie's head bobbed up and down as he strained to pull the wagon with the brake set.

Local drivers were masters of the whip. They could split a horse's ear with a flick of the wrist and a crisp crack. I never measured up. No matter how hard I tried, my whip always landed harmlessly.

One morning I was practicing my technique against a wall as Wang Lianfu squatted in the doorway gnawing on a lamb bone, his cheeks puffed out. "How do you expect to drive a wagon if you can't even crack a whip?" he said with a mocking grin.

I ignored him.

"Got the guts to take them to the regiment for a meeting?"

"Sure." Something like that didn't take "guts," did it? I hitched up the team and drove to the company compound, but as I was turning around, the shaft horse shied and the stepladder, which I had somehow forgotten to secure, banged into his rear leg. That startled the other three horses, and the team staggered forward. Qi Shuzhen, a girl from Tianjin, screamed and ran into the company office.

By now the wagon was streaking for the open steppe, and I wasn't sure I could catch it. Quickly stepping out of my felt boots, I ran barefoot through the snow, slowly gaining ground until I caught up and jumped aboard. The horses were galloping along; the wagon was bouncing violently in concert with the movements of the shaft horse. I crawled up to the driver's seat and had barely gotten my hands on the brake when we lurched upward, as if a wheel had hit a rock (I later learned it was a fire ditch), and I was launched. The wind whistled past me for the several seconds it took to hit the snowy ground, and by then the wagon had rumbled past. Lei Xia rode up, tossed me my boots, and lit out after the wagon.

I hobbled back to the company compound, dizzy and hurting. Just my rotten luck. The worst fall I'd ever taken.

The squad and platoon leaders, all gussied up in new army over-coats, white gauze masks, and fur caps, made the trip to Regiment Headquarters in the bed of Wang Lianfu's wagon that day.

When I learned that my felt rug and traces had been lost in the bumpy ride, I was so mad, I couldn't see straight. If I'd had a sword, I'd have sliced Blackie in two; I lay on the kang dreaming up punishments for the damned beast.

Two days later Lei Xia told me that Wang Lianfu had informed the political instructor that in my first few days on the wagons I'd lost two whips and three halters and was responsible for a belly strap that had snapped. He wanted me replaced, complaining that I wasn't up to the job. This was the same man who went around saying that driving a wagon isn't as easy as it looks and that a top wagon master could earn a hundred yuan a trip. "It's no job for the fainthearted," he'd say with a spirited glint in his eye.

Lei Xia's news came as I was pumping myself up to break the black horse and it hit a nerve. I wasn't some scrawny girl Wang Lianfu could replace anytime he felt like it, and I stayed up all night writing to the branch committee to make sure they knew I was determined to stick it out and not be reassigned. I'd break that horse if it killed me.

I asked around for some helpful hints, which ran the gamut from ty-ing a noose around the animal's jaw or above his nose to pulling his ears and tying him up before beating him. Since he had been spooked twice, just seeing the wagon was enough to set him off: He'd prick up his ears as his neck tensed and his eyes widened. So I tied him to the wagon day and night to keep him in a state of constant panic.

"Get another horse," Lei Xia urged me. "Why put yourself through all this over an animal?" But his advice fell on deaf ears. By then I'd lost interest in other people's plans. I'd find a way to tame him on my own.

He was mean by nature, and when spooked his favorite trick was trying to flatten me against a wall; so I put blinders on him. And when he wouldn't obey my commands, I cinched the bridle so tightly over his nose, it would cut to the bone if he tried to work it loose.

I asked one of the shepherds to weave a whip that wouldn't unravel no matter how hard I cracked it. Then each time the horse panicked, I beat him mercilessly. Lei Xia helped me. Thick whips, thin whips, coarse homemade whips, sticks, leather belts—*smack smack smack*— Blackie got a taste of them all. It was midwinter, and I wore only a thin shirt, yet my forehead was dotted with sweat. He whinnied and he bucked, but I kept at it until at last he stuck his head under the wagon, pissed all over the ground, and just stood there—conquered.

It was the most exhausting work I'd ever done, and I went to bed that night without even washing up. As I drifted off, my head filled up with lessons I'd learned from my misadventures on the wagon: Set the brake, secure the stepladder, make sure the crupper doesn't touch their rumps . . . That night I slept like a log.

Breaking that horse became an obsession. My voice was raspy from screaming, I was light-headed and sore from all that frightful bouncing, my feet were swollen from being stepped on and kicked, and my arms were so tired from wielding the whip, I could barely hold my rice bowl.

"What's so great about driving a wagon?" Jin Gang asked when he noticed my preoccupation with the battle of wills between man and beast. "It's hard, dirty, dangerous work with a bunch of animals. And it could kill you one of these days!"

But danger is the essential ingredient of courage. In Beijing my heart raced whenever I saw a horse. Out here they were common-place—except for this one, which sometimes seemed possessed. If his hooves had ever found their mark, I'd be dead, but I stuck to it, keeping a tight grip on his halter and letting him vent his anger without hurting me. It gave me a rush. Safety lives at the heart of danger, like the calm at the center of a typhoon. As I lay sprawled across his back, hands wrapped around his neck, I smelled the odor of his wildness and felt the blood coursing beneath his hide.

But the time and energy spent breaking Blackie wasn't wasted, for I finally managed to hitch up my wagon with a full team of four horses, as intended. Oh, they still bolted once in a while, breaking something or other in the process; but if I couldn't get the wagon going, I simply took cover from the wind by climbing underneath it.

"Don't you realize you're just asking for trouble by staying in the wagon team?" Lei Xia said. "Wang Lianfu hasn't forgotten that beating."

I nodded, knowing there would be a fight sooner or later. I could see it in his eyes. But I couldn't stand by and watch him make life miserable for the students without doing something about it, could I? Besides, I didn't want all my hard work with the black horse to go down the drain, especially now that I was seeing results.

I ignored Lei Xia's warning and worked like a madman in order to be declared a "Five Good" trooper at the end of the year. That would please my mother. Every night I fed thirty-four horses, then watered them in the mornings. Wang Lianfu helped me pitch the hay at first but soon stopped showing up, since it was such hard work. Tightly packed to begin with, the hay was even heavier with all that snow, and I could lift only a little at once. In no time I was soaked to my underwear from sweat and melted snow.

But being declared a "Five Good" trooper would make it all worthwhile.

Meanwhile, Wang Lianfu, a squint in his eyes and a cigarette dangling from his mouth, listened raptly to Old Gigolo talk about getting into women's pants. A pall of smoke settled over the toasty room, from which laughter emerged from time to time. These "teachers" of ours never talked about anything except food, women, and profiteering.

As the new year approached, Wang's mood soured even more, and anything could set him off. The political instructor was about the only person spared his outbursts. Apparently, Wang's fiancée had threatened to break off their engagement if she didn't get a dowry, and he was an emotional wreck. He drank and stuffed himself with meat all night long, then slept all day. When he was suppose to take his wagon out he complained of a stomachache. But put a plateful of braised meat in front of him, and he could go through a double portion with no ill effects at all.

As I passed his room on my way back from feeding the horses one night I heard him say, "So what if they've spent ten years in school, what's it got them? They can't hold a candle to my forty-three fifty-seven." (At the time we were getting thirty yuan a month.)

"Lianfu, don't sell those students short. They can be a real pain in the ass. A slip of the tongue, and you'll never hear the end of it."

"I don't care. I expect an honest day's work from them."

"Lei Xia and Ma Bo are the worst of the lot."

Their voices grew softer.

It was 1969. The communications media were exhorting the students to present themselves to the workers, peasants, and soldiers for reeducation, which well served demobilized soldiers like Wang Lianfu, who still fancied themselves members of the "worker, peasant, soldier" contingent. They found fault with everything we did. They sneered as they appropriated our clothing. Sanctimoniously forbidding all contact between the sexes, they hung around the women's dorms. They stole the fruit, candy, and other luxuries our families sent, and more. Objections were met with "Wise up, and don't be so cocky! You're here to be reeducated!"

Nineteen-sixty-nine. If intellectuals were deemed to be "stinking old ninths," members of the lowest social caste, then we were "stinking old tenths," since we were even lower on the social ladder than the older intellectuals.

7

BLOOD

FEUD

THE MORNING OF January 7, 1970. Biting winds. The company commander ordered us to haul rocks down from the mountain. Wang Lianfu had another stomachache. I envied him: As soon as the weather turned blustery he headed straight for bed and stayed there. That way he didn't have to suffer from the cold, and his horses could take it easy.

Old Gigolo's wagon was the first out, followed a half hour later by mine, since I still hadn't gotten the knack of hitching up my team. He was on his way back by the time I arrived, so I loaded up quickly and started down the mountain at top speed, in hopes of catching him before he reached camp.

Sweat glistened on the broad, muscular flanks of the black horse, while the other three pulled so hard, the traces were taut as bows, and we sped silently down the snow-covered road. We negotiated a mountain pass and were about to ford the river when I caught a glimpse of Old Gigolo's wagon up ahead. Glaring at the team, I clutched my whip tightly, just waiting to lay into the first horse that slackened off.

I had shortened the distance between us to half a mile or so when the wagon shuddered as if it had hit a wall, launching me a couple of feet into the air and onto the rocks in the wagon bed. Unsure of what had happened, I thought I heard the hissing of a tire, and by the time I reined in the horses and stopped, we were about a hundred feet past whatever it was we'd hit. I climbed down. One of the tires was flat as a pancake, which meant I'd have to unload the rocks by the roadside and head back empty.

It was dark by the time I reached camp. "Where's your load?" Old Gigolo asked me. I told him what had happened, then unhitched the horses and rushed over to the office to make my report. The PI had gone to a meeting at Division Headquarters. While I was explaining to Company Commander Wang what had happened, the door flew open, shielding me behind it. "Ma Bo blew out another tire!" Wang Lianfu bellowed. "I don't suppose he told you yet. Said it was a rock, the fucking liar! You couldn't cut one of those tires with a goddamned knife!"

"Bullshit!" I stepped out from behind the door, cut to the quick by his outburst. He was stunned to find me there. "Hmph," he grunted in a lowered voice. "One day the traces snap, the next day it's a broken axle. This time a punctured tire. Who knows what's next? You call that driving a fucking wagon?" He stormed off angrily. I was tongue-tied. I'd frozen my ass off that day just so I could come home and have that shitty little malingerer snitch on me.

Company Commander Wang patted me on the shoulder. "Go get something to eat," he said. "We'll talk about this later. And don't worry. We can tell if it was a rock. The authorities are interested only in the facts."

In the mess hall I learned that Wang Lianfu had picked up my dinner that night—five stuffed buns—but when I got to my quarters, no dinner. It didn't take a genius to guess its fate in the hands of Wang Lianfu, who was always on the prowl for a meaty snack. So I dragged myself back to the mess hall and scrounged three cold steamed buns and some leftover potatoes, which I dunked in boiled water, just to get some hot food in my belly before turning in.

Back in the dark room I tossed and turned, but couldn't sleep. In my agitated mood, I nearly bit through my lip. Is this what we were here for, to be fucked over by these people? I rushed around feeding and watering the horses, sweeping out the room, and cleaning out the stove just like an old-time apprentice—overworked and harassed to boot. Wang Lianfu, on the other hand, the old "master," while reluctant to pass on his skills, was only too happy to call me an asshole. I put up with it in order to become a decent wagon master, earn a little respect for students generally, and make a contribution.

But now, as if falsely accusing me of sabotage weren't enough, Wang Lianfu had the gall to steal my dinner. I shook with anger. I'd had all I could take from him. I'd be a slimy maggot, a no-good bastard, a piece of shit, if I let it go on any longer. I had been too tractable and had let myself get all tangled up in the bonds of "reeducation." Now it was time to put him on notice that future attacks would be met with swift retaliation.

Most students wouldn't dare translate their anger into words or action, but I psyched myself up by recalling some of the loathsome things he'd done:

One night he went to Second Platoon, where he stretched out on one of the bed mats and bragged to the girls about his strength and terrific appetite. At ten o'clock he was still at it, and Li Xiaohua, who wanted to turn in, tried to get him to leave. That pissed him off. He called her a witch. "You should talk," she chided him. "Hanging around a women's dorm in the middle of the night and refusing to leave." That made him so mad, he picked up a pole and threatened her with it. When Liu Yinghong and some other girls rushed up to stop him, he filled the air with the vilest epithets in his repertoire, calling Xiaohua a slut, a soldier's whore, and a rotten piece of goods. She was in tears, tears of anger.

A few days earlier he fought with the kitchen help, accusing them of skimping on his portion and not giving him the meat his diet required. His tendons nearly popped out of his neck when the kitchen squad leader smiled and said, "We barely have enough for the two squads that haven't eaten yet." *Smack!* He slapped the man. "You dumb motherfucker! Make more."

Jin Gang once helped him slaughter a sheep, and when one of the animal's legs got loose and kicked him, he railed, "Are you some kind of asshole or just plain stupid? If you can't even hold a sheep's leg, your dad sure wasted a hard-on making you!" He kicked Jin Gang viciously.

These incidents were like ticking bombs in my mind. I had to stop thinking about them. The time had come to warn him. If he raised a hand, I'd be on him like an avalanche. Right after breakfast tomorrow. You brought it on yourself, Wang. We students would really be up shit creek if we settled for your brand of "reeducation."

A fight seemed inevitable. I knew that the students couldn't wait to see him get his just deserts and that even Company Commander Wang would be pleased. But I also knew that I was setting out alone on a path of danger and uncertainty, and that Mother would be unhappy if she knew what I was up to. She had told me to stay out of fights, but this time what else could I do? I was confused and disheartened. What were we guilty of? Why were we being singled out for abuse? It was time to act. If standing up to Wang was wrong, I'd accept the consequences in the name of all students in the company.

Breakfast time, January 8, 1970. I was feverish, my heart raced, my teeth chattered from nervous excitement, and the blood surged through my veins. Wang Lianfu was squatting beside the rice barrel, intently slurping his noodles. Holding the contents back with his spoon, he poured the liquid onto the floor, leaving behind half a spoonful of noodles and some slices of meat.

Everyone was watching when I confronted him: "Why did you take my dinner last night?"

He was immediately on the defensive. "I didn't."

"Liar."

"Who'd want your goddamned dinner?" His tiny eyes were frozen in a rounded glare.

"You, that's who." I was sure the kitchen crew hadn't lied.

"I'll take your old lady's cunt if I feel like it!"

"I'll take *your* old lady's cunt!"

"Fuck you!" he thundered as he stood up. He was livid, and his tiny eyes blazed.

"Fuck you too!" I accepted the challenge.

"Motherfucker!" he screeched as he landed a right cross on my jaw.

I staggered backwards. Explosions went off inside my head and chest. Hatred penetrated the marrow of my bones. I charged.

"Goddamned dog turd, I'll tear you limb from limb!" I looked into his hate-filled eyes as he grabbed a hatchet from beside the stove. Scooping up a metal bucket half-filled with noodles, I swung at his head, splashing hot soup all over him. Then, before he could get his bearings, I swung it again and heard it clang against his head. As soup clouded his vision, I grabbed him in a headlock, hooked his leg, and flipped him to the ground. Then I jumped on him and wrenched the hatchet out of his hand.

That was when Old Gigolo and another demobilized solder, Ma Dashan, from the wagon team, came and pulled me off, giving Wang Lianfu a chance to roar to his feet, pick up the hatchet again, and charge me. My arms were pinned so tightly, I couldn't move. Wang raised the hatchet. "Let me go, damn it!" I shouted, struggling to get free.

At that critical moment Lei Xia rushed up and snatched the hatchet out of Wang's hand, then screamed at Old Gigolo and Ma Dashan, "Lived long enough, have you?"

I broke free, ran up, and kicked Wang back down to the floor, then pinned him. His face was twitching madly. He tried to gouge out my eyes, choke me, or grab hold of my pecker—lucky for me I was wearing thick leather pants. Then he tried to bite my hand, but again he failed. In fact, as his right hand brushed past my mouth, I bit *his* thumb. He screamed in pain, which only made me bite down harder, and I didn't stop until I'd taken a chunk out of it.

Steam that had built up for a month blew like a volcano. My fists flew furiously, ripping screams from between his clenched teeth as he tried to protect his head with his hands. Wanting to do more than just pound him with my fists, I looked around for something else to use. There beside me was a dark bottle filled with insect repellent. I scooped it up and aimed it at his head. "Don't, Ma Bo!" he cried out fearfully, his face paling, "don't do it!" Luckily for him, I flung it so hard, it sailed past him, missing his head. Summoning all his strength, he knocked me down, roared like a wild animal, and threw himself on top of me.

He tried to choke me, but I wasn't worried, since Lei Xia and I had practiced getting out of this hold dozens of times. Two quick feints, a sudden arching motion, and I was straddling him.

Since fists were useless at that distance, I let go and jumped to my feet. He followed and reached out to grab a stick, but by then I was thumping him so hard, I had him backed into a corner, where I really let loose. He buried his head in his arms. There was no fight left in him.

Company Commander Wang walked in just then, and when Wang Lianfu saw him he crumpled to the floor. I kicked him. "Get up, you faker!" Not a sound. I slapped him. Still no sound. Here was a man who boasted he could lift two hundred pounds and take on three men at a time lying crumpled on the floor like a sack of potatoes, his eyes closed. Stray noodles and flecks of cabbage decorated his hair and neck.

I still wasn't finished, even though my knuckles felt as if they were on fire. It took two people to drag me away. By then nearly the whole company had rushed over to see, and the Tianjin student Liu Fulai giggled as he patted me on the shoulder. "Good for you," he squealed. "Amazing." Jin Gang handed me a towel and watched reverentially as I wiped my bloody face.

Company Commander Wang called me outside to find out what was going on. "It was Wang Lianfu's fault. He started the shouting match and threw the first punch. And he came at me with a hatchet. He had no right to steal my dinner. Or to say I lied about how my tire got punctured. Is that what reeducation means, taking shit from people like him?"

Company Commander Wang patiently tried to get me to promise I'd stop fighting. I agreed on the condition that if Wang Lianfu started anything, I'd protect myself any way I had to.

"BE CAREFUL, Ma Bo. Someone as mean as Wang Lianfu is sure to want revenge," Li Xiaohua warned me.

At dinnertime the kitchen-squad leader filled my bowl until it looked like a little mountain. Later that night I felt light-headed, and my knuckles throbbed—Wang Lianfu's head was hard as a rock. Although it had lasted only a few minutes, the fight had worn me out, so I went to bed earlier than usual and lay there, my ears ringing and my jaw numb. As always after I fought, I was feverish.

"Bed so early?" Lei Xia asked as he walked into my room.

"I'm so tired, I can't stand."

"That was some leg sweep," he said enviously, with a smile.

Lei Xia hadn't changed a bit. Back in the spring of 1968, when I was supposed to fight someone named Liu Ming, Lei Xia took him on first so I could see if he was any good, and he paid for his loyalty by being knocked down several times.

I squeezed his hand with heartfelt gratitude.

On his way out he said softly, "When Wang Lianfu was being patched up by the medic, he vowed, 'It's not over between us. There isn't room in Company Seven for Ma Bo and me!' Be careful."

My blood ran, but not as vigorously as before. I had taken a hell of a punch, better than any I'd landed, and my temples ached when I chewed. I probably lost a hundred ccs of blood from where the hatchet must have glanced off my head, while he'd lost hardly any at all. Feeling more like the loser than the winner, I fell asleep making plans for the rematch.

Early the next morning I put on a pair of lined trousers and cloth sandals. Satisfied that I was wearing the right clothes for the situation, I did some limbering-up exercises, then punched myself lightly in the face a couple of times. A good night's sleep had put me back in peak fighting condition.

It was about seven o'clock, and the sky was turning light when I kicked open Wang Lianfu's door. He was in bed smoking a cigarette, his head wrapped in gauze. He sat up quickly.

"Wang Lianfu, are you planning on getting even?" I demanded.

"No," he replied hoarsely.

"Don't bullshit me." I picked a wagon slat up off the floor and jumped onto the kang. His hand slid under the pillow and emerged holding a pair of shears. "You must have a death wish!" he hissed.

I brought the slat down hard. He jumped up, dressed only in a pair of underpants, and growled, "You motherfucker, this time only one of us leaves here alive!" The shears came at me, light glinting off the blades.

I rained blows down on his head, his face, his neck, his shoulders, his arms, and his hands, quickly putting him on the defensive. He jumped off the kang. I followed. Mindful of the fact that he needed to connect only once with those shears, I pounded him with the slat to keep him from taking the offensive.

"All right, let's see how your blood looks on my kang!" He lashed out with the shears, and before I knew it he was holding the other end of my slat. I grabbed his wrist and tried to flip him, but it didn't work. The shears were getting closer and closer. Since he was nearly naked, I couldn't get a grip on him, so I twisted and jerked and tugged to keep him off balance and make it impossible for him to stab me.

As we grappled in the narrow space beside the kang, the shears hit my hand once, making a small gash. Gasping for breath, we clinched so tightly that we could land only an occasional glancing blow. Finally I grabbed his weapon hand. Realizing the gravity of his predicament, he tried to kick me in the groin but was wide of the mark.

Just then Lei Xia ran in and tore the weapon out of Wang's hand. I picked up the slat and started beating the shit out of him. The complexion of the fight had changed dramatically. He jumped onto the kang in panic. I followed. He backed into a corner and frantically threw his comforter over his head to ward off the blows. I launched another frenzied attack, but this time he'd had enough. "Don't hit me, Ma Bo!" he pleaded from under the bedding. "No more. We're even. It's finished."

Enough for him, maybe, but not for me. Finally Lei Xia stopped me. "Okay, he's had enough."

I was dragged outside, the sound of his mumbles and sobs in my ears: ". . . can't stay in Company Seven! Oh . . . sprained my back . . . motherfucker, all bloody . . ."

At noon snowflakes swirled in the air. Wang Lianfu was sprawled on the bed of Old Gigolo's wagon under three blankets, his eyes clamped shut. They were taking him to the regimental hospital.

Company Commander Wang sent for me. Stroking his beard, he

said sympathetically, "Why couldn't you leave well enough alone? This time you really screwed up." I was ordered to write a self-criticism.

But first I wanted to write a brief note to Lei Xia:

Dear Lei Xia:

When the chips were down you stood firm, and for that I'm grateful. Friendships born in the heat of battle are the true ones. I'm proud to call you a friend. Our friendship, forged in a bloody struggle, will last forever.

Ma Bo

January 10, 1970

As I said earlier, society is too complex for me. In order to guard against retribution by Wang Lianfu, I made a pair of knives out of his shears and kept them under my bed mat, just in case.

8

FORTIFIED

DEFENSES

P OLITICAL INSTRUCTOR SHEN was fit to be tied when he heard about my fight with Wang Lianfu. He had no sooner returned from a meeting at Division Headquarters than he was screaming at Company Commander Wang for not implementing emergency measures. A nasty argument ensued.

A few days later Company Commander Wang was transferred to a "Mao Zedong Thought Support" unit in Baochang. I remember his departure as if it were yesterday: I fetched his chestnut colt from the stable, watered it, and led it over to Company Headquarters. Call that buttering him up if you want, I don't care, but I saw it as a chance to express my gratitude for his having sided with me over the fight.

"Ma Bo," he said, "work hard, study hard, and be as self-critical as possible. And no more flying off the handle."

I nodded. "I'll give them whatever they want, Commander."

He had always gotten along with his subordinates far better than the PI had. More obliging and less officious. Now that he was gone, I was losing a backer, and I wished he could have stayed.

Not long after the company commander left, the PI called everybody together to brief us on political work and summarize a report entitled "Everything Revolves around the Red Sun" [Chairman Mao] by the Commissar of the Beijing Military District.

As the meeting neared its end I stood up to criticize myself for giving Wang Lianfu a second beating. Political Instructor Shen stared at me without betraying any emotion, but when I finished he said, "Fighting is a perennial problem in this company, one we can't seem to solve. This latest fight was the worse yet, and stern measures are called for." His bloodshot eyes were glued to me.

Blame Wang Lianfu, I was thinking, not me. I only went back the second time because he threatened to get even. His behavior was worse than mine and should have been dealt with. It's as simple as that. Obviously I'd wasted my breath by being self-critical.

ONE DAY THE PI ordered a bunch of us Beijing students to fill out some forms, and in the blank reserved for background I wrote "Revolutionary Cadre." He exploded: "What do you mean, revolutionary cadre? Your father's background. Put that down!" I looked at him, a gloating, petty man, and saw what he was up to. "Your parents were investigated after the Cultural Revolution, so what gives you the right to say 'revolutionary cadre'?"

I'd had bad feelings about Political Instructor Shen since hearing of his activities in a "Mao Zedong Thought Support" unit in Taiyuan, where his "support" included swelling a local girl's belly. He was only a company-level political instructor (cadre rank nineteen), but he swaggered around, bulging paunch in front, hands clasped behind him, like a regiment commander. He was a master at chewing people out, an addiction that needed constant feeding. Nothing escaped his attention: the way we wore our caps, the way we slurped our food, even the way we took a leak in the backyard. He was also a notorious junk collector who never went out walking without picking up every rag, remnant of felt, bottle, or tin can he saw and taking it home with him.

I expected things to improve after the fight. They didn't. I had struck a blow for all students, only to realize that some of them held me in contempt *because* of my fighting. Naturally, it was worse with the demobilized soldiers. Things were looking so bad that I knew I had to set up a positive agenda. First, I would throw myself into my work to make up for my blunders and eliminate any bad influence it might have had on others. Second, I'd improve my relations with the masses, particularly people like Old Gigolo and Xu Zuo. Third, I'd get as close as possible to Liu Yinghong, since she was on good terms with the PI and could provide me with a measure of safety.

Getting friendly with Old Gigolo would be easy. All I had to do was sing the praises of his horses and snigger when he boasted about all the women he'd laid. But Xu Zuo was a different matter altogether. He rebuffed all my attempts to rekindle our friendship, so I stopped trying.

"How do people feel about my fighting?" I asked Lei Xia.

"They don't like it. They say you've got a mean streak."

A mean streak? I had no choice but to fight. "Aren't you afraid to be seen with me, since I beat up one of the PI's pets?"

He smiled and punched me playfully. "Don't needle me like that. I never turn my back on a friend, and I hate people who do."

Lei Xia's bravado was legendary. By helping me get even with Wang Lianfu, he had offended the PI and all the demobilized soldiers, who really ran things. I had nothing to fear with loyal friends like that around.

Then a letter arrived from my sister. Things were getting worse at home. Father, accused of treachery, was under detention, and Mother was being attacked from all quarters. Since I kept this news to myself, I was surprised when Lei Xia dropped by a few days later to inform me that my father was a traitor and that my mother's party membership was being called bogus; the campaign against her as author of a poisonous novel was gearing up. He said one of my Beijing relatives had written him.

I didn't want to believe this startling news, but what could I do? People's attitudes toward me had always been linked to my folks. When my father was an ordinary citizen they treated me one way, and after he became a vice minister they treated me quite differently. When my parents were high-ranking officials at the Central Committee level, people respected me and were always there if I needed something. But now that my folks had fallen out of favor, there was no longer any reason to butter me up.

At first Political Instructor Shen was just another crummy little bureaucrat to me, since my father's rank was the equal of an army commander. But now that my father was a traitor, the PI could have a field day with me. Panic and depression set in.

Father had joined the party in 1930; Mother, six years later. Now, after a lifetime of revolutionary work, they were a traitor and a bogus party member.

Following the 1969 general criticism, not only did I fail to become a "Five Good" trooper, I didn't even receive a basic commendation. Everyone else in the company did, everyone but Lei Xia and me. That was my reward for working like a slave in the wagon team. How could I ever face my mother?

Meanwhile I maintained close ties with Liu Yinghong, always taking my troubles to her. She was friendly, apparently unconcerned that I was awaiting punishment for fighting. She even washed my soiled bedding. Yinghong was a typical self-sacrificing woman. A fire always roared in the stove in her place, which she kept clean and well supplied. She even patched other people's clothes with her own. She treated everyone the same — great.

Shortly after she arrived on the steppes, her attention was drawn to a lone old Mongol woman who dressed in rags and was bothered by a bad stomach. She immediately wrote home to have her family send rice, with which she made congee for the woman. She also gave her the fourteen feet of fabric and five pounds of fluffed cotton she'd planned to use for a lined jacket for herself. Eating rice congee for the first time in her life, the woman sobbed in gratitude, and Yinghong's stock soared as word of what she had done spread.

Even the most progressive, most exemplary of her peers deferred to her. At the Seventh Battalion Activists Congress she was elected by acclamation to represent the division at the Inner Mongolian Production Corps Activists Congress to study the works of Chairman Mao. Printed copies of her address were distributed to all regiments.

She was not, however, particularly attractive. Dark-skinned, she had tiny eyes set in a large face, a thick waist, and stubby limbs. Unlike so many of her progressive peers, she avoided larding her speech with quotes from *People's Daily* and heroic exhortations. She was, in fact, her own worst critic, frequently given to publicizing what she considered her dark side: vanity, borderline hedonism, timidity, and selfishness. She always chose the dirtiest, most exhausting jobs for herself; she never fought over tools and worked unstintingly.

I invariably came away from one of our visits feeling ashamed. Compared to the natural, pure, selfless, and unpretentious Liu Ying-hong, I was little more than garbage. She was highly regarded by the masses, favored by those in charge, and spared from attacks by Political Instructor Shen.

9

SYMPATHY

ONE NIGHT I went to ask Liu Yinghong to mend some pants for me, but she wasn't in. Wei Xiaoli, who was alone in the room, stared at me wide-eyed. This daughter of a provincial first secretary piqued my curiosity, so I sat on the edge of the kang and asked her, "How did you get here?"

"My sister and I came on our own. But we had to cool our heels for four months at Corps Headquarters and got permission to come only after writing Vice Chairman Lin and Premier Zhou."

"Why come here?"

"To fight, naturally."

"Why aren't you and your sister in the same company?"

"How much fun would that be?"

Wei Xiaoli could not be considered pretty, with her oval face, tiny nose, and stumpy neck, but that doesn't mean she was ugly. There was something elegant about her neat features, her delicate lips in particular. Her eyes were clear, and it was immediately obvious that there was nothing hidden behind them. You didn't have to be on your guard with someone like her.

"Did you really fight Wang Lianfu over some stuffed buns?" she asked, avoiding my eyes.

"No. It had nothing to do with stuffed buns. There's bad blood between the students and the demobilized soldiers from Shanxi, who have taken over every position of authority. They think they're better than everybody else and are always taking advantage of the students. Wang Lianfu's the worst of the lot. The stuffed buns were just the spark that set it off."

I also avoided *her* eyes, as she concentrated on the Chairman Mao quotation pasted on the wall. "Why did *you* come here?"

"To fight. If there's war between China and the Soviet Union, this will be the front line."

"Why not go to Vietnam?" She kept her eyes on the quotation.

"I tried crossing the border three times in April of '67. I made it twice. But they sent me back, and I never got to fight."

"We were planning to go to Vietnam, too."

Political Instructor Shen walked in just then, his paunch covered by a brand-new army overcoat. He was looking for Liu Yinghong, but when he saw it was us he turned and walked out.

"My pants are torn. Would you mend them for me?"

She nodded and took them without a word.

Three days later I returned to fetch my pants. The stitches ran all over the place where she had sewn on a couple of green patches. It was a terrible, unfeminine job, but at least they'd hold up.

Xiaoli, who came to the Company in September of '69, wasn't much of a talker. After her father was beaten to death in 1967, his abdomen was split open and stuffed with big-character posters before the body was sent to the crematorium. Xiaoli's home was ransacked, and the family was evicted from the secretariat compound; all seven surviving family members were then crowded into an apartment so small that the kids slept on the table or in a trunk.

Words fail me when I try to describe what it was like to see her all alone on the snow-covered steppe. I always believed that children of senior officials were leaves from the same tree. She and I didn't meet often, but I considered her a friend. One day some people were talking about her when I entered the mess hall.

"She's worthless. It takes her forever to draw half a bucket of water from the well."

"She can't even peel an onion. She's worse than worthless."

"What do you expect from a pampered brat like that?"

I had seen her out in the snow with a pickax, trying but not succeeding to dent the icy ground, which anyone else could have managed with a few well-placed swings. Yet she stuck to it, even after her hands were blistered and raw. She was no pampered brat.

"Was her father one of those anti-Maoists who took the capitalist road?"

"Yes," the company clerk said. "Her introduction letter made that clear. But his offspring are salvageable through reeducation."

I couldn't keep quiet any longer. "I've heard soldiers say there were no problems in his past and that he wasn't as bad as his accusers say."

They glanced at me but said nothing.

It was the first time in my life I'd come to the defense of a child of high-ranking officials, most of whom truly are spoiled brats. But like the children of bureaucrats and landlords who joined the revolution decades earlier, some of those children abandoned lives of leisure to search for truth and turn their energies to the well-being of the common folk. There are always people who gloat when officials fall from grace and would stone their children in a well if they had the chance. I see no honor in that.

Rumors about my fighting had spread by now: I had threatened a poor and lower-middle-class herdsman with a knife; I had sicced a dog on a PLA soldier (anyone in an army overcoat suddenly became a PLA soldier); and I was a member of the counterrevolutionary Capitol United Action Front who had skipped to Inner Mongolia when it got too hot for me in Beijing.

It was my background. My mother sealed my fate the day she became a writer. People from literary families were among society's foulest outcasts, and in the corps they topped the commanders' shit lists. Revolutionary soldiers hate cultured people, writers especially, so naturally they had no use for me.

Over the spring holiday of 1969, I wrote to Liu Yinghong to thank her for her help, for not avoiding me, for lending me her prestige, and for raising my stature in the eyes of others. I signed off by asking her to look after Wei Xiaoli, contending that she shouldn't have to suffer because of her father.

Xiaoli eventually saw the letter and wept when she read it.

10

OPEN-DOOR PARTY
RECTIFICATION

IN LATE JANUARY 1970, an open-door party rectification took the Forty-first Regiment by storm. Work was halted so we could discuss directives read to us with somber devotion by Political Instructor Shen. As party representative, he welcomed criticism of the leaders, promising no reprisals. He smiled. "You can begin with me, your political instructor. If I make any of you wear tight shoes for what you say, you can do the same to me." His gaze calmly swept the audience; sincerity oozed from his pores.

In the toasty interior of one of the sod huts housing Company Seven, sixty or seventy students hotly debated this remarkable turn of events.

"An open-door party rectification is a great idea. We can avoid getting engulfed in the unhealthy trends and evil practices of the corps inner circle."

"If any party committee ever needed rectification, it's ours. Talk about problems . . ."

"But we mustn't settle for cosmetic changes."

The boys proceeded cautiously, but not the girls.

"They keep sending up inflated reports. Everyone knows we didn't meet our production quotas, but they reported bumper crops!"

"The PI has no respect for the indigenous Mongols. When someone from Company Four borrowed his horse without telling him, he told our groom, 'Next time you get your hands on one of their horses, ride it till it drops. I'll take the heat!' What kind of talk is that from a political instructor?"

"How come a peasant has to pay twenty yuan for a wagonload of cowchips, but the PI gets it for free?"

"How come he gets to keep the company transistor radio in his house?"

"He appropriated Daoerji's best horse and gave it to Director Li of the Regimental Political Section. Is that what you call proletarian behavior?"

Even Lei Xia fired a salvo:

"The PI turned a blind eye to the appropriation of our loot by some demobilized soldiers, and that pissed me off. He makes out like a bandit. Look at the stuff that winds up in his house. And not all junk, either, but even rugs and furniture. Doesn't he care how that looks?"

Unconcerned about whether or not the PI heard him, he continued after clearing his throat: "And that's not all. Since nobody's assigned housecleaning duties, we're forced to live like pigs. Until the brass comes, that is. Then we have to drop everything for inspection. Everything has to be just right. We can't even sit on our kangs until the VIPs are gone."

He was on a roll, speaking at the top of his voice. Just then a shadow passed beneath the window, and everyone looked over nervously, afraid that the PI might come barging in.

Now it was Liu Yinghong's turn. Wrapping her arms around her knees, she leaned back and said softly, "I think the political instructor is superficial and careless. If anybody does something wrong, instead of trying to reeducate him, he flies off the handle and makes a big show of his authority. He's not above getting physical, either. If there's sugar or steamed buns missing from the mess hall, he organizes a search of the students' quarters. Of course he never listens to us. What he says, goes. Like that well we dug in the vegetable garden last summer. Everyone said it was too close to the old one, and we should dig farther away. But no, he had to have his way. We wound up with so little water, we had to dig a third one."

Progressive members of the company were on good terms with the leaders and wouldn't dream of criticizing them in front of others, at least most wouldn't. Liu Yinghong was the exception: She always spoke her mind.

The recorder was scribbling like mad.

Most of the other students had bones to pick with various party members.

"Party members don't act in accordance with Chairman Mao's standards of party membership."

"Medical Officer Wang has two professional standards, one for male patients and another for females. He either dismisses the men's complaints or gives them minimal treatment, but he fawns all over the females and gives them the best medication."

"Jiang Baofu [Squad One commander] loves to tell dirty jokes to the male students, but he's all smiles around the girls. He's always boasting about how he did it to his old lady the first time, and you can tell when he's horny by the way he cuddles the guys in bed. He's a selfish, manipulative schemer who never pays his debts. And boy, does he have sticky fingers! He walks off with socks, underpants, soap, handkerchiefs . . . takes our biggest Chairman Mao badges and sells them to the herdsmen. He also snoops through our stuff and reads our diaries and letters, then sends up bogus reports."

"All Wang Lianfu knows how to do is chew us out, like a tin-horn dictator. Banging heads is a way of life with him, and the wagon team is his personal fiefdom. He never attends study sessions and works only when he feels like it. All kinds of public property—jackets, sheepskin blankets, rugs, boots, boxes, you name it—winds up in his hands. His work is sloppy and he spends half his time on sick call. But there's always a pot of meat on the stove—at public expense, naturally—and he admits he's in the wagon team mainly because it's so profitable."

67

BLOOD RED SUNSET

In their naïveté the students frequently saw only one side of an issue, but there was no denying the courage it took to criticize their superiors, instead of kissing up to them as some did. Yet our rectification schedule was a farce. We spent two weeks studying documents, improving ideological purity, and stuff like that, then were alloted two half-day sessions to criticize the party branch committee. It was over almost before it began, so Lei Xia and Liu Yinghong decided to write a protest letter.

Lei Xia's draft met with everyone's approval, even that of Qi Shuzhen, who admired his sincerity and admitted that his points were well taken. That was very significant for someone so hell-bent on joining the party that she took the PI's side 99 percent of the time. Every couple of days she reported on her own ideological progress in order to cozy up to the organization.

On the day the letter was to be delivered, Liu Yinghong and Lei Xia walked staunchly into the company office, where Political Instructor Shen merely glanced at them through his cigarette smoke. After declining Medical Officer Wang's invitation to sit down, Lei Xia read the letter in a clear, strong voice, standing stiffly at attention. When he finished he handed it to the PI like an ambassador presenting his credentials.

Shen snorted to show his displeasure as he accepted it.

Meanwhile, the rest of us put together an "out with the old, in with the new" list, demanding that Wang Lianfu and Jiang Baofu be ousted and that Liu Yinghong be admitted into the party.

The demobilized soldiers could barely contain their rage over this development, and poor Political Instructor Shen never dreamed that his little students would turn on him with such ferocity; the campaign was barely under way when he took to his bed with what seemed to be apoplexy. Summoning the party members to his sickbed, he put his experience from the 1957 antirightist campaign to good use by assigning the demobilized soldiers to observe and report on our activities. They would bide their time until the snake was lured from its hole, then strike.

His minions sprang into action, recording in their notebooks every expression of dissatisfaction with the company command, even enlisting the help of progressive students, telling them to keep their eyes peeled for anything out of the ordinary. To the girls' platoon they revealed that some people had muddied the water during the party rectification to catch their own fish and were joining forces to smash the party committee.

Qi Shuzhen, in her quest to join the party, was a perfect little secret agent, putting her ear to the cracks in doors to eavesdrop, then reporting what she heard.

When finally it came time to sum up the campaign, Political Instructor Shen delivered a forty-five-minute postmortem, in which he devoted forty minutes to accomplishments and five to defects. He then pointed out that Company Seven was infected with the poison of anarchy, mentioning Lei Xia and Liu Yinghong by name. They were called on the carpet for anarchistic tendencies—circumventing the standard organization procedures for submitting criticisms. He announced that Qi Shuzhen would replace Liu Yinghong as leader of the Second Platoon.

We couldn't believe it. Our small, out-of-the-way company quickly became the locus of a campaign against anarchy. Our blackboard displayed the following slogan in red chalk:

Strengthen Centralized Party Leadership!

Beneath it, in white chalk:

Down with Anarchy!

The fervor of party rectification was reduced to a hush. We could only swallow our rage as we watched the three-week campaign grind to a halt.

Things gradually returned to normal: There were no changes in the ranks of party members; the PI continued to swagger around, proudly preceded by his paunch. A large Mongolian rug was still spread across the head of his kang; a red cabinet inlaid with Mongol designs still rested beside it. The Red Lantern transistor radio, which had cost the company 150 yuan, remained on his table so he and his family could get the latest news and listen to their beloved Shanxi folk songs.

11

LEI XIA STRIKES
A BLOW FOR CLEAR
THINKING

AFTER THE RECTIFICATION campaign I asked Wei Xiaoli what criticisms her squad had made.

"Check with headquarters!" she snapped, walking off in a huff.

She had been avoiding me ever since our last conversation, and I wondered why. Was I a backward element because I'd "fought over some stuffed buns"? Was I too ugly for her? Seeing nothing in her eyes that might help me understand her aversion, I thought back to that day when the PI had walked in on us. Maybe he had warned her about me afterward. And of course there were the demobilized soldiers, who never had anything good to say about me. I desperately wanted her to know what I was really like and hoped she would stop believing those bastards. So I decided to write her a letter. I didn't want her to assume that I had any ulterior motives; I would never take advantage of a weak, abused, unhappy girl like that. I felt sorry for her, in fact.

I decided to reveal everything I'd done from the beginning of the Cultural Revolution up to the time I came to the steppes so she could get a clear picture of my "problem." Tense and feverish, I sat down and began to write, as carefully and neatly as I could manage, not even stopping to go to work. I labored over each word, racking my brain to get it just right. I wanted to be sincere without sounding vulgar. For days I did nothing but write, obsessed with the need to translate my sympathy into words, a gift she could treasure always. I must have rewritten the thing at least ten times, but still I wasn't satisfied.

There is more to me than mean looks, a belligerent attitude, and the ability to draw a knife across a sheep's throat, which is why my need to be liked and understood was stronger than ever after the fight with Wang Lianfu. "A bird sings to get a friendly response." No wonder thoughts of Xiaoli popped into my head with increasing frequency. I was on pins and needles if I didn't see her for two or three days; then a brief glance was enough to ease my anxieties. In the mess hall I kept my eyes glued to the window until she walked by, then slipped out to "accidentally" meet her on the road.

But she would just lower her head and walk on.

I thought of nothing but her. I'd had crushes before, some quite fanciful and lustful, but never this powerful. I tried to control my feelings, but emotional buds were already sprouting from the branches of sympathy. Of course, I wouldn't say so at the time, and I was even ashamed of my feelings.

Downy snowflakes fluttered in the air. I could hear their song and smell the redolent dry grass where they landed. How could one girl light up the world like that? Life was wonderful; life had meaning. Life, no matter how bitter, won out over the sweet call of death. I was in the grip of a mysterious emotion. Sweetness all around: the huts, the stable, threshing machines, even frozen cabbage. It filled my head.

One February day in 1970, right after breakfast. I was on my way out to feed the horses when Lei Xia slipped into my room and shut the door behind him. Something was up.

"Big trouble," he said gravely. "The PI is forcing me to write a self-criticism and admit to forming a conspiracy. Regimental Commissar Chen announced at the party rectification summing-up session that Company Seven was the scene of a political incident. How can those motherfuckers call a simple protest letter a political incident? And that's not all. Liu Yinghong has been replaced as representative to the Corps Congress."

Rumors had been swirling for some time, but I'd been so caught up in writing to Wei Xiaoli that I'd ignored them.

Lei Xia paused, then looked straight at me and said, "The way things are now, I'd appreciate it if you wouldn't send Wei Xiaoli that letter. They're saying that weapons were involved, and I'm going to try to talk to Political Instructor Shen. You can send it after I've cleared things up with him, okay?"

So, he'd been reading my letter to Wei Xiaoli! That was the first unhappy thought that flashed through my mind. But given the circumstances and Shen's mean streak, how could I refuse my friend's request?

"Okay, I'll hold off for now."

"Great!" He gave me a friendly pat on the shoulder. "Be careful of old Shen. He's out to get us. Watch your step, and if you take my advice, you won't ever send that letter to Wei Xiaoli. After all, her father was blacklisted, so you'd be well advised to stay clear of her. Remember, they can still nail you for that fight."

I told him there was no problem with Wei Xiaoli's father.

"Maybe so, but if Shen sticks a label on you, there won't be a damned thing you can do about it."

I nodded and held my tongue.

"Things are tangled enough as it is. Add her to the mix, and I don't know how you'll ward off the attacks."

I smiled. How could I refute his arguments?

"You haven't told anyone about your folks, have you?"

"No, but some people seem to know anyhow."

"Don't breathe a word. I mean it!" he exclaimed excitedly. "You'll really be in the soup if you do."

12

THE

AVENGING PI

HE WAS A BIG MAN with bloodshot eyes and a long, hooked nose dotted with blackheads. The only thing sticking out farther than his chest when he walked was his paunch. Even Battalion Commander Jiang came in second on that score.

We called him Beer-Belly Shen when he was out of earshot.

He greeted the news that some Company Three wagons had carried off our stones by thundering angrily at a meeting of platoon leaders, "If they do that again, beat the fuckers up! And I mean really lay into them! See me if anything goes wrong." His face was scarlet.

Of course, he could reel in his temper when he had to. Like the time a regimental guest-house attendant yelled at him for dumping a basin of dirty water into an open furnace; he merely smiled apologetically.

He was a veteran political worker. The walls of his house were plastered with portraits of Mao, a statue of the Chairman sat on the table, and except for some family photos, the frame of his mirror held nothing but Chairman Mao badges. His daughters were named Weiguo (Defend the Nation), Weihong (Defend the Red), and Weidong (Defend Mao Zedong). He had eaten his fill at the trough of "recalling past sufferings," and his wife complained to anyone who would listen, "Your political instructor didn't have a bowel movement for three days after that."

Now he controlled the fate of more than three hundred people. Narrow-minded, vengeful, and vindictive, he went out daily to supervise and inspect our work.

If you offended him, sooner or later he'd make you squirm. To him, not seeking revenge was an insult to the party. He would cast his net as wide as necessary and was a master at getting you to lower your defenses by making you think he'd forgotten the offense.

Lei Xia learned this the hard way. One day he was cutting some horse mane for shoe inserts, and the PI didn't say a word until he'd finished. Then he launched a withering attack at a company meeting, catching Lei Xia completely by surprise. What had he done to offend the PI? Then he recalled an incident from the previous summer, when he was riding past the PI's home around noon—galloping, actually— and the hoofbeats had startled the PI out of his nap. "Who's the prick out riding like that in the middle of the day?" came a thunderous shout from inside. Lei Xia rode on, assuming he was going too fast for anyone to get a good look at him, and mimicked the shout in his best Shanxi accent: "Who's the prick out riding like that in the middle of the day?" This seemingly trivial incident had stuck in the PI's mind for three long months.

Shen worked at the unhurried pace of a man enjoying a leisurely meal. He didn't care if it took six months or a year to get revenge. And he never settled for an eye for an eye: He wouldn't be satisfied unless he paid off a blood debt ten, even a hundred, times. If you had cut off one of his fingers, he would set out to sever your arm.

You say a student is goofing off? Okay, this year he loses home-leave privileges and his work goes uninspected, which means no monetary allowances. Or he's sent up the mountain to freeze his ass off for a winter, making little rocks out of big ones. If that doesn't work, there's always the threat of demerits in his dossier.

A peasant is trying to beat the system? Okay, his right to work is canceled, which means no wages. He's not allowed to sell winter meat, no cowchips are delivered to his home, and he gets no subsidy. If that doesn't work, he's sent up the mountain to lug rocks all winter long, until he wears out at least two pairs of felt boots.

A herdsman is out there acting like a coward? Okay, he attends company study sessions: no work, no wages. He get no milk cows, and has to pay the replacement cost for any animals that die. He's alloted no grazing land and must dig his wells by hand. If that doesn't work, we'll find out how many whores he's slept with and fucking report him!

Confident that his turn was coming, Lei Xia busied himself digging up dirt on the PI by eavesdropping beneath his window. Once, he informed me of a meeting in the PI's home where squad and platoon leaders sat around drinking and talking until their cigarette smoke was so thick, they could barely see.

"Drink up, Instructor. It's been a tough year. A toast to the PI!"

"This motherfucking bunch of students is turning things upside down. They've raised so much hell with party members, we're starting to look like the walking dead."

"We'll have to get that bunch from Beijing, the ones who stirred things up during the rectification campaign. They may be young, but they know what they're after."

"Do they really think they can undermine the party? They've got as much chance of that as a goddamned dung beetle has of going to heaven!"

"Instructor, the Communist Party can't be subjected to that. We've got to put them in their place."

"Here, Instructor, here's to you."

"In twenty years of soldiering nobody ever talked to me like they do," Shen said, sounding drunk and weepy. As soon as his crying jag was over, he said, "We'll do it by the book. There's a spy in Lei Xia's family," he went on. "Jin Gang's folks were capitalists, and Ma Bo's father has been arrested. They snuck out of Beijing and found their way here, but this is the end of the line."

"Right," Jiang Baofu added spiritedly. "The ones from Beijing are the worst. Those fuckers nearly beat old Wang to death."

"What about that cocky Liu Yinghong? She actually thinks she became a progressive without the help of the branch committee."

"Don't worry, we'll fix their wagon, every one of them."

"What makes those fucking students think they're such hot shit, anyway?"

Shen was still trying to get a fix on his enemies late that night as he planned his counterattack. Blessed with the stamina of a peasant, he didn't care how long it took or how hard he worked when he was on someone's trail.

The lamp inside his smoky room was still blazing at two A.M.

13

SNEAK

ATTACK

"WRITING A PROTEST letter is a serious crime? Horseshit! We'll see what the Central Committee has to say about that."

"Shh," Lei Xia shushed me nervously. "Not so loud. Someone might be listening." He paused. "Our little angel, Qi Shuzhen, spends half her time outside our window, so be careful."

"If I didn't know better, I'd say we've lost our freedom of movement."

Lei Xia nodded. "I'm going to make myself scarce around here. Remember the last time? The PI knew about it the next day. Is that fucking weird or not? It had to be Qi Shuzhen who reported me."

"The little cunt! Damned spy!" I swung a haymaker in the air. "Let's get her, what do you say? We can pelt her with mud. No one'll know if we do it at night."

"No way. Wang Lianfu is running around trying to stir up public opinion against you!"

"Did you go see the PI?" I asked him.

"We talked once, but he's taking a hard line. He says I have to reveal the origins of my stance. My so-called lack of feelings for the branch committee is supposed to show disdain for the party, and criticizing the branch committee is the same as criticizing the party. We're supposed to talk again in a couple of days, so wait till then to send your letter, okay?"

I nodded. What could I say?

He opened the door, looked up and down the street, and slipped into the darkness.

By then I'd finished my letter to Wei Xiaoli, and the longer I had to wait to give it to her the more agitated I became. Lei Xia thought of no one but himself. Finally I decided I'd waited long enough, since the letter had nothing to do with him and couldn't possibly complicate his situation. He was overreacting. The very next day I asked Liu Yinghong to give the twenty-one-page letter to Xiaoli. She was eager to help. "Can I read it?"

"Sure. It's my life story."

Somehow I made it through the next couple of days, but just barely. At the first opportunity I slipped into Yinghong's room. It was an overcast day, and despite the blazing stove, the room was dark. She sat with her legs tucked under her as she studied the works of Chairman Mao.

"Did you give it to her?"

She smiled weakly. "She wouldn't take it."

Thunderstruck.

"How . . . how can that be?" I barely got the words out.

"I handed it to her yesterday afternoon and said, 'This is from Ma Bo.' 'So?' she said. 'I don't want it.' I felt like a jerk standing there with that letter in my hand. You're in the same company, so if you have something to say to her, just say it. What's she supposed to think when you write her a letter?"

"It seemed like the best way to tell her I felt sorry for her." My heart was thumping. Lying always made my nose sweat.

"I read the letter, remember? It was very touching. I don't think you're such a bad person," she added softly.

I gaped at her, my mind a blank.

She handed me the letter and said sympathetically, "I can talk to her for you, if you prefer."

I shook my head and dragged myself out the door. I didn't feel the biting cold. Yinghong ran after me to hand me my cap.

She wouldn't even read it! My face was burning as if I'd been slapped. I walked home, shut the door behind me, and threw myself onto the kang, where I lay without moving. I didn't even get up to eat.

I had squeezed my brain dry over those twenty-one pages, and she hadn't even glanced at them. Well, fuck her! What a sorry excuse for a woman! What ever happened to human decency? I clenched my teeth as I nervously planned my revenge. It had all happened so fast.

One minute I was chilled, the next I was burning up. I went from feeling like tearing her limb from limb to wanting to howl at the moon over her burdens. That night I tossed and turned, unable to stop thinking about what had happened, unable to understand what was going through her mind.

The next day was the twenty-seventh of February, 1970. After wolfing down some breakfast, I dressed hurriedly. I hadn't slept all night. The image of Wei Xiaoli was burned into my aching eyes.

Lei Xia materialized in front of me, his eyes blazing as he bolted the door behind him. He had been staying away so as to keep the PI from linking us in some dark conspiracy.

"I've had my talk with the PI. You can send your letter if you want."

I shook my head absently.

"What's wrong?"

"I already did, but she wouldn't take it."

There was a moment of silence.

"I told you it was a mistake. She hasn't been here long enough to adapt to her new surroundings. How could you expect her to accept a letter from someone she hardly knows? I wouldn't if I were in her shoes."

"Well I sure as hell wouldn't have acted like that," I said angrily. "I'd have taken the letter, then figured out what to do. It wasn't a goddamned love letter, you know. Why don't I just stick it up on the bulletin board and let everyone read it?"

"Okay, let's lay our cards on the table. Ma Bo, were you trying to take advantage of her or not? Like make friends with the daughter of a capitalist-roader, then when her father's released, you're in. A provincial first secretary's son-in-law, sitting on top of the world." He was looking straight at me.

"I feel sorry for her, damn it!" I thundered. "That's all! Even rehabilitated, her father would never be a first secretary again. A man dies, the tea turns cold, don't you understand that? There's just some tragic attraction there, and old man Wei is not 'sitting on top of the world'! If Xiaoli's old man were still in power, I wouldn't give her the time of day!" I glared at him.

The doubt written on his face turned to a smile. "Okay, then I read you wrong. I feel sorry for her, too, if you want to know the truth. But this is no time to be associated with her. Old Shen's just looking for an excuse to nail us. I'll help get you two together afterwards, but back off for now, okay?"

I said okay, remembering our school days in 1968 and the vow we had taken to never place any female before a comrade-in-arms. It would have been unseemly not to agree to his request, since he not only displayed no jealousy over my having written to Xiaoli but was even offering to help.

"Ma Bo," he said gravely, "the situation is getting more serious every day. The Central Committee has launched the One-Smash and Three-Oppose campaign, which is aimed at smashing counterrevolutionaries, opposing corruption and theft, opposing speculation and profiteering, and opposing extravagance and waste. Active counterrevolutionaries are the main target. It's going to be a major campaign, the party's central mission for 1970. Old Shen hates us so much, I guarantee you he sees this as his chance to get even."

"Can he really pin a counterrevolutionary label on us?"

"They're stirring up public opinion against us. All this talk about blind ambition, failed attempts to overthrow the branch committee, non-organization-sponsored activities . . . They're out for blood, and they won't stop until their purge is complete."

"We're not antiparty or antisocialism, so let the fuckers purge on!"

Lei Xia sighed. "You're really out of touch. At a meeting yesterday, the PI said we're next. He told them that I'm more reactionary and sneakier than you and that I instigated the fight between you and Wang Lianfu. He's really been on my case the past few days. He used to say hello to me, but now he ignores me. Something's bound to happen, so be on your guard."

"You're overreacting. He wouldn't try anything over a letter, would he?"

No response.

"I'm going to write the Central Committee and get to the bottom of this."

He nodded to show his support. After a moment of reflection, he looked me straight in the eye and said, "Ma Bo, when the chips are down, you're the only person I can depend on. Xu Zuo avoids me because of my friendship with you. Besides, he's in Beijing on sick leave. Jin Gang's too young and timid to be reliable. I haven't forgotten how you carried me on your back that time I got sick in Lhasa, or how you came to my defense during the December seventh brouhaha, or how you demanded to be locked up with me when I was arrested for carrying a gun. But the big test is ahead of us. Old Shen's out to get me this time. Why did I have to be born into a family like mine?"

"I don't think it'll be as bad as you say."

"You don't know what they're up to."

People with bad backgrounds tend to be oversensitive.

"There's one thing you have to keep in mind," Lei Xia added.

"What's that?"

"Never mention our conversations about the Central Committee leadership. Just pretend we never had them, okay?"

I grasped his hand. "Don't worry," I said.

"One more thing. Wang Lianfu has been in the hospital for three weeks and refuses to leave. He's pleaded his case against you to the commissar several times. If I were you, I'd burn all my letters and do something about my diary. The less they have on you, the better."

"But how do I defend myself if they decide to attack?" I asked mournfully.

"Don't worry," he said with a smile as he patted me on the shoulder. "I'll be right there with you."

"Honest?"

"Honest."

As he stood there, his handsome face as red as the god of war, I knew he'd be as good as his word.

"All they have against you is that fight," he said with a frown. "A personal squabble. My problems are political, tied up with class struggle and class vengeance."

Why, I'll never know, but I was actually jealous of Lei Xia for becoming the principal target of Shen's attack. It was gratifying to know he was my friend. Our friendship was a tank that had withstood an artillery barrage. Jail, armed struggle, and fisticuffs had created a unique bond between us. This would be one more test of our friendship, another thrilling episode in our relationship. Not bad!

After a long pause, he asked, "What's the filthiest object you can think of?"

What was this all about? I didn't know what to say.

"A fly?"

"A maggot?"

"A whore's you-know-what?"

He shook his head, clenched his teeth, and said, "A turncoat! There's no dirtier word in any language."

I could have kissed him.

He grasped my hands, his eyes blazing.

"Together through thick and thin!"

"Together through thick and thin!"

Our vow was barely audible, but our souls were united.

14

OLD SHEN GETS
WHAT HE WANTED

AFTER LEI XIA LEFT, I put on some hot water to wash up, and as I sat on an upturned bucket staring at the basin, Wei Xiaoli's face gradually took shape in my mind and wouldn't go away. Steam was rising from the basin when Jiang Baofu walked in. "Ma Bo, the PI wants to see you."

"I was just about to wash up."

"You can do that later," he said smugly. "He wants to see you now."

Political Instructor Shen rolled his eyes and forced a smile as he ushered me into his office. "Sit down."

I sat across from him and asked with trepidation, "What is it, Political Instructor?"

He gazed up at the ceiling and said casually, "I just want to talk, that's all."

"About what?" I was wary.

He laughed drily. "At the company meeting you examined your mistakes." He coughed self-consciously. "Let's begin with your family." He opened a red notebook.

Taking stock of the situation, I decided not to say anything about the current struggle against my parents. I knew that sooner or later they'd be off the hook, and I didn't want the PI to think I was the son of traitors. I hadn't forgotten Lei Xia's comment. So I started with my grandfather during the period before land reform; but I'd barely begun when Jiang strolled in.

"A regimental car has driven up, Political Instructor. Shall I call muster?"

"Yes, have the company assemble at Team Four."

Jiang ran out, blowing his whistle.

A car from Regimental Headquarters. Probably bringing a directive. Or maybe one of the leaders was here to give a speech. Since everyone else was at the meeting, that left just me and the PI. My tough luck. I'd rather have gone to the meeting, where I could see Xiaoli for the first time since her refusal to accept my letter, which I was still carrying around.

The door opened and seven or eight sullen uniformed men armed with assault rifles entered. I was the immediate focus of their gazes, not to mention the muzzles of their weapons.

The soldiers were followed into the room by Commissar Chen, Regimental Commander Qi, and Director Li. The ruddy-faced commissar pointed to me. "Is that him?" he asked the PI.

Old Shen jumped to his feet. "That's him."

"What's your name?" Commissar Chen asked.

"Ma Bo."

"Cuff him!" he growled, a frown creasing his brow.

Two of the soldiers rushed up, as the regimental security-section staff officer, Zhao Shigui, approached me holding a pair of brass handcuffs. In two seconds they would be snapped around my wrists. My temples throbbed, my fists were clenched, my taut muscles were hard as rocks.

My first thought was to resist. If I started swinging, there would be plenty of bloody noses and black eyes to mark the occasion. But the impulse quickly passed. What chance did bare knuckles have against assault rifles?

I unclenched my fists, and the soldiers held me as Staff Officer Zhao snapped the handcuffs around my wrists.

"What's this all about, Commissar Chen?"

"You'll know soon enough."

My spirits, deflated by Wei Xiaoli's rebuff, were quickly revived. I was tense, and I was invigorated. Emotional numbness and self-loathing vanished the instant the cuffs were snapped on. If Commissar Chen expected me to give up meekly, he was in for a surprise. I glowered at him, just so he'd know.

The look was too much for him. He turned and walked out, leaving Staff Officer Zhao and the soldiers behind.

"Why am I being arrested?"

"Have you read the Constitution of the People's Republic?" Zhao asked blandly.

"I've read it."

"Then you know it's illegal to physically abuse people."

"I know."

Without another word, he reached over, unbuttoned my jacket, and emptied my pockets. There it was, my letter to Wei Xiaoli. After glancing at the first page, he stuffed it into his small satchel.

The tragicomedy that ensued is something I won't forget as long as I live. The entire uniformed complement of the Forty-first Regiment, led by the commissar and regimental commander, had been mobilized to arrest me in the name of an insignificant wagon master. The humor of the situation dispelled the last vestige of tension, and I wasn't scared at all. It was so comical, I felt like crying.

I carefully planned what to say when they paraded me in front of the company. I wanted my captors to know that justice was on my side.

"What did Lei Xia tell you this morning?" Jiang Baofu asked triumphantly.

"Nothing."

"None of that, now," he said with a grin.

I stood at attention.

Staff Officer Zhao held up my handmade knives. "What are these for?"

"Cutting meat."

"Bullshit! Part of a secret conspiracy, aren't they?"

"No."

"You deny it? Don't tell me you forgot what you said."

Shit! Which little bastard had overheard our conversation?

Staff Officer Zhao sneered. "Were you planning to get your revenge against Company Seven with these? Got any more?"

"No."

Political Instructor Shen walked in and glared at me. "What about the Mongol knife?"

"I don't have it. You never gave it back."

"I most certainly did." His bloodshot eyes nearly popped out of his head. Angry creases appeared beside his hooked nose.

"No you didn't, you sure as hell did not!" I was so angry, I nearly saw stars. The sly old fox wanted to get me on a concealed-weapon charge, even though the knife was now a permanent fixture on his kitchen table.

I was about to get a taste of his political skill. He had let me cool my heels for two full months after the fight, until the One-Smash and Three-Oppose campaign was launched. Then he struck, the vindictive SOB.

The commissar and regimental commander returned. "Commissar Chen, why am I being arrested?"

He avoided my eyes. "You damned well know."

"No I don't."

"Take him away," he said with an impatient wave of his hand and a scowl on his face.

"Aren't we going to the meeting?"

"No."

Damn. I wanted to look into the eyes of Lei Xia and see Liu Yinghong and Wei Xiaoli. But it wasn't to be, for I was led past a gantlet of soldiers to a waiting ambulance. Bandoliers were draped across the soldiers' chests; hand grenades hung from their belts; their bayonets glinted in the sunlight.

It was an awesome display out there on the remote steppes, proof of the might of the Forty-first Regiment's dictatorship of the proletariat. It would have put even Beijing to shame.

Not wanting to appear cowed, I walked casually between the rows of glinting bayonets up to the ambulance. Not too fast, not too slow. I jumped into the vehicle without any help.

The Forty-first Regiment used ambulances to haul prisoners.

The only person I saw out in the biting cold was Li Xiaohua. Astonishment, curiosity, and fear merged in her eyes. Her face was pale, her lips slightly parted. All that attention from a pretty girl made me feel by turns sad and smug. I wasn't afraid, but she was, and a sense of muted pride swelled my heart. She stood frozen to the spot as the ambulance pulled away.

Staff Officer Zhao sat next to me, earflaps down, hands encased in shiny black gloves; his red cap insignia was nearly blinding.

As we sped through the cold air, instead of tucking my neck into my jacket and curling up, I sat straight and gazed somberly at the snow-covered steppe. I could still hear Lei Xia's words: "Together through thick and thin!" I took a deep breath and thrust my chest out as far as I could. Then I glared at my uniformed escorts, letting the gaze bore into each one's eyes until he blinked, before moving triumphantly on to the next man. They tried their stubborn best but were no match for me.

I wanted to take on Staff Officer Zhao, but he wouldn't look at me.

When we reached Regiment Headquarters I jumped down off the ambulance. A crowd of students quickly gathered. "Move on," Zhao grumbled, "there's nothing to see here."

Since I had an audience, I held my head high and walked calmly into the makeshift detention center set up by the Forty-first Regiment for the One-Smash and Three-Oppose campaign. The lock clanked, then silence. Old Shen had gotten what he wanted, I thought to myself, but he'd better not be carried away with his victory, because sooner or later history would vindicate me.

15

A LETTER
IN BLOOD

IT WAS the northernmost building in Regimental Headquarters, right on the edge of the steppe. The sole window did little to abate the darkness, but the roof, made of four thick planks, let a few weak rays of sunlight in through the cracks. A thick layer of dust on the walls showed how long it had been since the departure of the former occupants. The smoke-blackened ceiling was infested with cobwebs. An armed sentry guarded the locked door.

I had two fellow prisoners: A Tianjin student named Ren Changfa from Company Two sat on the felt rug in his leather cap and army overcoat, a blanket wrapped around his legs; Yan Shu, also a Tianjin student, sat cross-legged on the table, a padded coat draped around his shoulders, making him look like a perched owl.

We three gloomy prisoners ignored each other, which only increased the icy atmosphere. Since the room had no kang, we had to sleep on reed mats covered by a felt rug. I curled up under my sheepskin coat and tucked my hands between my knees to keep warm; eventually the manacles lost their icy edge.

The earthenware stove, never used, was like a block of ice.

The winter night was deathly still but for the occasional howl of a northern wind; I squeezed my eyes shut and commanded myself to go to sleep. It didn't work. My ears rang, and I saw stars. In my twenty-two years I'd never had to sleep handcuffed and fully dressed.

What was I guilty of? Why had I been arrested? I'd had worse fights than this at school, and nothing had ever happened. I was no angel, I had my faults, but arresting me and clapping me in manacles for fighting was going too far.

My arrest coincided with the final wrap-up of the party rectification campaign. Coincidence or a payback? Shen apparently had me arrested in order to squelch the "evil winds and noxious influence" of someone who had been critical of him.

Owing to my obsession with Wei Xiaoli, I had misread the delicate situation in the company and had failed to predict the direction of Shen's attack. Now I realized that, contrary to Lei Xia's assumption, the target had been me all along, not him, and I began to worry that my arrest was the first step in labeling me a counterrevolutionary. He was going to make an example of me—kill the chicken to scare the monkeys—and my only chance was to appeal to the commissar and regimental commander.

It was letter-writing time again.

Late that night I formed an idea of what to say. The cold, dark night wrapped itself around me. Ren Changfa moaned in his sleep from time to time.

Early the next morning I awoke and surveyed my jail cell. A sliver of brittle yellow paper was stuck to the window opening. I tore it down and ripped it in half. I'd use half now and hide the rest under the reed mat.

Since they had taken my fountain pen, it would have to be a letter in blood; and since I didn't have a knife, I would have to use my teeth. Without hesitation, I bit down on my nearly frozen left forefinger but couldn't break the skin. I had to be careful not to bite down so hard that I'd mangle the thing.

It hurt. A knife would have been quick and painless, and there would have been enough blood for my purpose. Instead I had to rely on my dull teeth, and all I could manage was four deep indentations. Then it dawned on me that warming the finger would make the job easier, as I knew from my culinary experience. So first I breathed on the finger, then stuck it into my mouth to soften it with saliva. Ren Changfa rolled over; Yan Shu coughed. Were they waking up? That was bad news. Knowing I had to finish quickly, I took my finger out of my mouth and put myself into the mood by invoking history: Xiang Yu cut off his own head, Wang Zuo cut off his own arm, Nie Zheng sliced off his own nose, an anonymous prisoner gouged out his own eye. Do it! I bit down hard, ripping off a chunk of flesh, and immediately tasted something salty.

I began to write on the scrap of paper:

Long Live Chairman Mao!

Dear Commissar Chen and Commander Qi:

Since coming to the steppe I have been guilty of serious mistakes, owing to insufficient ideological reform, and for this I'm willing to accept any punishment the organization metes out. But I am neither antiparty nor antisocialism, and I am not a counterrevolutionary.

I beseech you, as respected regimental leaders, not to believe rumors about me or listen to only one side of the issue, so that I can regain my freedom as soon as possible.

Respectfully yours,
Ma Bo, Company Seven

Eternal Fealty to Chairman Mao!
Eternal Fealty to Mao Zedong Thought!
Long Live Chairman Mao!
Long Long Live Chairman Mao!
Long Long Long Live Chairman Mao!

P.S. Political Instructor Shen never returned the knife to me, I swear it.

The guard, a fellow by the name of Yang, brought in a basin with some cold rice for breakfast. No vegetables, just a sprinkling of meaty broth. Lacking the luxury of a bowl, I held the basin up to my mouth with one manacled hand and a pair of chopsticks in the other, and shoveled the rice into my mouth. It was a new way of eating, and I wasn't very good at it.

As Yang watched me eat, sympathy crept into his eyes. He was a demobilized soldier from Company Three who had seen me beat the Tianjin wrestlers from his company during the autumn harvest. He had always treated me okay. I pondered my situation briefly and decided to exploit his sympathy.

"Would you take a letter to the commissar for me?"

"Sure, no problem." He seemed happy to oblige.

I removed a piece of cloth from under my shirt and handed it to him. I'd scrawled the words "For Commissar Chen and Commander Qi" on the cloth. The purplish words shocked him. The white cloth, which I'd ripped from my shirt, served as an envelope for my letter in blood.

16

ALL KINDS
OF PRESSURE

YEARS LATER I found out what happened in the company after I was taken away.

On the night of February 26, 1970, Director Li of the Regimental Political Department notified Political Instructor Shen over the telephone that I was to be arrested the following day. They kept me under surveillance that night. At nine in the morning the company leadership was summoned to hear a Central Committee directive read by Director Li, a stocky man whose dark face was inlaid with a pair of shining eyes above and black, bristly whiskers below. Casually smoking a cigarette, he squinted and began to read, slowly and deliberately:

Central Committee Document
Number Three, 1970

To Be Carried Out on
the Orders of Chairman Mao:

A Directive Regarding Counterrevolutionary Sabotage

The national situation remained excellent in the wake of the Ninth People's Congress. But class enemies, foreign and domestic, stung by a series of defeats, have increased their acts of sabotage. Some engage in military terror, fabricating rumors to mislead the people; some steal state secrets in the service of our enemies; some seize every opportunity to have verdicts overturned and refuse to accept supervision; some link up secretly to create havoc; and some try to sabotage the policy of rural work assignments. In order to implement correct strategy and consolidate national defense, we are determined to attack—swiftly, accurately, and relentlessly:

1. The masses must be fully mobilized.
2. Key elements must be targeted, in this case active counter-revolutionaries, who will be resolutely suppressed.
3. We must distinguish between the two different types of contradictions.
4. We must publicize and mobilize on a grand scale. Before sentencing or carrying out capital punishment, the masses must hold meetings. Then, once the verdicts have been handed down they must be carried out at once.
5. The limits of sanctioning jurisdiction must be unified. In accordance with Central Committee provisions, only provincial/municipal/autonomous-region revolutionary committees can approve capital punishment, and they must report directly to the Central Committee.
6. Public-security leadership in revolutionary committees and military control commissions at all levels must be strengthened.

January 31, 1970

(Distribution of this document is limited to the central leadership of provincial and army commands, who will propagate it verbally to subordinate commands. It must not be distributed in written form, especially in print or other communications media.)

Secretariat of the Central Committee
of the Chinese Communist Party
Released February 2, 1970
Number of copies: 1827

Director Li's sharp eyes swept the faces arrayed in front of him. "The Regimental Party Committee has decided that Ma Bo, a member of your company, must be sequestered for interrogation. We will hold public meetings to unmask him."

Those two terse sentences landed like a bombshell. The students waited anxiously for Li to go on. But he just sipped his tea without saying another word.

"The meeting is over," the PI declared. "Squad and platoon leaders stick around."

Staff Officer Zhao had turned my room inside out while I was out: A clutter of books lay on the floor, tattered clothes were draped all over the kang, and the stuff in my bag—my diary, my letters and photos, "Mao Zedong Anti-U.S. Iron and Blood Corps" insignia, even a tiny Chinese flag I'd taken with me to Vietnam—had been confiscated.

The next day the PI announced, "The Regimental Party Committee has declared the case of Ma Bo a serious matter, a pivotal point in our One-Smash and Three-Oppose campaign."

He also announced some personnel changes: Liu Yinghong was temporarily relieved as acting squad leader and was to be investigated, although she would remain in the group. Lei Xia and Jin Gang were transferred out of the maintenance brigade and sent to the agricultural workers' platoon. Wei Xiaoli was assigned to the mess detail to slop hogs.

You could have heard a pin drop, since everyone knew exactly what it all meant. Lei Xia left the meeting feeling as if his heart were weighted down with a stone. He stood in the snow looking confused, not sure where to go. Political Instructor Shen called him over to the company office. "You're Ma Bo's best friend," he said brusquely, "so there are two paths open to you. You can break with him completely and expose and unmask him, or you can continue your stubborn resistance and wallow in the filth with him. It's up to you. You were the ringleader of the political misadventure during the party rectification. So in addition to exposing Ma Bo, you'll have to come clean about your activities back then. Do you understand?"

Lei Xia glared at the PI without saying a word.

Everyone's nerves were frayed now that the arrests had begun, and the situation was changing fast: Lei Xia's room, once a gathering place for students, was now deserted. In the past surrounded by a jovial crowd when he went to the mess hall, he now came and went alone; no one dared to be seen with him. Knowing that he and Ma Bo were sworn buddies, that his father had been a Nationalist spy, and that he could be arrested at any time, people avoided him like the plague.

Some even said that Jin Gang was a Ma Bo follower, since he had boasted about my prowess, had taken wrestling lessons from me, and had modeled his lifestyle—seldom bathing, always wearing tattered clothes, and so on—after me. This talk threw him into a panic. He tearfully defended himself against the rumors, but the PI saw through his self-serving lies and read him the riot act, forcing him to come clean about carving official seals at my behest and forging letters of introduction back when we first came to Inner Mongolia. Naturally he blamed everything on me.

Jin Gang also distanced himself from Lei Xia, who spent most of his time writing confessions and self-examinations. He needed permission to participate in outside activities, and his wages were suspended, although he still received his meal stipend. His face turned gaunt, his eyes were constantly bloodshot, and he hardly ever spoke. At one point he went to the PI and said, "Why stall like this? Arrest me and get it over with!"

The PI just grinned. "Don't get carried away. You must trust the organization."

17

I KEEP
MY COOL

SO MANY PEOPLE came up to gawk at us that the guards had trouble maintaining control. Not wanting to be a caged monkey, I lay on the floor most of the time under my sheepskin coat. Now I knew why zoo animals sleep so much: It is the only way to maintain their dignity.

"Which one's Ma Bo?"

"The one on the floor, I guess."

"I hear he put up a hell of a fight when they arrested him."

"He's feisty, all right. They say he beat the shit out of a demobilized soldier."

"Over there. Look."

"It's too dark. I can't see a thing."

"They're on the floor. That's them, over there. Wonder why they're sleeping in the middle of the day."

"Poor guys."

I watched their heads sway past the cracks.

I remember seeing a bear in the Chengdu Zoo during the Red Guard linkup. It was in a cage not much bigger than itself, and since it couldn't move, it just lay there staring back at the people watching it.

Now I was that bear. The locked door, the sealed window, my handcuffs, the cold glints of the bayonets, and the twenty-four-hour guard posted at the door kept a vigil over me.

The three of us ate twice a day, mainly millet, except for an occasional steamed bun. The only vegetables were in a broth mixture. The portion never varied, a basinful at each meal. The rations were extremely generous; and though we did nothing but lie around all day, we never failed to finish them off, even though a basinful of millet was more than an entire squad's quota.

Maybe it was nervous energy, since boredom is such a frightful drain on physical strength. Whatever the reason, we were always waiting impatiently for our next meal. The arrival of breakfast was proof that we had made it through another night. Seeing dinner delivered proved that we had endured another day.

There was, it seems, no coal in the regiment, so we went without heat. Indoor fires were permitted only for the six winter months in Inner Mongolia, but it was still cold even in March, and we kept our earflaps down the whole time. Our noses ached from the cold, our faces had a waxen look, and we spouted steam when we talked.

The guards permitted us three trips to urinate and one for a bowel movement each day, and we had to adapt our eating and drinking schedule to our toilet privileges. At other times they wouldn't open the door for us. For them it was a matter of convenience, but for us it meant resetting our biological clocks.

I alone was manacled morning, noon, and night, even in the toilet. Taking a leak was no problem, but the final act of taking a shit was beyond me, and I had to enlist the aid of Ren Changfa. I'll bet nothing like that ever happens in capitalist prisons.

Ren Changfa was a petty young man whose squad leader had constantly bullied him. When he finally complained, the squad leader and some of his pals beat Ren up on New Year's Day. That was the last straw. He asked for a transfer and threw a tantrum when that was denied. His company commander tried to talk him into returning to his squad, but he said he'd go to jail first. "Would you lock me up if I said something reactionary?" he asked his apathetic company commander.

"Such as?"

"Such as 'Chairman Mao stinks'? Such as 'I like Chiang Kai-shek better'?"

"What did you say?" The company commander thought he was hearing things.

Ren Changfa repeated his comment loudly and tearfully.

The company commander's expression changed dramatically, and he ordered his clerk to tie Ren up. When the squad leader heard that Ren had maligned the great leader, he and some of the other students beat him senseless, leaving a gash in his head, two black eyes, and a lot of spilled blood.

He had already begun to regret his actions by the time he was delivered to Regiment Headquarters, where he wept and stood dumbly, wrapped in a blanket. He was all of seventeen years old.

My other cellmate, Yan Shu, sat around all day with his head scrunched down into his padded coat, hands thrust up the sleeves like an old peasant. According to him, a friend had fought a demobilized soldier when they were making New Year's dumplings. Seeing that his friend was getting the worst of it, he whacked the soldier over the head with a rolling pin, knocking him senseless. Yan was cuffed and locked up.

During the 1970 One-Smash and Three-Oppose campaign we were the only three students in the regiment to be singled out. Our average age was nineteen.

One day passed, then another, and a third. No one came to see me. I was the regiment's forgotten man. But my brain slipped back into gear as the nervousness abated. Even though I was manacled, I stuck to my guns that criticizing the branch committee during the open-door party rectification had been just and proper. Calling me a "careerist" was a bald-faced lie. That was no way to get ahead in a place like this, and who wanted the chickenshit job of political instructor, anyway?

But I began to miss my fellow students, miss them a lot, and I knew things were not going well for them, either.

I tossed and turned all that night. Who would interrogate me? The regimental commander? The commissar? I could almost see them:

bloated figures sitting under a bright light; dark, bushy eyebrows; bright red insignias; stern, vigilant looks.

How should I behave during the interrogation? I decided to keep my legs straight, spread slightly in defiance; stick out my chest, hold my head high, and stay poised like a coiled spring; keep my lips tightly shut with the hint of a snarl at the corner to show how I'd suffered; and stare daggers at them—get them to blink first.

Just thinking about my tough-guy act gave me a rush. The silence outside was broken only by howling northern winds. Ren Changfa moaned in his sleep like a dying man. I couldn't tell if it was real or if he just wanted some sympathy. I nudged him.

"What's wrong?"

"Cut out the noise, I'm trying to sleep."

He was soon at it again, one agonizing moan after another. Jail had been his only refuge from a bullying squad leader, but now he was eaten up by remorse. All night long he was at it, making it impossible for me to sleep. Finally I whacked him with a broom. He grunted "Fuck you" a couple of times, then quieted down. No more moans.

I tried to escape the bitter cold by curling up into a ball.

When I awoke the next morning, Ren was looking into a mirror. A patch of dried blood showed on his right cheek.

"I've got a splitting headache," he told the guard who brought breakfast in, glowering at me.

The guard took him out.

He returned at around nine o'clock, and I was summoned to Staff Officer Zhao's office.

18

THE

HAYMAKER

STAFF OFFICER ZHAO'S room was bare except for a washbasin by the door, some cowchips stacked beside the kang, and an old filing cabinet in the corner; a towel and a pair of nylon socks were drying on a line.

No bright light, no whitewashed walls. In fact, a very dark room. Neither the commissar nor the regimental commander had shown up. The only other person in the room, a swarthy, rough-looking demobilized soldier, sat on the kang. I had expected something different for my interrogation and was disappointed not to be facing a dyed-in-the-wool inquisitor.

A cigarette dangled from Zhao's lips as he chatted with the other man. When I entered, he looked up without skipping a beat in his conversation. He was a tall, lanky man with a large head, big ears, and a long face. His nose hung in the center of his face like a gourd. The asymmetry of his features made his expressions seem unreal, and it was impossible to determine his mood by just looking at him. At first I didn't know if his smile signaled pleasure or disdain, whether it represented goodwill or ill.

I assumed the practiced posture: legs straight, chest out. Standing gave me a slight advantage over the seated men.

It took Staff Officer Zhao only a moment to realize that I'd thrown down the gauntlet. He turned to face me, and as our eyes met, a silent battle of wills was launched. We stared each other down, his face growing longer, his nose thickening. Deep creases showed at the corners of his mouth as the battle raged. Then he blinked, and I knew I'd won. I turned off the power.

"Why'd you hit him?" he asked in a heavy Shanxi accent.

"I didn't."

"Fuck your ancestors! Stop lying!" The soldier jumped off the kang, looking very cross. Before I knew it—*smack*—he slapped me across the face. My ears rang.

"Don't do that," Zhao warned. "Now, did you hit him or not?" he repeated.

"No." I forced myself to answer calmly but was already a bit light-headed, and my nose felt bent out of shape.

"Then what happened to his cheek?"

"He kept me up all night moaning, so I nudged him with a broom."

"Fighting in jail. You've either got real balls or no brains."

"I didn't hit him."

The soldier came back and stuck his finger under my nose. "Say that one more time, you fucking wild animal, and I'll show you what it's like to be hit!"

I held my tongue.

Staff Officer Zhao opened a drawer and took out an assortment of handcuffs, including those I'd worn the first time. They were shiny from wear and, owing to a few links of chain between the two cuffs, not all that uncomfortable. Now it was time to choose another pair, smaller and coarser. The soldier wrenched my arms behind me while Zhao snapped the pair he'd chosen over my wrists. But he couldn't get them closed; they were probably meant for children.

"Stop squirming!" he bellowed.

The soldier took over. Forcing my wrists onto the table, he took aim and banged down with his fist. The cuffs snapped shut.

Taking out a handkerchief to wipe his sweaty face, Zhao said through clenched teeth, "Now we'll see how hard those dog bones of yours are."

The cuffs dug into my wrists, and the surfaces were rough and pitted; the absence of any chain between them made it impossible to move my hands independently. But I wasn't about to beg. The world scorns weakness.

"Why have I been arrested, Staff Officer Zhao?"

"You know why."

"No I don't."

"How many fights have you had here? If we arrested you on that alone, you'd have no complaints."

"But somebody else always starts them."

"You listen to me. The Party Committee sent you here in response to demands from the masses at Company Seven. Now go back and think about your problem. A letter in blood isn't the answer. The only way you'll get anywhere is to come clean."

So he knew about my letter to the commissar.

When the guard escorted me back to jail, Ren Changfa kept his head lowered and didn't dare look at me.

The rough manacles, crudely fashioned by the regiment blacksmith, would rub my skin raw if I wasn't careful. Since the pain was unrelenting whether I stood or lay down, I paced the floor. The pain spread from my deltoids to my biceps: not a sharp pain, but the dull ache of a blunt knife, which was even worse in the long run.

Somehow I made it to dinnertime. When the guard carried in the basin of millet and realized I couldn't eat with my hands behind my back, he went to get the key from Staff Officer Zhao. No dice. Someone would have to feed me.

After Ren Changfa and Yan Shu were finished, they volunteered to feed me. But I shook my head and asked them to put the food on top of the stove. Then I squatted down and lapped it up, chasing the elusive clumps, some of which stuck to my nose and chin. Finding my predicament unbearable to witness, Ren moved the millet around with his chopsticks and offered to shove it into my mouth.

Accept pity from a little snitch? No way! By moving my head up and down and sliding the millet around with my tongue, I managed to finish it.

The guard's eyes oozed pity.

By nightfall the pain in my arms made me want to cry out. I had never experienced such discomfort in my life. Later in the night, when the regiment was asleep and my fellow prisoners were snug in their beds, I lay prone on the rug; but the pain was more than I could bear in the surrounding quiet. So I got up and paced the room some more, like a caged wolf.

The guard flashed his light on me. "Try to get some sleep." I turned around to show him my cuffed hands.

He walked off, but soon returned and said, "Sorry, Staff Officer Zhao won't let me take them off."

I looked up and sighed, which caused my cap to fall to the floor. I just stared at it lying at my feet, knowing there was no way I could put it back on. But then the glacial air made my ears ache. So I got down on all fours, picked it up with my teeth, stood up, and carried it to the windowsill, where I pulled back the earflaps with my teeth to make a nice round hole. Then, squatting down, I aimed my head at the hole and thrust it forward like a rocket ship linking up in space, but this was more difficult, since the cap was so soft.

I missed the first time and the second. By then I realized that Ren Changfa was sitting up. "Here, let me," he said softly.

"I can do it myself!"

He mumbled something before sliding back under the covers.

After rounding out the hole once more, I managed to get my head in. But now it covered my eyes, and I had to adjust it by rubbing my head up and down against the wall.

By then only an occasional sharp pain disturbed the numbness in my shoulders. I was forced to sacrifice the skin on my wrists and shrug my shoulders forward to ease the pain a little. Ouch! It hurt like hell. Every few steps I cursed, "Fuck you!" I don't know whom I was cursing. Then I remembered reading somewhere that strenuous physical activity can reduce the impact of pain, so I began walking in circles, raising a cloud of dust on the dry floor.

Now the pain in my shoulders was joined by matching pains in my neck, chin, and the back of my head. It felt as if scorpions were dancing on my arms and burying their stingers in my skin.

My cellmates slept on as I paced the darkness in excruciating pain. I pointedly stomped my feet and raised the decibel level of the "Fuck you!" curses I spat out with each step to disturb their sleep. They needed to be reminded that someone was suffering in their midst. I paced all night long and cursed until I was hoarse.

The next morning I lay on the felt rug and let Ren Changfa pour water into my mouth; it had little or no effect on the pain. Yan Shu urged me to go see Staff Officer Zhao, for by then he was deeply troubled by my suffering. But I knew I mustn't go crawling to Zhao. Knowing how much I was suffering with my hands cuffed behind my back would only encourage him to prolong it.

At breakfast time on the third morning the guard led me over to Zhao's toasty room. My eyelids drooped from exhaustion.

He eyed me up and down, a cigarette dangling from his lips, and sneered, "Well? Are you going to keep on fighting?"

"No." It was time to give in.

"I thought you said you never fought."

"No, you're right, I did." My eyes were closed.

He laughed.

My shoulders ached, my head was splitting, and my nose was so dry, it felt as if it would crack. All I wanted was to have my hands freed so I could get some sleep.

Zhao puffed his cigarette casually, gloating over my newfound tractability, before removing the handcuffs.

The first thing that occurred to me after my hands were free was that I couldn't move my arms. It took forever just to slide them from the middle of my back down to my buttocks, then to my thighs; the bones seemed so brittle, I was afraid they might snap at any moment. Gradually I moved my hands out in front, where I gingerly rotated the wrists, and finally screwed up the courage to flex my muscles. It felt so good, I sighed with relief and smiled, overwhelmed by the satisfying sense of freedom regained.

Zhao watched me curiously, a faint smile on his lips.

The skin on my wrists had been rubbed raw and bloody.

He let me limber up for a few moments. "That's enough." He snapped the original pair over my wrists in front.

"Okay, let's hear it."

I yawned, then repeated what I'd said in my letter to the commissar: "Since coming to the steppe I have been guilty of serious mistakes, owing to insufficient ideological reform . . ."

" 'Mistakes'? Try 'crimes'!" he bellowed. His eyes bored into me.

"What crimes?"

"You've read the Constitution, so you ought to know that assault is a criminal act. Soon after your arrival you beat up a poor herdsman, and this time you mauled a demobilized soldier. A pretty impressive list of crimes in itself. But you also sicced your dog on a soldier, bragged you were going to knock out a herdsman's teeth to avenge the dog, threatened a poor herdsman with a knife, sabotaged your wagon, and conspired with Lei Xia to beat up someone."

I responded to each of the charges. The dispute with Old Gigolo had been disposed of by the Military Control Commission; the fight with Wang Lianfu had been his fault; threatening the poor herdsman with a knife was a scurrilous rumor; siccing my dog on a soldier was slander, pure and simple.

"Enough of your damned lies! You can defend your actions till Hell freezes over, but we'll get to the bottom of this." With a testy look, he continued, "Okay, let's say you're right, that you've done nothing wrong. Then tell me why you ignored corps policy that no one is to get romantically involved for three years? I'm talking about your love letter to Wei Xiaoli."

"That was no love letter. I wrote because I felt sorry for her."

"Felt *sorry* for her? We know you better than that. You've got the dirtiest mind of anybody I know."

"'My feelings for her are absolutely pure, and they won't change just because she'll have nothing to do with me."

His fishy eyes crinkled in a smile. "Pure? Is that why your diary is filled with disgusting comments about sexual desires, masturbation? Pure, my ass! All you've got on your fucking mind is whoring around."

This haymaker made my heart pound and my skin crawl.

"You assume that all we know how to do is feed our faces, don't you? That diary of yours is more than just garbage, it's a reactionary document. This time we're going to settle *all* accounts, old and new, with you."

Shivers ran up my spine and my legs began to tremble. But I tried not to show it.

"Go on, get out of here. Think about what I just said. Don't you mess with Mr. CCP!" he shrieked.

I was dragged back to jail, feeling groggy; I lay on the floor in a daze.

When I first arrived I made a point of writing self-criticisms in my diary, and now that so-called "garbage" made me a marked man. If they went public with their accusations, I wouldn't be able to hold my head up around anyone. What would people like Liu Yinghong, Lei Xia, and Wei Xiaoli think of me?

Staff Officer Zhao's reputation was well deserved. He had broken down my defenses by focusing on relations between the sexes. I wanted to howl. After two days and nights with my hands cuffed behind my back, I had been hit right between the eyes and had no idea how to deal with it. Too exhausted to ponder the situation further, I settled in to sleep.

Nights on the steppe were dark and cold, but compared to people like Zhao, they were warm and cheery.

19

VITALITY

SAPPED

AN APRIL MORNING in 1970.

An armed guard stood at the door. When Staff Officer Zhao saw me walk in, he slid a stack of documents to the side of the desk. "Have you thought things over? What do you have to say?"

I repeated what I'd written in my letter to the commissar: "Since coming to the steppe I have been guilty of serious mistakes, owing to insufficient ideological reform . . ."

Bang! He pounded the table. " 'Mistakes'? Try 'crimes'!"

I paused, then replied softly, "I've committed no crimes."

"You arrogant little bastard! This is no local precinct, and unless you start telling the truth, you can forget about getting out, ever! To us evidence is what counts, not statements by the accused. We'll reach a verdict whether you confess or not."

"Staff Officer Zhao," I said earnestly, "drawing a clear distinction between friend and foe is a cardinal revolutionary principle. I admit I've made mistakes, but I am *not* the enemy."

"You are not a good person, Ma Bo."

"Staff Officer Zhao," I replied courteously, "won't you listen to my side of the story?"

"Are you going to come clean or not?"

"I'm not an antiparty, antisocialist element, I've never stolen anything, and I've never committed murder or arson. What am I supposed to come clean about?"

He jumped to his feet and said with a snarl, "You asshole, tell me why you've been listening to enemy broadcasts."

A shiver ran down my spine.

"Speak up! Why were you listening to enemy broadcasts?"

"I was worried that China and the Soviets might go to war, so I listened. I wanted to know what was going on."

"Aha! Now it comes out. You listen to both sides to see who's right and who's wrong. That's open defiance."

"Chairman Mao said to avoid one-sided approaches to issues, like understanding the Chinese side but not the Japanese side, or understanding the Communist side but not the Nationalist . . ."

"Are you telling me that Chairman Mao said you could listen to enemy broadcasts?"

"He never said I couldn't."

"Reactionary! Vice Chairman Lin said that military units are forbidden from listening to enemy broadcasts. The 1960 enlarged session of the Military Commission stipulated that it is strictly forbidden. You're aware of that, aren't you?"

"No."

"Listening to enemy broadcasts is a counterrevolutionary act. You compounded the crime by disseminating what you heard."

"But lots of people in the company listen."

"You mean it's okay for you to be a counterrevolutionary because they are?"

I broke out in a cold sweat. My heart was racing. I had seen posters that labeled the act of listening to enemy broadcasts counterrevolutionary.

"And that's just the beginning," he went on. "There's also the business of attacking our great leader . . . You'd better start using that head of yours. After a mass trial in Xilinhot recently two people were shot, both counterrevolutionaries. One was younger than you."

By now the mental strain was taking its toll. I had been lulled into thinking it was just a matter of fighting, nothing to get too excited about. But now that it was political, I figured I was in real trouble.

"Go back and think some more," he said, handing me ten sheets of paper. "Then write an honest and complete confession—nothing more, nothing less. Do you hear me?"

The knowledge that I had become a political prisoner was numbing. In 1970, when the net of class struggle was thrown over the entire country, counterrevolutionaries were dealt with severely, while thieves and hoodlums ran wild. The authorities would rather arrest a thousand innocent people than let a single counterrevolutionary slip through. A reactionary comment could prove fatal.

I learned from the guards' conversations that public trials were being held all over Inner Mongolia. Counterrevolutionaries had been shot already. I'd have been a fool not to be worried.

There were objective standards for weighing the severity of criminal cases, but no such standards for political crimes; verdicts were handed down based upon the judges' moods. People who opposed Liu Shaoqi before the Cultural Revolution were counterrevolutionaries; once the Cultural Revolution was under way, they became heroes. Politics were extremely elastic: If someone was out to get you, you could shout "Long Live Chairman Mao" and still be accused of "displaying the red flag to attack the red flag." Anyone could be purged. Sparrows were considered counterrevolutionary, and the whole country was mobilized against them; so what chance did someone like me have?

Over the next three days I filled ten pages with responses to the issues Zhao had raised, and what it boiled down to was they had no justification to label me a counterrevolutionary.

How had he found out about the enemy broadcasts? Someone must have snitched. But who? After going down the list, Jin Gang seemed the most likely. But then it could have been Lei Xia.

When the chips are down, it's every man for himself. I wrote a note to Lei Xia warning him about Staff Officer Zhao's question and my response, reminding him of his comment that the dirtiest word in any language is "turncoat." What I was hinting at, of course, was for him to be discreet in what he revealed.

Yan Shu, who seemed to hold me in some regard, had nothing good to say about Ren Changfa. So when he whispered one day that he was getting out and wondered if there was anything he could do for me, I asked if he'd pass my note to Lei Xia. Happy to do it, he said. Now we had to find a way to smuggle it out. He came up with the idea of wrapping it in a ball of thread.

"Thanks, Yan Shu."

"Glad to do it," he replied bashfully.

He was too excited to talk, but he remembered to hand me his fountain pen as he walked out the door.

Now it was just Ren Changfa and me. We leaned against the window and gazed longingly between the cracks, not exchanging a single word the whole time. One down, and two to go. I wondered how long they'd keep me there.

Political problems weighed me down like a boulder. Had I responded to Staff Officer Zhao's accusations consistently? Were there quotations from Chairman Mao I could use in my defense?

Mentally shot, I lay under my coat and hummed a tune:

> *Wild goose soaring,*
> *Fly quickly, quickly,*
> *A message to Beijing.*
> *The Red Guard defender*
> *Thinks only of Chairman Mao . . .*

It was a popular ditty during the Cultural Revolution. My eyes watered, and before long tears were slipping down my cheeks.

I thought back to the days when our revered Chairman Mao had thrown his support behind the young Red Guards as we fought revisionism. In February 1967, at a meeting in the Beijing Exhibition Hall held to denounce the "Three Hus" (Hu Yaobang, Hu Keshi, and Hu Qili), I personally escorted the First Secretary of the Communist Youth

League, Hu Yaobang, onto the stage, and stood proudly in front of thousands of people. I forgot that after the mantis devours the cicada, the sparrow is on its way. Now I was Public Enemy Number One in the Forty-first Regiment, handcuffed and locked up.

Staff Officer Zhao was livid when he read my report.

"You're like an oily dog's prick, treacherous and slippery. What is this? Have you no sense of shame? Who said you could give such a glowing account of yourself? I wanted a list of your reactionary words and deeds. What's the big idea?"

"Staff Officer Zhao, I'm not guilty of reactionary words or deeds."

"No reactionary words or deeds?" His eyes were wide with disbelief. "Enough of your lies!" He glared at me, then thundered, "Your letter to Wei Xiaoli was filled with reactionary ideas! When the revolutionary masses ferret out capitalist-roaders within the party, you call that unfortunate. Is that reactionary or isn't it?"

"If an old cadre is purged because of a mistake, that's nothing to gloat over. That's what I meant by unfortunate."

"Then tell me, was it unfortunate that the revolutionary masses ferreted out Liu Shaoqi?"

Silence.

"Stand up straight!"

Reluctantly I stood at attention.

"Speak up!" He pounded the desk.

"I wasn't talking about Liu Shaoqi, I was talking about Wei Xiaoli's father. There was no problem with him."

"Who said so? Did you read her letter of introduction to the corps command?"

"No."

"Then where do you get that bullshit? How do you feel about the Cultural Revolution? How about mass movements?"

"There are problems with mass movements."

"Who said so?"

Having no reply, I kept my mouth shut.

"How come your legs are always bent? Stand up straight!"

I did as he said.

"Speak up! What about your crimes against Chairman Mao and Mao Zedong Thought?"

"Staff Officer Zhao, I'm not opposed to Chairman Mao or Mao Zedong Thought. What do you want me to say?"

"You're not? Ha ha!" His fishy eyes narrowed to slits. "I think you'd better stop lying. I'm telling you, Ma Bo, I've taken down high officials, grade seven and eight, so I know what you're going to shit the minute you squat."

"Staff Officer Zhao, I am honestly not opposed to Chairman Mao." Tormented at not being believed, I would have ripped out my heart and shown it to him if I could have.

"Are you refusing to confess, you motherfucker?"

Silence.

Bang! He slammed a pair of handcuffs down on the table and barked, "Did you or did you not say that Chairman Mao has his faults?"

I was stunned. "That doesn't mean I oppose Chairman Mao."

"It's a smear against the Chairman!"

"But Chairman Mao himself said that everybody but the dead and unborn has his faults."

"Chairman Mao is the exception, according to Vice Chairman Lin. Every word spoken by Chairman Mao is the truth. One of his sentences is worth ten thousand uttered by others."

"But Chairman Mao himself said he has his faults."

"Chairman Mao was being modest. Vice Chairman Lin's comment is the one we must accept as true." He banged the desk to show there was no room for debate.

"But Chairman Mao himself said that all people have their faults. And his words are the truth."

"Shut up! Vice Chairman Lin's comment is to be accepted as true. You're reactionary through and through, as your vicious attack against the Chairman proves. I've never seen anyone so arrogant!" Then he barked at me, "I told you to stand straight! Who said you could bend your knees? Bow your head!"

Reluctantly I stuck out my chest and stood at attention, my legs as straight as a ramrod. I lowered my head.

"Speak up! Admit your crime of opposing Chairman Mao and Mao Zedong Thought!"

Silence.

"Speak up!"

"I didn't, so what do you want me to say, Staff Officer Zhao?"

"Shit, do you really think all we know how to do is feed our faces? Speak up!"

Silence.

"Okay, then let me ask you this: The revolutionary masses express their devotion to Chairman Mao in every imaginable way because of their profound feelings for their leader. But you call this a personality cult. Am I right?"

I nodded. "Yes, because the party never approved of worshiping any individual."

"Vice Chairman Lin says we are to worship Chairman Mao without reservation."

"In 1956 the Central Committee pointed out in 'On the Historical Experiences of the Dictatorship of the Proletariat' that a personality cult is contrary to the tenets of Marxism-Leninism."

"Shut up! Chairman Mao has said that a degree of personality cult is necessary. Did you or did you not say that 'Vice Chairman Lin doesn't speak as amiably as Chairman Mao'?"

I admitted that, in order to show I had the right attitude.

"Vice Chairman Lin has called upon everyone to implement the 'Three Loyalties' and 'Four Eternals.' Don't you think they need to be forced on the people? Why must you always sing a different tune than Vice Chairman Lin? How many heads do you have?"

I was lathered with sweat. His aggressive questioning was having the desired effect on me.

"I asked you how many heads you had. Answer me!"

"Just one."

"Then it's time to come clean. It's party policy to be lenient with those who confess their crimes and severe with those who refuse to do so. Your attitude will determine what happens to you. You're a young man, so don't take the road to ruin."

"I want to come clean," I said softly.

"Now you're talking. I've just scratched the surface of your reactionary theories. There are plenty more."

During the earlier interrogation his accusation that I was a womanizer nearly destroyed my morale. But this swift and powerful attack on my politics all but drove the soul out of my body.

"What did you say about Qiu Huizuo?"

"I . . . I said he'd slept with over a dozen girls."

"What else?"

"I said he was an old thug."

The recorder took down every word.

"When? Where? Who'd you say it to?"

"WHAT DID YOU say about Lu Ping?"

"I said his political record is clear, so he'll probably be released."

"When? Where? Who'd you say it to?"

"What did you say about a personality cult? When? Where? Who'd you say it to?"

MY HEAD WAS swimming. I was like a wrestler being lifted into the air and slammed helplessly to the mat.

The night had grown late, and everyone else was asleep. The Public Security Office of the Regimental Political Section was the only room in which a light burned.

Lei Xia had divulged everything from our conversations. "Chairman Mao has his faults," "Vice Chairman Lin doesn't speak as amiably as Chairman Mao," "The 'Three Loyalties' and 'Four Eternals' don't need to be forced on the people." He was the only possible source. I could understand, since his survival was at stake, and as long as *I* survived, I could deal with it. But I had a premonition that the point of the knife would soon be pressed against my back—by the hand of a friend.

Nothing—including being locked up, having my hands cuffed behind my back, being slapped across the face—was as terrifying as being sold out by a friend.

I was like a terrified rat in the clutches of a cat.

TWO NIGHTS LATER I was called outside by the demobilized soldier who had slapped me. He led me to a dark corner of the wall.

"What are you doing?" I asked softly.

"You son of a bitch!" He smacked me across the cheek. I stumbled and fell.

He kicked me. "Get up!"

I got slowly to my feet, holding my face in my hands.

With his attacks on my politics, Staff Officer Zhao had sapped my vitality, and all my bravado was gone.

"Put your hands down!"

Grudgingly I dropped my hands. He slapped me across the other cheek, jerking my head ninety degrees.

"Face front!"

I forced myself to face him. Another sharp crack, and my right ear was ringing. I hit the ground, pretending I was out, just like Wang Lianfu.

"Aren't you the tough guy? Get up, you scumbag!"

Tucking my head in and covering my face with my hands, I curled into a ball, like a whipped puppy.

Then the kicking began.

I lay there and took it without a murmur.

"Hey, who's out there?" A disembodied voice somewhere.

The startled soldier stopped kicking and answered as though nothing were wrong. "It's me, Jiao Jun. Is that you, Commissar Liu? Pretty late for you to be up, isn't it?"

"What are you doing there, Jiao Jun? Fighting?"

"N-no."

A slim figure walked up. "Who's that? Get up."

"Ma Bo, a criminal."

"Have you been beating up on him? You'd better watch your step. Now take him back."

"I wasn't beating up on him, Commissar Liu. He tried to get tough with me, so I pushed him, and he won't get up."

Liu nodded. "Take him back this minute."

As he dragged me back to jail, he muttered. "Those people don't give a fuck that Old Wang was damned near killed!"

The image of Deputy Commissar Liu stuck in my mind.

When Squad Leader Yang took the next watch outside my door, he exclaimed indignantly, "That fucking Wang Lianfu is bad news. He doesn't know when to quit. Having you arrested wasn't enough, so he had Jiao Jun give you a beating. I'll have a talk with Jiao. Put up with it a little longer. Tell the truth and confess to whatever they say. Don't try to be a hero. A few days ago at a mass meeting at Western Ujimqin Banner they shot another one, a counterrevolutionary."

20

SIX

COUNTS

MY SITUATION WAS grim. Granted, I wasn't on death row, but being known as having a bad attitude was perilous enough. During the Cultural Revolution people were beaten to death for less. I knew I had to show a willingness to cooperate. I'd never have room to maneuver if I didn't gain my opponents' trust. It would be folly to go up against Staff Officer Zhao.

The sentry escorted me to Zhao's room.

An enigmatic smile played on his lips.

"Well, ready to talk? It's your last chance."

"Yes."

"Okay, did you kill anyone during the Cultural Revolution?"

"No."

"Start any fires?"

"No."

"Rape?"

"No."

"How about robbery?"

"No."

"Did you and Lei Xia ever gang up on anyone?"

"That was his idea. He called it a workout. But it was too much for me, so I went home. He said I was chickenshit."

"Be man enough to admit what you've done," the student taking notes piped up.

"I'm not going to say it was my idea if it wasn't."

Staff Officer Zhao grinned. "Pretty slippery. Right out of a vat of grease. Whose idea was it to forge an official seal?"

"Mine. We had no authorization to stay in guest houses along the way, so I told Jin Gang to forge one."

"What sort of tricks did you pull with your bogus letters?"

"None."

"The truth. The revolutionary masses, including some of your co-horts, have exposed and unmasked you, so we know everything. I'm only asking you these questions to check your attitude. If you tell the truth, you'll be treated leniently. But if you refuse to cooperate, we have ways of bringing you around. Severe treatment awaits those with bad at-titudes. A sentence of fifteen years, for instance, could be stretched to twenty." He fiddled with his fountain pen. "How old are you?"

"Twenty-two."

"How old will you be in twenty years?"

"Forty-two."

A sympathetic look appeared on his face. "One life shot to hell, wouldn't you say?"

I frowned, then nodded.

"I expect you to tell the whole truth. I'm not trying to scare you, but forging an official seal could put you away for quite a while. But if you come clean, you can count on leniency. It all depends on your attitude."

Silence.

"Tell me about 'The East Is Red'?"

Jin Gang and his big mouth! "I . . . I don't think 'The East Is Red' is much of a song, and I've said so."

"And?"

"And I don't think it should be sung all the time. There are limits to how often you can sing *any* song."

" 'The East Is Red' is the revolutionary masses' favorite song. They'll never tire of it, not after a thousand, even ten thousand times!"

Silence.

"Let's hear about how you smeared Comrade Jiang Qing."

"I never smeared Comrade Jiang Qing."

"According to my sources, you smeared her pretty good."

"Staff Officer Zhao, I tell you I never smeared her. You asked for the truth, and that's what I'm giving you."

"Since you appear to have amnesia, let me jog your memory. What was it you and Lei Xia talked about in your aunt's house in early 1968? Can't recall?" Vigilance showed in his eyes. "Didn't you say that Jiang Qing was a 1930s movie star?"

He scored again. Like a thief caught in the act, I was so panicky, I didn't know what to do. I could see the eerie, cold glint of Jiang Qing's glasses and was scared witless. There was no escape this time. "I just re-peated something I had heard from the United Action Committee in late '67."

"You knew it was a vicious smear, and still you repeated it? That's even worse. What else?"

"I can't . . . uh, can't remember."

"Got grease on your brain, too? Real slippery. Every time there's a crucial question you get amnesia."

He paused to let his sarcasm sink in, then went on: "Speak up, what else did you say about Comrade Jiang Qing?"

My head drooped. I was deflated.

"You can stick garlic stalks up your nose if you want, but you'll still be a pig, not an elephant. Out with it!"

"Nothing, honest," I answered hoarsely.

He banged the handcuffs on the desktop. "I want the truth!" he thundered. "Stand up straight!"

"Stand still!" the sentry commanded from behind, prodding me in the leg with his rifle.

"Speak up; what else did you say about Jiang Qing?"

"I don't know. You can't expect me to remember every casual com-ment I ever made."

With a tightening of his lips, Staff Officer Zhao said, " 'Jiang Qing has so much power, the commanders won't speak up no matter how mad they get.' Did you say that or not?"

"I forget. I might have."

"So you not only maliciously smear Jiang Qing, but you smear the commanders in the same breath."

"The Beijing United Action Committee said that in early '67. I just repeated it in a casual conversation."

"Repeating counterrevolutionary comments is forbidden."

Knowing he wouldn't listen to reason, I held my tongue.

"Snap out of it, Ma Bo. Lei Xia, Liu Yinghong, Jin Gang, and the others are trying to be revolutionary. That's why they exposed and unmasked you. What good will it do to conceal things?"

He farted loudly a couple of times, filling the room with a stink like rotten eggs.

"There's nothing to tell, Staff Officer Zhao, honest." I put more feeling into my voice and eyes than I thought possible.

"You know if there is or isn't."

"The truth, Ma Bo!" the student shouted.

"Now!" The rifle nudged me in the rear.

"Out with it!" Deafening shouts from three throats, mean glares from six eyes, the lingering stink of rotten eggs.

"Okay, go back and think hard about the Jiang Qing affair."

I nodded dejectedly.

"You can't fool me with that pitiful look. I know what you are. You're like a woman who wants to be a whore and still have a memorial archway erected in honor of her chastity."

On the way out the door he stopped me. "What's this?" He took a ball of thread and a slip of paper out of the drawer.

I was stunned.

"The first thing Yan Shu did when he got out was turn these over to us. Everybody wants to be revolutionary. No one wants to wallow in the muck with you."

I maintained my composure as I recalled something Yan Shu had said: "If they made me live in a doghouse to get out of here, I'd do it."

"Listen up. If you try to smuggle another message out, I'll snap the small cuffs on you again and leave you to rot," he snorted.

I THOUGHT LONG and hard that night. I mustn't let them destroy me. I was shaken and I was scared, but strong survival instincts instilled me with courage and imagination. That's when the idea of running came to me.

I'd begun scrutinizing my cell the minute they locked me up, so I knew that two of the windowpanes weren't fastened down. Not much room, but enough. All I had to do was crawl through the window at night, steal a horse from the stable behind the regiment mess hall, and make my getaway. Once I was in Beijing, I'd be okay. But first I had to shed my handcuffs.

"Ren Changfa, give me a hand. These things are killing me."

He jumped at the chance, willing to do anything to relieve the boredom. So on one of our trips to the toilet he picked up a piece of wire, which he later flattened with a brick, then notched with a shard of broken glass.

To keep the guards from seeing what we were up to, we covered ourselves with our coats when he began working on the lock with his homemade key. Just inserting it in the hole proved to be a tougher job than we had figured, but he wasn't easily deterred; flatten, notch, flatten some more—he threw himself into it. But three days of failure finally wore him down. "It won't work," he said glumly.

I'd have smashed it with a rock if I'd had a free hand. A saw blade would have worked, of course, but how could I get my hands on one of those? Running away was out of the question as long as my hands were cuffed like a common criminal's.

Our days were deadeningly monotonous. Sometimes we would press our faces up against the window to gaze at the outside world for two or three hours at a stretch. Just like watching TV. Our "programs"? Chickens shitting on the ground, pigs rooting at the base of the wall, people going in and out of the toilets, anything that moved, anything to pass the time.

Puffy clouds drifted silently toward us, naked branches rustled in the wind, regiment loudspeakers blared news of Prince Sihanouk's national salvation declaration. What glorious things were going on beyond the wall.

The road to Company Seven ran south of our little prison cell. Although I never caught sight of Lei Xia, I did see Jin Gang once as he passed by in a tattered army overcoat cinched at the waist with rope; he was leading a camel cart. "Jin Gang!" I shouted (the guard was away at the time). He looked around before spotting me through one of the cracks in the window, then tensed visibly. A smile—that was a good sign—a brief nod, and nothing more.

I once memorized a prison poem by a revolutionary martyr, but it took the loss of my own freedom to appreciate it:

> *A piece of ground the size of my hand, a slice of sky as big as a*
>   *basket.*
> *Fresh air. Sunlight. Water. A little at a time*
> *Beyond the wall the mountain turns yellow, then green.*
> *How many days? How many months?*
> *Time creeps by in the midst of my longing . . .*

Written in a Nationalist prison twenty years earlier, it now created an intimate bond with a prisoner in socialist China. Same difference.

During the chilling months of the One-Smash and Three-Oppose campaign, jails were being built all over China, thousands upon thousands of them. Those were dark days, indeed.

Finally, after two months of collecting and organizing evidence, plus plenty of hard work by Staff Officer Zhao, they indicted me on six counts:

1. Slandering Chairman Mao and Mao Zedong Thought
2. Slandering Vice Chairman Lin and the PLA
3. Slandering Comrade Jiang Qing
4. Demanding that the verdicts on unrepentant capitalist-roaders be overturned.

5. Listening to enemy broadcasts and disseminating the information
6. Writing reactionary letters, making lewd diary entries, and spreading promiscuous bourgeois thought

On the basis of these six counts, the Forty-first Regiment Party Committee reported me to Fifth Division and the Inner Mongolian Production Corps as an active counterrevolutionary.

21

Betrayed

SPRING ARRIVED on gusts of warm southern winds.

One night in mid-May, 1970, a guard led me into a room where a military man was sitting on the kang. Stocky, early fifties, he had the look and carriage of someone important.

Seven or eight soldiers filled the room, including two at the desk—scribes, by the look of them.

Staff Officer Zhao cleared his throat. "Ma Bo," he said gravely, "Director Fang of the Corps Public Security Section has come to adjudicate your case. The organization is right here, so if you have anything to say, now's the time. We expect you to act in accordance with the principle of seeking truth from facts."

I raised my head to get a glimpse of the newcomer; wearing an army overcoat, he struck a casual pose as he leaned against his bedroll.

"Are you Ma Bo?" Hebei accent. Genial.

"Yes." His features were square [*fang*] and boxy, just like his name. "Sit down."

I sat stiffly on a stool in the middle of the room.

"How are things these days? Getting enough to eat?"

I nodded. "No complaints."

He looked down at my handcuffs. "Do those chafe your skin?"

I raised my wrists to show they had been rubbed raw.

"Take him to the clinic when we're finished and have that attended to," he said to Staff Officer Zhao. Then he turned back to me and said amiably, "You don't have to wear those anymore. But I expect you to reciprocate by doing what's right. They put them on you because of your reputation as a fighter. It was their responsibility to the party and to you."

A rush of warmth flooded my heart. No wonder he'd climbed so high in the organization.

He started by asking about my family, and once the climate was relaxed, he said, "Ma Bo, tell me what you've been thinking lately."

That old feeling of grievance caught in my throat again. My cheeks began to ache. With a trembling voice I said, "I . . . I'm not a . . . a counterrevolutionary."

"No one said you were. We've investigated your case, and our conclusions benefit you and the cause of revolution at the same time. Thirsty? Somebody pour him a glass of water."

Staff Officer Zhao handed me a mug of water.

During the previous two months my interrogations had been characterized by angry shouts. But with Director Fang it was different: He spoke softly and even made sure I had water. I was afraid to look at him in case he was repulsed by the wolfish glint in my eyes. I'd given so many mean looks to so many people that my eyes had taken on a permanent wildness.

"Don't be afraid, Ma Bo, just tell us what you've done."

So I told him about my experiences during the Cultural Revolution, how I'd gone to Vietnam and Tibet, about my fighting, about how I'd stolen the knife and gotten a pistol. I was so nervous, it came out all jumbled up, sort of breathless.

He listened with obvious interest, as to a storyteller spinning a yarn.

The two soldiers at the desk were writing furiously.

I talked on and on, from seven till ten-thirty that night, and on my way out Director Fang told Zhao to remove my handcuffs. "Go back to your room and clean up," he said solicitously. "Do you have soap and a towel?"

"No."

He turned to Zhao. "Have the guard buy some for him."

The first thing I did back in the cell was guzzle pints of cold water. Then I danced around the room. No more handcuffs. For two months, taking a shit had become a real chore. Because of those cuffs I'd had to forgo the final nicety, and because of them I couldn't take off my coat at bedtime. The collar had been rubbed shiny by constant contact with my chin. He was all right, that Director Fang.

They didn't come for me the next day or the day after that. Ren and I spent most of our time leaning up against the window to gaze outside. Since we never saw Director Fang use the toilet, we assumed he'd gone off to the company.

A week passed before he summoned me again. As I'd guessed, he'd been gathering evidence back at Company Headquarters.

"Ma Bo, you must trust the organization. Tell us the whole truth so we can make everything come out right. As nearly as we can ascertain, your parents aren't in big trouble. We're all members of one big revolutionary family, and no one wants to see you become a counterrevolutionary."

My nose began to ache from the emotion of the moment. Old Shen and Staff Officer Zhao had long since disowned me from that "big revolutionary family," but to Director Fang I was a "comrade." To hold back now would be a slap in his face.

Unlike other public-security personnel, who are in the business of screaming and intimidating, Director Fang nodded in agreement when I said something sensible. Staff Officer Zhao, on the other hand, called me a liar no matter what I said.

A sixth sense common to all prisoners told me that Director Fang had a soft spot in his heart for me, possibly because of my parents. He treated me far better than he treated Ren Changfa. So I tried to answer his questions in a way that would satisfy him and justify his feelings toward me, reminding myself that I had to seek truth from facts but not get so carried away that I'd confess to anything just to show a good attitude.

I made a show of unburdening myself of everything, keeping my head down, my waist bent, my voice weak, low, and slightly hoarse. I knew it was safe to confess to stealing fruit, using a forged bus pass, and lifting a bedsheet from the guest house. Comments about Jiang Qing, on the other hand, were dangerous—no sense in meekly laying my head on the execution block. I avoided political issues as much as possible but couldn't gloss over them altogether. I knew I had to admit to a "real" problem once in a while. In other words, sacrifice an arm for the sake of survival. Everything hinged on a good attitude.

During the 1970 One-Smash and Three-Oppose campaign, Chairman Mao personally approved a policy of selective capital punishment as a deterrent. Thus the threat of execution hung over the head of every imprisoned criminal. With a bad attitude, you could be sacrificed as an example to others.

"What exactly did you say about Jiang Qing?"

"Nothing." I grimaced. Just the mention of her name evoked disgust and fear, like having a snake wrapped around my neck.

"We want the truth. You're not a bad kid. Get it off your chest, and you'll feel better. No more dribs and drabs. Stop squeezing the toothpaste from the top."

"Think hard. What did you say about Jiang Qing? Your friends have already told us plenty. See, it's all right there." He pointed to a stack of papers on the desk. "I'm not joking when I say we know everything about you. But we want to hear it from *you*."

Staff Officer Zhao rolled his fishy eyes. "We even know how you stole two eggs from Company Three's chicken coop during the fall harvest," he said smugly.

Director Fang walked up with the stack of papers in his hand. He held up the top half. "See here, these are Lei Xia's statements. Now do you believe me?"

I read the top sheet: "Accuser: Lei Xia. Date: 18 May 1970." His fingerprint in red ink was affixed.

He handed me another sheaf, then another . . . all together, six thick sheafs of paper, each signed by Lei Xia, the "accuser."

He'd sure had a lot to say.

I opened my eyes as wide as possible to hold back the tears. But a couple broke loose and slid down my cheeks.

"Why are you crying?" Director Fang asked sympathetically. "The poison runs deep. You're so blinded by your sense of loyalty, you no longer know right from wrong."

Zhao couldn't nod his agreement fast enough. "That's right," he said. "In his diary he called his own father a sly old fox."

"Why do you think so highly of Lei Xia? You fell smack into the trap of a secret agent's son. Done in by your own sense of loyalty, don't you know that?"

More tears slid silently down my cheeks. I'd suspected betrayal but was shaken by the stack of evidence in front of me.

Director Fang and the others gazed at me with curiosity as they sucked on hard candies. The paper window covering rustled.

FOLLOWING THE ARMED struggle on August 21, 1967, Lei Xia had become a thorn in the side of the opposition and was forced to leave school. He decided to go with me to Tibet. When I asked if he wanted to arm himself with a knife, he said he'd been thinking of getting a pistol. I asked why.

"To come to the aid of my country," he said in dead earnest.

I was delighted.

At the Chengdu station I said I wanted to slap him to test his loyalty. When he said okay, I narrowed my eyes and slapped him as hard as I could. He didn't flinch. Good boy! I stepped back and took a fighting stance. Another slap. He stood his ground, even though his face looked like a granite bust with five red welts on each cheek, hard and unyielding, encasing the unsullied soul of a warrior.

After we returned from Tibet, he was so intent on wiping out the disgrace of the August 21 debacle, he volunteered to become my punching bag during workouts. Day in and day out he let me punch him without asking anything in return.

When Old Gigolo knocked me down with an ax handle, it was Lei Xia who came to my aid. When Daoerji and his pack of Mongols were about to kill Ingush, it was Lei Xia who rescued him. When Wang Lianfu came at me with shears, it was Lei Xia who stopped him. He was the first person I ever loved. On April 26, 1968, he was arrested for carrying a pistol. Unable to bear the thought of losing my best friend, I went to the jail and demanded to be locked up with him.

One friend like that was enough for a lifetime.

He said I was Napoleonic: somber, eccentric, suspicious, and short-tempered. To me he was Lenin's bodyguard Vasili: loyal, incorruptible, and fearless. Our friendship was the union of a tank and a cannon, useless separately but a formidable weapon when united. It had weathered many bloody battles already but none like this, and its survival would be a story worth telling.

But to all appearances, an intrepid young man had become a piece of traitorous dogshit. The red fingerprint was a smear of blood, bequeathed to me by the person who had urged me not to become a turncoat. "Together through thick or thin!" A knife to the heart. Memories and tears.

What sort of age were we living in, when all loyalties were abolished, except devotion to one man? Constantly encouraged to turn against our own, we were caught up in a frenzy of betrayal. Not even our own parents were to be trusted.

22

THE

GRILLING

"REFLECT ON WHAT you said about Jiang Qing. Now get some rest, it's late," Director Fang said with what I took to be genuine concern. But I don't think I slept a wink that night, unable to get Lei Xia's betrayal off my mind.

One day in 1968, he said, "Jiang Qing keeps the Chairman on a short leash. Like house arrest." To which I replied, "She's worse than the fucking Empress Dowager!" Serious business, much too risky to confess. But Lei Xia must have told them. If not, why was Director Fang so intent on asking me about Jiang Qing?

Admit it or not? I asked myself all night long, finally deciding to stall a while longer. I'd have to stonewall it on this one.

They sent for me the next morning.

"Ma Bo, you look like a man burdened by his thoughts. Speak up, lighten your load. It's foolish to hold back now, since Lei Xia has already told us everything. Break free of that loyalty mumbo jumbo. Your attitude will determine the degree of leniency. We want to hear you repeat what you said about Jiang Qing. We already know what it is, we just want to give you a chance to unburden yourself."

I looked at Director Fang, a man who held the power of life and death over a hundred thousand students in the Inner Mongolian Production Corps, and was assailed by doubts. If I clammed up, they'd say I had a bad attitude, and I could forget about a light sentence. But if I told them what they wanted to hear, I'd be confessing to the crime of "viciously smearing Comrade Jiang Qing," and anything was possible. Comparing the wife of Chairman Mao to the Empress Dowager could earn me a bullet in the head.

I couldn't, I just couldn't say it. Maybe Director Fang was trying to trick me into confessing something he wasn't sure of. I wished I could forget I had ever said it, but I could actually hear it echoing in my head. I clenched my teeth and kept the words inside me all that day.

They sent for me again that night.

"Ma Bo, you're starting to worry me. What keeps a clever boy like you from turning the corner? Remember, we're comrades in one big revolutionary family, and no one wants to hurt you. Just say it, and we'll help rid you of the poison."

I kept my head lowered and my mouth shut.

"Let me read you part of a directive from Vice Chairman Lin," Director Fang said, putting on his reading glasses. " 'The height of stupidity,' " he read, very deliberately, " 'is refusing to acknowledge your mistakes. The smart person is one who jumps at the chance to rectify his mistakes. Anyone who won't face his own mistakes is not only stupid, but a coward as well.' "

He handed me the booklet and told me to read it aloud. I did as I was told.

"Come on, Ma Bo, bite the bullet and say it."

By this time I'd confessed to every bad thing I'd done since childhood, everything but that one damning utterance.

My head hung from exhaustion: four hours of interrogation in the morning, another four in the afternoon, and four more at night. Answering Director Fang's questions was hard work, since I had to make sure everything I said would stand up to scrutiny and not contradict what I'd said before.

It was getting late when he yawned, looked at his watch, and said, "That's enough for now. You need to think harder."

We were back at it at eight the next morning, me on a stool in the middle of the room, surrounded by eight uniformed men.

Director Fang had interrogated me for two days without the desired results, but he was patient as always, his attitude as genial as when he'd begun. "Ma Bo, have no misgivings. When it's time to dispose of your case, we'll take into consideration the facts that your parents are veteran comrades and that you're still young. It's a person's complete history that counts, not an isolated comment or two. Don't you agree?"

I nodded.

"Then go ahead and say it." His voice dripped with sincerity and with hope.

"I really don't remember, Director Fang."

"Not true. You're still weighed down by your thoughts, I can see that."

"I really don't remember, Director Fang," I said dejectedly. The gentler he became, the harder it was for me to do what he wanted. My heart was in shreds.

I managed to hold out till noon; break time, I thought. But less than two hours later I was back on my stool being grilled. I was losing my voice and my ears were ringing. I grew increasingly tense as exhaustion set in and was afraid I'd say the wrong thing. By taking turns they wore me down until I saw stars.

The minute I entered the room I sensed that something bad was about to happen. I felt naked, totally exposed. My forehead was all sweaty.

"Ma Bo." The dulcet voice of Fang. "We've done everything but get down on our knees and beg. Why do you think we're going to all this trouble? For you, that's why. We must fulfill our responsibilities to you and to the party. That's the only reason we keep asking you these questions. If we felt like it, we could slap a counterrevolutionary label on you so fast, it'd make your head swim."

That bowled me over. All that time, all that energy spent on me, grilling me until their lips were cracked, their tongues dry, their eyes red and puffy; and still I clammed up. Why?

Should I tell them? Being known as someone who "viciously smeared Comrade Jiang Qing" was not pleasant to contemplate. Not tell them, then? What if Director Fang lost his patience? A battle of indecision raged inside me.

My will was bending to the concern in Director Fang's eyes.

It must have been past nine o'clock, and I was so sleepy, I could barely keep my eyes open. Director Fang smiled. I could no longer resist the power in that smile.

Slowly but surely my ears began to fail me, and the sounds of their voices drifted farther and farther into the distance. After nearly fifty hours of interrogation my mind was a blank, except for the constant buzzing. Say it and be done with it. Let them do what they want with me. I need rest, I need sleep.

Utterly disheartened, I asked hoarsely for pen and paper. Zhao handed me his fountain pen and a clean sheet of paper. I wrote, "In early 1968, after hearing Lei Xia say something about Jiang Qing, I said, 'Jiang Qing is the new Empress Dowager.' "

My tears flowed as I wrote, for I knew I was fitting the noose over my own neck and that Director Fang would be my hangman if he chose to. The room was deathly quiet. Eight pairs of eyes followed the movements of my right hand.

When I finished, Director Fang picked up the paper without a word and handed it to the man beside him.

I bowed my head and sobbed.

Finally Director Fang broke the silence. "All right," he said gently, "you did it on your own. I'm proud of you."

Staff Officer Zhao pointed to the paper. "Your fingerprint."

With one final effort I added my fingerprint in red, like the red mark on a list of the condemned.

The guard took me back to my cell. It was after ten o'clock.

———

THEY DIDN'T SEND for me again.

For two solid days I lay on the floor in a semitrance, my head buried under my sheepskin coat. My brain wouldn't function, and I ached from head to toe.

Now my fate was in someone else's hands.

23

DIVIDE
AND CONQUER

As NEARLY AS I could piece it together afterwards, this is what happened in the company during that period:

Political Instructor Shen went looking for all who knew me and got them to snitch on me (he got them to snitch on each other while he was at it). He was determined to ferret out every so-called antiparty activity that had occurred during the rectification campaign. The pressure was greatest on Lei Xia. For two solid months he was summoned time and again by public-security cadres from the corps, the division, and the regiment.

"Let's lay our cards on the table. You've got problems of your own, some more serious than Ma Bo's, so by not calling you on the carpet we're giving you a wonderful opportunity. Don't forget, your father was a Nationalist secret agent."

"He ran off before I was a year old!" Lei Xia countered angrily. "My mother raised me by herself. If it's background you're looking for, check her out, not him. In 1966 I went to the State Council Reception Center to clear the mess up, and they agreed it's my mother who counts, not my father."

Staff Officer Zhao responded with a phony smile, "Well, that's what it says in your dossier. What counts is that while you can't choose your past, you *can* choose your future. The regiment wants to be absolutely correct in dealing with you. You could have been arrested long ago for conspiring with Ma Bo to beat up a demobilized soldier. That was no ordinary fight, it was an act of class hatred."

"Go ahead, arrest me."

"Don't get moody on us," Director Fang replied genially. "Ma Bo has already confessed to everything you two did. It's all right there in his diary. There's nothing you can tell us that we don't already know. You'd be well advised to say it anyway."

But he refused to snitch, even in the face of strong political pressure. It was time for them to divide and conquer: The Regimental Political Office sent a telegram to his mother, who rushed to Inner Mongolia from Manchuria to beg for leniency. As proof that Lei Xia should not be considered the son of a Nationalist agent, she brought the documents from the 1967 trip to the State Council Reception Center.

"Xia," she pleaded tearfully in the regimental guest house, "tell them what they want to know. What else can you do?"

Lei Xia glared at her.

"What if they arrest you, too? I have no connections, no backing. Don't try to be a hero, you'll break my heart."

Lei Xia was speechless.

"He's probably going to be sent away no matter what, so why not expose him? Because he might come back? Think about yourself for once. And think about me."

She was soon sobbing piteously. The trip from Heilongjiang had taken seven days, owing to all the late and missed trains, and she was ill by the time she arrived. Her drawn, ashen face nearly broke his heart. She was his sole protector. Yet his reputation meant everything to him, and he couldn't do what she asked. They could turn him into a pig or a dog if they wanted to. But a turncoat? No way!

When his mother saw that her words were falling on deaf ears, she climbed out of bed, kneeled on the floor, and begged, "Why won't my 'little baby' do as I say? It would kill me if they arrested you!" She banged her head on the floor.

He picked her up and put her back in bed. "Don't make a scene, okay?"

Her tears were wasted on him.

In the end it was Director Fang who won him over.

My confessions had filled ten thick notebooks. After showing him my signature, they told him I'd revealed how he listened to enemy broadcasts and egged me on to beat up Wang Lianfu the second time. When the subject turned to my letter to Wei Xiaoli, Director Fang said he was of the opinion that I had broken my vow to Lei Xia by writing her without his knowledge. And by divulging our activities during the Cultural Revolution I'd given Political Instructor Shen ammunition to punish him. It was obvious that his well-being was of no concern to me.

Poor Lei Xia didn't sleep a wink that night, as he agonized over what to do. The word *turncoat* tormented his soul. On the other hand, who could blame him for giving up a "turncoat" who was already beneath contempt?

In the spring of 1970, when the One-Smash and Three-Oppose campaign was in full swing, tens of thousands of people were attacked in huge open rallies. Announcements of verdicts were posted in public places like train stations, athletic fields, and storefronts, so large and so white that you couldn't miss them, each listing the names of "counter-revolutionaries" with red check marks to show that the executions had been carried out. That was the political climate in which Director Fang finally managed to undermine Lei Xia's stubborn will.

Normally his wit and daring were never more in evidence than during a crisis. Once he'd made up his mind, nothing could change it. He liked to boast that he could cut off a man's ear without a moment's hesitation and even manage a smile if he had to.

Once he finished the first notebook of accusations against me, our friendship was history. No need to be sad over the fate of a "turncoat," so if accusations were what they wanted, that's what he'd give them. Now that he was serving a new master, the first person he went to see was Liu Yinghong.

"What are *you* going to do?" he asked her unhappily.

"The damned PI wanted me to snitch on Ma Bo. Then he got everybody in Second Platoon to snitch on me. Arresting Ma Bo isn't enough for him. He won't be happy till he gets us all."

Lei Xia frowned and said softly, "Don't be swayed by your emotions. Just do what he wants."

"What do you mean?"

"I mean we should seek truth from facts. If there's something to report, report it. Why protect him?"

"Have you broken with Ma Bo?"

"Why get involved in his problems? He's the one who's already told them everything."

"Who said so?" she asked warily. "He wouldn't do that."

"The director of public security said so. He showed me a stack of confessions. Maybe he was trying to trick me, I don't know, but there's no question that Ma Bo sold me out."

"How?"

"In that letter to Wei Xiaoli he divulged things we'd sworn never to tell anyone. I asked him not to send it till I'd talked with the PI, but he wouldn't wait. He was mooning over a girl and he told her things that could put his best friend's head on the chopping block. Wouldn't you call that selling me out?"

Liu Yinghong lowered her head and said nothing.

"You don't know Ma Bo. He's not what he seems to be. I caught him admiring himself in a mirror lots of times. Staff Officer Zhao says his diary reads like an X-rated novel."

"You should look at the whole picture," Liu Yinghong said.

"I am. He fought one of his best friends over a dog. He told Wei Xiaoli about the incident with the pistol in spite of my warning not to, just so he could get into her good graces. Eating wasps, drinking the water he washes his feet in, using a rock for a pillow, it's all for show."

"By attacking him like this you're falling right into Shen's trap—he wants to get us fighting like a pack of dogs."

"I'm not afraid to say any of this to his face, but I didn't include it in my written report."

Jin Gang, of course, didn't need Lei Xia to do his work for him; he filled a dozen pages of accusations against me. He was scared silly over the fact that he had forged an official seal; with his dubious background, he went looking for Political Instructor Shen, Director Li, and Commissar Chen to plead his case, never missing an opportunity to "swear to Chairman Mao."

Together they gave Shen a mountain of damning evidence, and still that didn't get them off the hook. Ordered to make room in the dorm for a second group of Tianjin students, they wound up sleeping in huts next to the square, and the new arrivals were told, "Avoid the people in those huts. They're problem cases."

The PI referred to Lei Xia and the others as the Ma Bo Clique.

24

THE JURY

IS OUT

AFTER DIRECTOR FANG left, I went over the issues I'd dealt with, answering each charge with two or three rejoinders. I was fairly confident I'd be okay. If I had read him right, he wouldn't be too hard on me. I knew I was better off than Ren Changfa, who told me that Director Fang had pounded the table and screamed, "Stop lying! Why can't you be more like Ma Bo?"

As my dejection evaporated I stopped grieving over the loss of Lei Xia's friendship. I only wished I hadn't wept in front of Director Fang like that. Mother would have called me a sissy.

Being in custody was beginning to take its toll. Director Fang had told Staff Officer Zhao to let me out once in a while to stretch my legs, but he never did. So I did fifty push-ups and some deep knee bends every day to keep my muscle tone sharp, and Ren Changfa and I sparred every once in a while.

As the weather turned warm, the guards began restricting our water intake so they wouldn't have to escort us to the latrine so often. Their work ethic had deteriorated dramatically: They frequently made themselves scarce, leaving no one to open the door for us when nature called. And when we pissed in the room, the stench gave them yet another excuse to stay away. Which was okay with me, since I could do whatever I wanted.

We now had a new cellmate: the accountant from Company Ten, a favorite of his company commander but a sworn enemy of Staff Officer Zhao. He was charged with raping young girls.

"It wasn't rape," he defended himself dolefully. "They let me do it. And they weren't young girls, either. It's a way of life with those herdsmen. Some do it to seven, eight, as many as ten. Me, I only had six . . . Thirty or more isn't unusual. Why don't they arrest them?"

Ren Changfa and I made a chess set to pass the time, using scraps of toilet paper for the chess pieces. I won every game at first, but eventually he improved to the point where we were pretty evenly matched. Once, after seven games, he said I'd lost five, but I was sure it was four. An argument erupted.

"Four."

"Five."

"Cut the bullshit. It was four!"

"If you want me to hand the game to you, just say so."

We argued till we were red in the face. Finally he sneered and said, "You're not only a rotten player, you haven't got the decency to admit it when you lose." He touched his cheek—the old "shame on you" sign—and stuck out his tongue. That did it; I slapped him. He turned ashen before charging like a wild man. "Little bastard!" he screamed, picking up the water pitcher and whacking me over the head with it.

We really got into it then: hair-pulling, gouging, pinching, punching, growling like mad dogs, trying to get a grip on each other, panting, calling each other every name in the book. Our poor little rapist cowered in the corner.

It wasn't easy, but I pinned him. "Fuck your old lady!" he screeched as he struggled to his feet. It took a couple of meaningful rifle prods from the guard to separate us.

Staff Officer Zhao sent for me the next day and was as abusive as ever. I expected him to cuff my hands behind my back again, but when he merely screamed at me, I assumed there had been news from above. Something told me things had taken a positive turn.

———

WHEN JULY rolled around we were taken out by armed guards to work at jobs no one else wanted: hefting baskets of mud, digging holes, stacking coal, cleaning the latrines, sweeping the streets. Before long we were the most recognizable people in the regiment. But we didn't care what people thought, since working outside was better than being cooped up all day in a tiny room four paces from one wall to the other.

After a hard day's work we were asleep before our heads hit the pillow. "What a life," one of the guards said enviously. "Someone to watch over you when you sleep and bring you food when you're hungry. You're even protected in the crapper."

Each morning a group of cashiered senior officials lined up for work details. The Revolutionary Committee had been cleared of involvement in the "Inner Mongolian Party" in the summer of 1969, but the people charged with carrying out policy weren't happy about that, and as late as summer 1970 members of the Inner Mongolian Party in Injgan Sum were still spending half their time performing hard labor, the other half studying and being studied.

No one can imagine what it's like to be publicly denounced until it happens to him. I watched the line of doleful men with deepening sadness as they paraded beneath our window in single file, heads bowed, dressed in rags. Naturally I was reminded of how I'd ransacked Gonggele's home. I regretted doing it. So what if he was a herdowner? That didn't make him any less human. Why beat him like a common beast?

One day, as we were sweeping the Regiment Political Section compound, an old herdsman walked by. It was Gonggele. I smiled. "Hello there." He recognized me, bowed slightly, and replied, "Hello. Hello there," before continuing on his way.

Staff Officer Zhao burst out of his room and ran up to Gonggele. "Hey! What did you say to him just now?"

Poor Gonggele didn't know what to do.

"Don't you know he's a criminal? Want to join him?" The old fellow just smiled and nodded to show his remorse. I felt awful.

Guilt bothered me more than anything. Next came thoughts of Wei Xiaoli. My first love, and now she was gone. Just thinking about her broke my heart, so I tried hard not to. For a time I hoped to see her in my dreams, which might mean we had a future after all. I hoped and I hoped, but even several months later it still hadn't happened.

Then one night there she was, standing gracefully in the dark sky, wreathed in the stars, her face pale, her limpid eyes fixed on me. Were those tears? Her neck, longer than before, fit her body perfectly. Her lovely red lips trembled slightly, as if she wanted to say something. Her moonlit face was as fine as a piece of alabaster. She was the purest, loveliest girl I'd ever seen. Wrapped in a cloud like a sacred cloak, black one minute, white the next. The sun, the moon, and the stars swirled behind her; the Milky Way danced above her head. My heart was pounding. I'd have stepped forward but for the fear that my breath would foul the air around her. Sadly the light was too hazy to see the emotion hidden in her eyes.

Sadness mixed with joy, sweet yet bitter. Was I dreaming, or was this real? I awoke with a start. Darkness all around. I screamed in agony.

2 5

THE

VERDICT

STAFF OFFICER ZHAO burst into our cell one morning. "Today's the mass denunciation meeting," he said, crinkling his nose. "Do what you're told up there. Keep your heads down and your mouths shut. If you've got something to say, save it till later. Don't screw up, or you'll pay dearly." The overpowering stench in the room made him blanch, and he softened his voice a bit. "We have a responsibility to the masses to carry out party policy. You guys will get what you deserve."

Two armed guards escorted us to the meeting.

Since it was the first meeting of the One-Smash and Three-Oppose campaign, every company was represented, to which all the tractors and wagons parked in front of the assembly hall attested. A banner proclaiming DENUNCIATION MEETING hung above a platform lined on both sides by armed soldiers. The hall was packed; even the windowsills were occupied.

Six uniformed soldiers walked up behind us. This was no ordinary event; you could feel it in the air.

"I declare this denunciation meeting open," Director Li of the Regimental Political Section announced.

"Bring up the first defendant, the child-rapist Xiaowu Lata!"

Twisting his arms behind his back and grasping the nape of his neck, two soldiers dragged and pushed him up to the platform.

The slogan leaders—one male, one female—shouted in turn, "Down with the criminal Xiaowu Lata!"

"Long live the dictatorship of the proletariat!"

Echoed by the crowds, the slogans were deafening.

"Bring up the Company Two active counterrevolutionary Ren Changfa!" Director Li announced majestically.

Ren's head was pushed down below his knees. Two soldiers holding his arms and neck dragged him stumbling to the platform.

"Down with the active counterrevolutionary Ren Changfa!"

"Leniency for those who confess their crimes, severity for those who refuse to!"

"Steadfastly suppress all active counterrevolutionaries!"

Frenzied shouts reverberated throughout the hall.

Then came the words I'd been dreading: "Bring up the Company Seven active counterrevolutionary Ma Bo!"

Two grim-looking soldiers jerked my arms behind me, grabbed me by the nape of the neck, and pushed me through the crowd, one agonizing step after the other, my head no more than a couple of feet from the floor. Suddenly I was standing dizzily on the platform as the shrill voices of the slogan leaders rang out, followed by terrifying echoes from the crowd:

"Down with the active counterrevolutionary Ma Bo!"

"Never forget class struggle!"

All those glaring people reviled me with their shouts, and then Director Li read the formal charges against us, followed by the verdicts from the corps. This time our heads were jerked back by the hair until all we could see was the ceiling.

"Active counterrevolutionary Ma Bo, male, Han nationality, twenty-two, middle-peasant background. Came to the Injgan Sum pasture in October 1968 and joined Production Company Seven.

"Verified facts show that Ma Bo frequently, casually, and maliciously attacked our great Chairman Mao, Vice Chairman Lin, Mao Zedong Thought, and Comrade Jiang Qing. After careful investigation, the Corps Party Committee, in applying the principle of leniency for those who confess their crimes, severity for those who refuse to, concludes provisionally that Ma Bo is an active counterrevolutionary and is to be returned to his work unit for supervised labor."

"Down with the active counterrevolutionary Ma Bo!"

"Down with the active counterrevolutionary Ma Bo!"

The male slogan leader was hoarse from screaming, the tendons in his neck straining against the skin. The cheeks of his female companion, equally consumed by proletarian indignation, were bright red. Shouted invective from the students at the meeting made me cringe. Now the time had come for the company representatives to step forward with their denunciations.

"Bow your head!" A fist thudded into the back of my neck.

Liu Yinghong read the Company Seven denunciation. Caught up in the emotional climate, she reviled me fervently: hypocrite, loyal follower of Liu Shaoqi, fascist. Dishonest, base, shameless, immoral.

I was stunned that someone I respected could attack me with such ferocity. Her words cut like a knife.

I wanted to look up and proclaim my innocence, but I was afraid of stirring up the volatile crowd's emotions. I knew I'd have to stand there and let her dump her load of shit on me.

"Bow your head!" Another fist in the nape of my neck. I was nearly touching my knees already. How much lower did they want me to get? Bent nearly double, and not sure how much longer I could keep standing, I straightened up, a millimeter at a time, so they wouldn't notice. I wouldn't fall in front of all those people. My dignity was at stake.

As I strained to regain my balance, great beads of sweat, mixed with tears, dripped onto my shoes and the floor. I knew I was about to keel over. I had to straighten up.

"Bow your head!" This time the fist thudded into my kidney, hard and deep.

I was drowning in angry denunciations, vitriol, and self-righteous slogans. The pain in my lower back was nearly unbearable.

"Down with the active counterrevolutionary Ma Bo!"

Angry shouts bounced off the walls—these were the voices of our national-reclamation troops. Had it not been for the guards, who kept order, and Director Li, who represented authority, they would have rushed the platform and torn me limb from limb. Words cannot describe my terror at that moment. I was still dizzy and my ears rang long after I had been returned to my cell.

Ren Changfa received three years for being an active counterrevolutionary. Xiaowu Lata got seven years.

We lay on the floor like mummies, oblivious even to the flies swarming around our mouths. The next day we were taken on a circuit of the companies to be subjected to more denunciations.

Just before the Company Seven meeting began, Director Li glared at me and said, "Ma Bo, the masses have complained about your behavior during these denunciation meetings. Just because you weren't permanently labeled doesn't mean there isn't a label with your name on it. Labels are in the hands of the masses, who can stick them on you any time they want!" He ended his tirade with a spray of saliva that hit me full in the face.

The meeting was held in the front of the mess hall, right where I'd thrown Wang Lianfu eight times in a row. The wall was plastered with slogans: SUPPRESS ALL COUNTERREVOLUTIONARIES! DOWN WITH THE ACTIVE COUNTERREVOLUTIONARY MA BO!

They stood me in front of my Company Seven comrades, two armed soldiers forcing my head down until I was bent double. I was lathered with sweat under a blazing sun. Everyone had shown up, including old ladies who never attended meetings, farmers' dependents, babes in arms, even some old Mongols, all wanting to see what would happen to me.

Lei Xia was the first to speak.

I couldn't see his face, but I could picture the smug look. His cheeks, as rosy as they had been when I had slapped him at the train station that time, would be the proof of his anger.

"First I must thank the regimental and company commanders for giving me this chance to expose and unmask the active counterrevolutionary Ma Bo. Back when I still refused to remold my worldview, I engaged in many activities that brought shame to the party and to

Chairman Mao. But the One-Smash and Three-Oppose campaign, led by Chairman Mao and the party, has exposed an active counterrevolutionary hiding among the revolutionary masses. Yet while everyone else was shouting approval, I remained passive. Then our leaders patiently showed me the error of my ways, and I vowed to return to Chairman Mao's revolutionary line. Now I will take the lead in exposing the counterrevolutionary activities of Ma Bo.

"Like all hypocrites, he played the role of high-principled idealist to the hilt in order to hoodwink the young people around him. I worshiped him because he pillowed his head on a rock, wore filthy clothes, and ate wasps, and I was nearly sucked up in the quagmire of counterrevolution. He cleverly drew attention to himself by adopting an unorthodox lifestyle. He raided his own home during the Cultural Revolution to steal enough money to take him to Vietnam. It was all part of an ambitious plan. He once told me he revered Napoleon, who would go down in history as a hero or as a villain, one or the other.

"Politically he's a dyed-in-the-wool reactionary. On the pretext of conducting research, he vilified the great Chairman Mao and was always burying his head under the covers to listen to enemy broadcasts. He said we should listen to both sides to see who was right and who was wrong. He was so unhappy with the way the revolutionary masses investigated his parents that he said if he ever got his hands on the Red Guard who grilled his father, he'd kill him.

"His hypocrisy carries into daily life. He poses as a person of high morals, but goes around stealing anything he can get his hands on. He took a bedsheet from a guest house on the way to Inner Mongolia and an alarm clock from a photo studio in Western Ujimqin Banner. People who boast about being pure and high-minded really have nothing but sex and filth on their minds. Ma Bo's like that.

"The evidence proves he is an active counterrevolutionary in every way. I resolutely support the verdict handed down on him. I am determined to learn a lesson written in blood from this episode. No more false loyalty. I will follow Chairman Mao in revolution for the rest of my life!

"Down with the active counterrevolutionary Ma Bo!"

The shout, honed to a razor's edge with loathing, ripped through my eardrums.

Wei Xiaoli was somewhere in the crowd, I was sure of that. It was the ultimate cruelty, having to stand like a loathsome coward in front of a divine goddess. I felt I had been stripped naked.

Then I heard Qi Shuzhen's voice ring out: "Active counterrevolutionary Ma Bo, in the reactionary letter you sent to a certain person you indulged in unbridled propaganda on behalf of the theory of bloodlines. Chairman Mao has said there is no such thing as love or hatred without reason or cause. What Ma Bo loves or hates has class origins. His father is quarantined for interrogation, his mother is the author of the stinking poisonous weed *The Song of Youth*. His aunt once betrayed an underground party member who was her paramour. This is the sort of reactionary environment in which Ma Bo grew up, so his thoughts and emotions carry the brand of the reactionary class. Fish school and shrimps cluster. Sending a love letter to the daughter of a capitalist-roader was inevitable. They could join forces to give vent to their dissatisfaction with the party and with the Cultural Revolution."

My deepest, most treasured emotion, reserved for the divine creature who had bestowed a look upon me in a dream, was torn from my chest and displayed for all to mortify.

"Bow your head," Director Li said in a low voice behind me.

My chin was already touching my chest.

"I said, bow your head." The voice was still low, but this time it had a sharper edge.

"Bow your head!" Someone grabbed the back of my neck and forced my head violently downward.

"Down with the active counterrevolutionary Ma Bo!"

For an entire week we were dragged to each company to be paraded and denounced by the masses—chickens being sacrificed to frighten a regiment of monkeys. At night we lay on the floor of our cell without exchanging a word.

I'm done for! From that point on, I knew, I would be a political pariah. I was an enemy of the Communist Party, an enemy of eight hundred million Chinese citizens. An enemy even of my own parents.

I had been abandoned by *everyone*. The shadowy life of a counter-revolutionary, outside the protection of the law, someone to be beaten or killed with impunity. Chairman Mao, do you know what is happening to us out here?

I could hear Director Fang's comforting voice: "Trust in the party, trust in the organization. We don't want you to become a counterrevolutionary. Deep down you're a good person."

Naïvely I had offered up my heart to him, hiding nothing and expecting leniency. You tricked me, Director Fang. You lied when you said, "Leniency for those who confess their crimes, severity for those who refuse to."

Gradually I came to believe that his affability and intimacy belied evil intentions. Still, it was hard to link deception with the good looks, warm gaze, open emotions, and neat appearance of the old Eighth Route soldier. I hoped I was wrong.

Distinguishing friend from foe is a basic revolutionary principle. How could they so casually declare me the enemy? Was it really that easy to become the enemy of eight hundred million people? Was it really all right to publicly insult and vilify, even destroy, a counterrevolutionary, treat him like an animal in the zoo?

The questions were piling up fast. They tore at my heart.

We lay on the rug, hardly making a sound, for three days, interrupted only by the next dispirited meal. We were worn out from days of standing in the "airplane" position—bent at the waist, head up, arms straight behind us—yet lying there all day long didn't help. The cell was deathly quiet. A bowl of millet lay on the floor, untouched by anything but flies.

After three days, I was beginning to adapt to the harsh realities of my new life, and a thought began to form in the black void of my mind: You must survive! The darkness quickly swallowed it up. Then another thought: You mustn't die! Again the darkness swallowed it up.

Gradually yet another thought rose above the rest with growing intensity:

Appeal to the Central Committee.

The power of this thought was greater than the darkness. It swelled until it was a raging ball of fire, the fire of life.

I must write to the Central Committee.

No more lying down. I felt as if every second wasted by not writing that letter brought me closer to death. I wrote like a madman, all that day and night, for I had to let the Central Committee of the Communist Party know what had befallen me. I filled sheet after sheet of paper with the words that would save me.

THE GUARD ESCORTED me to Staff Officer Zhao's room. He pointed to a thick stack of documents. "We need your fingerprint," he said. Ten notebooks, everything I'd told them. They were numbered. I did as he said. He then went through them page by page, and had me place my fingerprint next to all the changes. Finally he took out a clean sheet of paper and told me to write: "The material contained herein is factual and given voluntarily. No coercion was used by the interrogators." When I finished, I signed it and affixed my fingerprint.

He looked at me and said, "We've followed party policy to the letter in carrying out our duties. No funny business. Is there anything you want to say?"

"Staff Officer Zhao, the penalty's too harsh for the crime."

"What? You get a slap on the wrist and still have the guts to say it's too harsh?"

"I never opposed the party, and I never opposed Chairman Mao, so why do they say I'm a counterrevolutionary?"

Deadpan. "Your problems are worse than anybody else's, yet they withheld the label. Here, read this report from the division."

He opened a drawer, shuffled some papers, and handed me one.

An Investigative Report by the Political Section,
Fifth Division, Inner Mongolian Production Corps,
Beijing Military Region, People's Liberation Army,
Regarding Criminal Activities by the
Active Counterrevolutionary Ma Bo

SUPREME DIRECTIVE

We must be prepared to expose counterrevolutionaries in hiding. They must be punished for their reactionary crimes.

Based upon irrefutable proof of criminal activity, the accused is to be known as an active counterrevolutionary, loathed by the people for reactionary thought and serious crimes. Refusing to confess to his crimes while under detention, he engaged in illegal activities. The Division Political Section therefore decrees that Ma Bo is to be expelled from the ranks of corps troopers and sentenced to a period of incarceration of eight years.

Forwarded for approval by
Political Section, Fifth Division,
Inner Mongolian Production Corps,
Beijing Military Region (seal)
8 October 1970

I was stunned. Eight years? For what?

"Director Fang checked with the Beijing Military Region Public-Security Section on your case. The decision was personally approved by a senior official."

"But I'm, I'm not a counterrevolutionary."

I sounded weak and diffident, and Zhao sneered. "I guess the term turns to ashes in the mouths of counterrevolutionaries. If you don't want to be a counterrevolutionary, you shouldn't act like one, right? This is a collective decision by the Corps Party Committee."

"But I am *not* a counterrevolutionary, Staff Officer Zhao!"

"Are you saying that the Communist Party has treated you unfairly?" His fishy eyes snapped open wide.

"No, no, I'm not," I protested.

"Good, because if you were to say something like that outside, you'd be advocating the overturning of a lawful verdict, which would only add to your crimes. Understand?"

As the guard escorted me out of the compound, I was gripped once again by fear.

Next to the gate stood a red "quotations wall" five meters tall and half a meter thick. On it, in Chairman Mao's own calligraphy, was the gold-lettered slogan SERVE THE PEOPLE.

26

LABOR

REFORM

LATE AUGUST 1970, the autumn harvest season. Even after sundown the place was as busy as a train station, the square lit up like daytime. Whirring winnowers tirelessly sent grain arching through the night air. Students swept up the husks; porters hummed as they carried sacks of grain into silos; noisy combines raced their engines in distant fields.

There were mountains of grain. That first year we brought in a bumper crop. It would be the last of its kind.

Some newly arrived Tianjin students breathed life into the company, their selflessness and rousing work ethic contrasting sharply with the passivity of those of us who had experienced the party rectification campaign. The newcomers vied to see who could leave the best impression on the steppe, on the leaders, and on themselves.

I lived a very different life, as my diary shows.

AUGUST 29, 1970

Last night Staff Officer Zhao told me to return to the company. I rode back this morning on Old Gigolo's wagon with mixed feelings. I was returning as a free man *and* as a counterrevolutionary, sort of like a fresh steamed bun with a maggot in it.

Old Gigolo shared his felt blanket with me. Reported to the PI first thing. He was supervising grain-storage work. "I'm back, Political Instructor."

"So I see. When did you get in?" He stood with his hands behind his back, grinning smugly.

"Just now."

"Okay. You'll work with Squad Three."

"Where do I bunk?"

He frowned. "We're kind of cramped, what with the newcomers from Tianjin and all."

"What about the new block of buildings?"

"No doors or windows yet."

"That's okay with me."

He gave his permission, and I walked off dejectedly. People stopped working to watch me pass. I retrieved my torn, moldy bedroll from the storeroom. The only clothes that hadn't disappeared were my wrestling outfits. After laying a mat on the floor of my new quarters—it was going to be awfully cold in there—I piled dirt on the threshold to keep the chickens and pigs from wandering in and shitting on my bed.

It's time to begin life as a counterrevolutionary, ready or not. I'll keep my mouth shut, hold my head up without seeming proud, and hide my feelings. I hear Wang Lianfu refused to return to Company Seven and was reassigned as a driver for Company Three. That's great news. With him around I'd be dead meat.

SEPTEMBER 1, 1970

Sweltering.

Spent the day making adobe blocks, stripped to the waist and work-ing as far from camp as possible, stopping only to eat and relieve myself. I don't dare take a break, not even to catch my breath, since I'm prob-ably being watched. Working alone all the time wipes all thoughts right out of your head.

Blood blisters on the palms of my hands, and my feet ache.

I was ready to drop last night but went looking for Squad Leader Jiang Baofu anyway. In the dim kerosene lamplight I told him that the charges leveled at me during the denunciation meeting were unfair, that I wasn't opposed to the party or to Chairman Mao, and that I'm no counterrevolutionary.

I could see flashes of interest in his tiny, darting eyes, even a little sympathy and curiosity. "It's no business of mine if you're a counterre-volutionary or not," he said with a shake of his head. "It's what the corps says that counts. We're to treat you in accordance with the party's revo-lutionary humanism."

I can live with that. Things could be better, but they could be a lot worse, too.

SEPTEMBER 3, 1970

Met Liu Fulai on the way to the brickyard: "Hey, you look okay, except for your color."

I sighed.

"Now that you're out you'll realize how easy you had it in there. Making these blocks will wear you out in no time."

"Maybe you should spend a little time inside and see how you like it."

"Don't you think you got off light? Everybody says you're lucky you're not serving time."

"Fuck, no!"

Employing all my persuasive powers, I explained my innocence. He was sympathetic. "You'll be okay if you let things take their course." When he shoved some crabapples into my hand, warm feelings flooded my heart.

His smile vanished as quickly as it had appeared. "Got any money?" he asked. "How about lending an old pal a tenner? I need new boots."

"Sorry, I'm broke," I said apologetically.

He walked off disappointed.

SEPTEMBER 7, 1970

I helped Liu Yinghong and her friends repair the mud walls of the pig sty. My hands bled and I couldn't straighten my fingers by the time I was finished. The hard work was made worse by the ache in my heart. Yinghong's friendly face reminded me of her spiteful attack at the denunciation meeting. Was this the same girl? I wanted to see if there was any sympathy hidden in her eyes, but she averted them.

I knew without looking that Wei Xiaoli was nearby, and when she hollered at the pigs, my heart nearly stopped. Even with my head down and my bad eyes, I knew where she was standing at all times.

We met at the well, but when she saw it was me, she backed off to let me go first, a painful rebuff.

SEPTEMBER 9, 1970

Went to see the PI today and got chewed out.

I opened with "I'm really not a counterrevolutionary . . ."

His face darkened as he cut me off: "They could have given you ten years for what you did. It was a slap on the wrist, especially considering that you refused to admit your guilt. People complain that all you do these days is run around saying that you're not a counterrevolutionary. Well, listen carefully, Ma Bo. We were told to denounce you anytime you're not acting right. So watch your step."

"What do you think I'm doing?" I protested nervously. "Every day I scrub pots and pans, sweep the streets, and carry dirt. I work overtime. Wouldn't you say that's watching my step?"

He sneered and rolled his eyes. "Are you telling me that scrubbing a few pots and pans and working overtime is serving the people? I always put in extra hours. That's what labor reform is all about. You're getting kid-glove treatment, so don't start confusing things. The regiment told us to hold a denunciation meeting against you on your first day back, but we called it off because we were too busy with the harvest. If you keep complaining about being framed, don't grumble when we get tough with you."

I stared at the tips of my shoes.

"I know you like the back of my hand," he added. "Don't think you can get away with something just because I'm not there to see it. The eyes and ears of the masses are on you. From now on, accept labor reform. Forget your wild ideas. Remember, the corps has had its say. That's all for now."

I shuffled back to my frigid room.

SEPTEMBER 13, 1970

Before anyone else was awake, I was at the well fetching water. Squad Leader Jiang assigned me the job.

A bleak, scary kind of autumn morning.

I work like a slave every day and sleep like a log every night. Sleep lets me forget I'm a counterrevolutionary and forget the cold looks. I even dream sometimes. But when my eyes snap open in the morning my freed soul is once again clamped. It's enough to piss a guy off. The first waking moment is always the worst.

At noon a tractorload of willow twigs was delivered. Lei Xia had hitched a ride on it. Instead of averting his eyes when I came up to start unloading, he looked straight at me. There was strength and confidence in his eyes, not what you'd expect from someone who could betray a friend. He was prepared to stare me down. I let him win that round. I'd only make things worse by throwing down the gauntlet. "Loosen the windlass and undo those ropes!" he yelled to someone, as if I weren't there.

SEPTEMBER 14, 1970

Ever since my talk with the PI, I've stopped protesting my innocence. Now I communicate only with my diary. I understand the power of informants. I just work work work. I talk to no one. Just me and the mud. I'm scared they might criticize me again.

For over a week I've been mixing mud for two squads making adobe blocks. It's impossible to keep up with them. Qi Shuzhen complains that the mud's too watery or that there isn't enough straw or that it's lumpy. She's one picky squad leader. If the mud has a lump as small as a Ping-Pong ball, she makes me remix it so she and her friends can take a break.

Under her influence the new girls from Tianjin don't give me a chance to catch my breath. And Liu Fulai, still steaming because I didn't lend him the money he wanted, has turned mean.

Since my hands are in the mud all day, they're covered with sores. I look like a leper. I've got open sores on the soles of my feet where straw gets imbedded. The pain is terrible. I go to bed without washing the mud off my arms because removing it hurts too much.

SEPTEMBER 16, 1970

When I was locked up, a big, swarthy guy was always taunting me through the window. I hear he's a newcomer in Company Seven by the name of Zhang Baofeng, although everybody calls him Dumbbell. Assigned as a driver to the transportation company, he strutted around like the cock of the walk. Everybody hated him. Then one day he got into an argument with a co-op clerk for wearing a gaudy sportshirt and dark glasses, and Director Li ordered him back to Company Seven.

He stuck out his hand when he saw me. "I owe you an apology, pal, I shouldn't have got on your case like I did." I shook his hand and exchanged some small talk. No sense in holding a grudge.

Jiang Baofu sent for me when he heard about our meeting, and work was halted in First Platoon to criticize Zhang Baofeng. I was summoned to give my side of the story, and as I entered the room, Jin Gang was holding forth: ". . . obviously hasn't learned to distinguish between friend and foe, apologizing to a counterrevolutionary like he was his best friend! A flagrant example of departure from the proper class stance." He stopped when he saw me standing in the doorway. "It was all my fault," I announced. "Bad attitude . . ."

"You can leave now," Jiang cut me off. "There's work to be done."

Dumbbell glared at me, his face all sweaty. I knew the sort of shit they'd throw at him after I left and how they'd gang up on me as a reactionary. But I didn't care as long as they didn't do it to my face.

SEPTEMBER 17, 1970

Director Li brought the regimental harvest detail over to Company Seven. We seldom see him, since he's usually hanging around the women's dorm trying to "get a handle on things." They say he eggs them into arm-wrestling contests, then pinches them to hear them squeal. I've never seen him do a lick of work. He's too busy hunting wild geese with his semiautomatic rifle. Whenever he comes toward me, I lower my head. He won't listen to reason, so why talk to him?

At this afternoon's meeting, he singled me out as an active counterrevolutionary, and immature, to boot. "When our blustery friend Ma Bo stands on the platform, you can hear his knees knock," he said. He might as well have slapped me in the face.

I work my ass off to make a good impression. Obviously I'm wasting my time.

SEPTEMBER 19, 1970

Ever since Director Li singled me out, everyone avoids me, especially the girls, who treat me like a demented rapist. The PI read my letter to Wei Xiaoli in front of the whole company as proof that I was out to seduce the women by hook or by crook.

When my quilt was torn I went to the Changs' to use their sewing machine. "Normally, I'd be happy to let you use it," the wagon master's wife said. "But Uncle Chang got into trouble with the PI the other day, and if he found out I let you use my sewing machine, he could make things very unpleasant for us. He's just waiting to catch us at something, and I'm scared."

Words failed me. She looked up and down the street, nodded, and smiled awkwardly as she closed the door, leaving me standing there with my quilt in my arms. They live on the southern edge of camp, where the PI couldn't possibly see them.

I took a break and went to the wagon yard to read the papers, but the team leader said icily, "It's not a good idea to come here all the time. There's a ban on casual visits because so many things have turned up missing."

I was told to work over at a place called Five Rooms, but the wagon left a few seconds before I was ready, and even though it was no more than thirty yards away, the driver wouldn't stop for me. The dozen or so passengers were equally unmoved by my plight. They just glared at me as I ran to catch up. I nearly made it, but then I heard the crack of a whip and the wagon left me in its dust. They really whooped it up then.

The looks I get burn the skin of my face like branding irons. I don't know how much longer I can take it.

SEPTEMBER 24, 1970

Stuffed buns for lunch today. Since normally only 10 percent of our grain ration is made up of bleached flour, it was exciting news. The Tianjin students started fighting over the food as soon as it was delivered from the mess hall, so I made myself scarce until they were finished. All they left me was some picked-over crust at the bottom of the barrel. I scraped it out and ate it, since I needed energy to work, but almost puked as I forced down those little bastards' garbage. I kept my eyes closed the whole time.

I was still hungry, so I went to the mess hall, where the kitchen helper Yang Shufen, whose big eyes sparkle in the dark kitchen, handed me a couple of plain buns. I was grateful, but didn't dare say so.

SEPTEMBER 29, 1970

At noon today Jin Gang was sitting alone playing a fiddle. No one else was around, so I sat down beside him. He looked at me without a word. At least he didn't get up to leave.

"When do you plan to go home, Jin Gang?"

Silence.

His face was set tight; the sun reflected off his glasses. "I was never wrong about anybody in my life until you came along. I still can't believe you'd be like that."

"Like what?" I asked nervously.

"Despicable, selfish, a hypocrite." He spat out each word.

I tried to explain, but he wouldn't listen.

"You sold out your best friend because of a girl," he said scornfully.

"My best friend sold *me* out!" I shouted.

But he was already walking away.

How had I sold him out? By giving Wei Xiaoli the letter a couple of days early? So what? Nothing happened to him, but I'm a counterrevolutionary. How could he turn on me like that? I was so depressed, I went without dinner.

OCTOBER 1, 1970
National Day

Snow is falling lightly under a dark sky. Freezing winds knife through the gaping door and windows as I huddle under my sheepskin coat and enjoy a rare break from work, the first in over a month. Lying here without moving is heavenly. I've been in this position all day, reflecting on the past month: slaving away, driving myself like mad, wearing myself out digging and mixing clay. Ten hours a day of back-breaking labor, which leaves every joint in my body swollen and painful. All to make a good impression and not give anyone a reason to find fault with me.

After being criticized, Dumbbell made a clean break with me. Now he reports me for everything under the sun. If I go into the woods, he reports me. If I buy a new quilt, he reports me. If I go to the mess hall for something to eat, he reports me. It would be comical if it weren't so sad and so dangerous.

Eyes everywhere—the windows, the walls, the corners. In this sort of climate hard work is my only chance for survival, and sleeping after an exhausting day of work, my sole pleasure.

Just before nightfall a big black pig came snorting its way into the room and started rooting around my bed. I picked up a broken piece of block and hurled it. A direct hit! It turned tail and ran, squealing loudly. I've been reduced to taking out my frustrations on pigs. A counterrevolutionary loses even his personality. He knows only obedience and servility. What a way to live!

Another quiet night. I'll bet things are really hopping in Beijing, with fireworks above Tiananmen Square, and the Great Hall of the People all lit up. Out here? Cracked and pitted walls surrounded by darkness, hard ground covered with clumps of weeds, and water buckets with hardened cement on the sides.

I spent National Day huddled under a sheepskin coat, with pigs as my sole companions.

OCTOBER 5, 1970

Worked overtime last night. Wanted to test my stamina. Dug dirt for nine hours, stopping only to eat once and take a leak twice. It's the most monotonous, tiring work there is. After a day in the clay pit the soles of my feet are so tender, I'm afraid to touch them.

As soon as I sat down for dinner, Jiang Baofu came to get me to work overtime carrying sacks of grain. My heart fell. After wearing myself out in the mud all day, I didn't think I had the strength. But I didn't have a good reason not to go, especially since the PI was supervising work in the silos.

I worked like a dog until midnight. I couldn't believe I did it and wasn't surprised that I felt like a rag doll. As I dragged myself back to my room, my coat over my back, I heard Dumbbell say, "He's a tough little motherfucker!"

Wrong. I'm not tough. It's the club the PI holds over my head. "You're at our mercy!" it says.

OCTOBER [date missing,] 1970

Got my pay and lost it, all 14.40 of it. In a shitty mood all day. Since I'm always worried about my political life and have to work like a dog, money doesn't mean much to me these days. So when they handed me my pay, I just stuffed it into my pocket like a wad of tissue. But losing it hurts like hell. I could kick myself.

The thief was no dummy, whoever he was. Who better to steal from than a counterrevolutionary? The people in charge don't give a damn, and the victim can't do anything about it. When I got out of jail, all I had were the clothes on my back and my bedding. Are a counterrevolutionary's possessions up for grabs? I asked the PI for help, but he looked me in the eye and said, "Lei Xia was supposed to watch your stuff. If anything's missing, see him."

Lei Xia, a one-time friend who won't even say hello to me now. But

I went to see him anyhow. "How the hell should I know? Nobody asked me to watch your stuff. The PI's full of shit!"

Haven't heard from my folks since my troubles began, so I'm on my own. Have to make do with what I've got. The bottom half of my sheep-skin coat is in shreds, but I wear it, I have to, since I don't have any long underwear. I was looking forward to buying leather workshoes with this month's pay to save the soles of my feet while I'm working in the mud pit. I was so close.

OCTOBER 19, 1970

It gets colder every day. Ice on the stable trough today.

Spent the day digging mud for the new mess-hall roof, working in my bare feet. Liu Fulai and Dumbbell stood around with their heads scrunched into their collars, stomping their feet and cupping their hands over their ears. But even the freezing cold didn't keep them from arguing.

"Fuck you!" one said.

"Fuck you!" the other said.

After I mixed a batch of mud, I worked with them tossing loads of it onto the roof, which was higher than the other buildings. But while the three or four of them took turns in this back-breaking work, I was a team of one, working as if my life depended on it.

I thought I heard Old Gigolo say to one of the farmworkers, "Ma Bo must be crazy to work that hard."

I worked until everything around me was a blur.

For lunch they served millet. Liu Fulai surprised me by dumping some vegetables into my bowl. But when I saw how much the others got—two or three times as much—my gratitude turned to anger. I pay as much for food as they do and work twice as hard. I scooped out some more. They exchanged glances, but no one said a word.

The afternoon was a repeat of the morning.

For dinner we were given three steamed buns each. I was still hungry, but when I went to the mess hall for more—mush if that's all they had—the new man in charge of the kitchen said, "Your platoon leader told us not to give you any."

I was too embarrassed to say anything.

Went out after dinner to unload wagons but was so hungry that I couldn't stand it. Is this your revolutionary humanism, Jiang Baofu?

OCTOBER 20, 1970

Since the wind was too strong to work, the others attended study sessions inside. I tacked a cowhide over the window to keep out the cold, then blocked up the worst cracks with a pair of torn leather pants. I propped a beat-up horse trough covered with lime against the door. The room is dark as hell now, but at least there's no wind.

Curled up under my coat and stared at the ceiling. All kinds of confused thoughts. They can have their study sessions, I'll just lie here and take it easy. I've never been much good at talking or socializing. All I ever needed was a few friends. But now I'm all alone, and since there's no one to pour my heart out to, I write things down and send them to Mother. But even she ignores me.

A counterrevolutionary, disowned by his own mother!

I don't know how I'm going to make it.

OCTOBER 22, 1970

The slack season has been turned into a busy season by the "Learn from Dazhai Commune" campaign. Even in this cold weather the company has turned out to dig a canal. Everybody else has a personal daily quota of three yards, but mine is five. Jiang Baofu came to check my progress when it was time to knock off.

"Finished?"

I nodded.

"The sides are uneven. Smooth them out with your hoe."

"This isn't what you call precision work." I patted down the sides anyway. "Why all the fuss? They'll just start collapsing when the water hits them, anyway."

Liu Fulai came running over. " *'Why all the fuss'*? Is that what learning from Dazhai means to you?"

I shuddered.

"That's reactionary, Platoon Leader Jiang. Nail the fucker!"

Jiang frowned and waved him off.

"The PI said that if the fucker won't toe the line, we're supposed to nail him!"

I prudently kept my mouth shut and my hands at my sides. I knew Staff Officer Zhao was waiting to snap the cuffs back on me.

Even after Jiang nudged him away from the scene, Liu Fulai kept it up: "The little fucker isn't toeing the line. Don't be fooled by his arrogant silent treatment!"

How could somebody who once gave me some crabapples and who places so much importance on loyalty hate me with such vehemence?

OCTOBER 25, 1970

This morning I was watching Li Xiaohua try to cinch up a horse that wouldn't stand still. It kept trying to nip and kick her. Her face was flushed. But when I went over to give her a hand, she said, "It's okay, I can manage." Figuring she was just being polite, I tried again, which spooked her worse than the horse. "I don't need your help," she insisted, "I don't *need* it!"

Doesn't a counterrevolutionary even have the right to help someone? I stopped in my tracks and gazed into her pretty eyes. "Li Xiaohua," I was thinking, "I fought Wang Lianfu to avenge you, and this is the thanks I get?"

Letting me live among other people but forbidding them to have anything to do with me is worse than dropping me off in the middle of a desert. I'd love to find some sympathy somewhere; even pity would do.

But both are in short supply in this climate. People who scorn sympathy and pity, saying that anyone who accepts them should be ashamed of himself, probably get all they need. They have no idea how it feels to be a beggar or an outcast or a criminal.

I haven't seen a single smile since returning to the company. Even Dumbbell only apologized to me because he was afraid I'd kick his ass.

27

STONE

MOUNTAIN

GREAT NEWS! I was being sent up the mountain to the rock detail. My ticket out of this place. Better to be cut off from society and live a spartan life on the mountain than be subjected to the scorn and surveillance of a bunch of jerks and turncoats.

One December morning I went up Stone Mountain carrying all my belongings: bedding, the clothes on my back, and a broom.

Company One was closest to the mountain, a peak with gentle outcroppings in the middle of nowhere. The ground was sparsely covered by a layer of dead grass, with bare patches honeycombed by rat holes. Two yurts had been thrown up on a slope three hundred yards from the peak. Old Jiang, Daoerji, the herdowner Gonggele, and I shared one; Liu Fulai, Dumbbell, and a couple of Tianjin students shared the other.

Jiang had been sent up for accidentally saying "Down with Chairman Mao" when he had meant "Down with Liu Shaoqi" during a heated argument. He was made the leader of our work detail.

I was surprised to meet up with Daoerji and Gonggele again. Daoerji's speedy sorrel colt had caught the PI's eye, and when Daoerji wouldn't swap with him, the PI found an excuse to confiscate it as a mobilization precaution, then promptly turned it over to Director Li. Daoerji called the PI everything from a bootlicker to an ass-kisser. Shen let him rant on.

Then one blustery November day Daoerji was herding his sheep when his camel tripped and broke its leg (his own leg was also bunged up in the fall). The vengeful PI struck like lightning, making him write a confession, deducting thirty yuan from his wages, and refusing to call his injury job-related. When Daoerji tried to reason with him, a shouting match ensued, and his herd was confiscated. Then he was given a choice: Work on the mountain or give up his wages. With a family to support, that was no choice at all. Once there he spent most of his time in bed, since his game leg made work all but impossible.

Payment for calling the PI a bootlicker.

It did my heart good to see the swaggering murderer of Ingush, the rumormonger who had accused me of threatening him with a knife, brought low like this. But as one of Political Instructor Shen's victims, he earned my sympathy as well.

The old herdowner Gonggele hadn't changed a bit—always ready with a self-effacing smile, whether you were a party functionary or a criminal. There was kindness in his clouded eyes. Although he hardly ever spoke, he coughed incessantly and wiped his mouth so often with his sleeves that they shone.

To no one's surprise, Jiang worked us pretty hard, since that was the only way for him to regain the position his slip of the tongue had cost him. He roused us out of bed before sunup, jerking the covers off anyone who was slow getting up.

The herdowners and I took turns lighting the stove, then worked until breakfast at nine o'clock. The rocks we wanted were at underground level, and even though digging them out was hard work, the quarries were warm and toasty no matter how low the thermometer fell. While Jiang swung his sledgehammer relentlessly, the herdowners and I sweated. Meanwhile, Liu Fulai and Dumbbell kept up a running argument, calling each other every name in the book.

No one slacked off.

Our pile of rocks grew and grew.

On New Year's Eve, Jiang, who had gone down to report to the company, returned beaming. "Well, we're making quite a reputation for ourselves. We were singled out for praise at the meeting."

New Year's Day, 1970. Urging me not to spend the holiday alone on the mountain, Daoerji said he'd find a place for me to stay. But I didn't want to go down there where I'd be at the mercy of the dictatorship of the proletariat. Anyone, the nerdiest guy or bitchiest girl, could have a field day with me. If I did something wrong, intentional or not, I would be reported, and no holiday meal was worth that. I'd rather spend my time with the grass and rocks on my barren mountain. At least they left me alone. So what if my New Year's dinner consisted of hardtack and pickles?

Gonggele led a wagon carrying the semireclining Daoerji, wrapped in two sheepskin coats.

Jiang and the others cheerfully changed into clean clothes—they'd been up half the night washing them—and rubbed scented cream on their faces, then waited for the tractor to take them down the mountain.

"Ma Bo," Jiang said softly just before he left, his brow knitted, "it's my wife's lying-in period. I haven't been paid this month, and I need the money. How about a loan?"

How could I say no? He held my fate in his hands.

As the sky darkened I tossed some cowchips into the stove, which flared up and cast my shadow on the wall of the yurt. A pot of rice gruel simmered on the stove. It was a huge relief to be all by myself. No one condemning me on behalf of the dictatorship of the proletariat. I did what I wanted. It was so quiet, I could hear the blood flowing in my ears.

The New Year's celebration was scheduled for six days, which would constitute my longest holiday since returning to the company. That meant I could take my time copying out the letter to the Central Committee.

I hung up my broom for the time being.

One day.

Two days.

Three days. I copied the letter, carefully and neatly.

Six days into the new year I walked down to Regimental Headquarters and sent the letter, registered mail. That brought me peace of mind. And it wrapped up my New Year's holiday for 1970.

On the seventh day, the others returned. They couldn't wait to tell me the hottest news about Dr. Wang.

It began with Yang Lanlan, probably the most delicate of the Tianjin students, who had complained that making adobe blocks and working on new construction was too hard for her. In her search for lighter work she lit upon the job of nurse, and the clinic became her home away from home. Dr. Wang agreed to recommend her for an apprenticeship at the regimental hospital. Late one night, when she had sentry duty, she stepped into the clinic to warm up, and he talked her into staying. So began the clandestine affair. When their secret was discovered—in that environment it was only a matter of time—the PI sent for Dr. Wang, who broke down and wept pitiably, pounding his chest and vowing to turn over a new leaf. For days he did virtually nothing but cry and publicly wish he'd never been born.

Fearing a scandal, the PI decided to hush the matter up and give Dr. Wang another chance. But the lovers were soon back at it, and this time Yang Lanlan became pregnant, which nearly sent Dr. Wang off the deep end. He tried everything to abort the fetus: having her ride a galloping horse and making her swallow all sorts of concoctions. Finally, he sent her to Tianjin for an abortion, on the pretext of a rest cure for hepatitis. But when her parents discovered the real story, they wrote to the regiment, where Dr. Wang devised a scheme to blame the pregnancy on an anonymous Mongol herdsman who had assaulted Yang on the steppe.

Married and the father of one, Wang had the sophisticated, genteel air of an educated physician. I never once heard him utter a dirty word, and he always wore a carefully pressed uniform, inside or out of doors.

The graying Deputy Commissar Liu came to Company Seven to personally dispose of the case, announcing gravely at a mass meeting: "Wang Wanping has committed a serious offense. What he did was immoral and constitutes a smear on the army's reputation. In addition, by attempting to pin the blame on a member of a national minority, he has weakened our political influence. Even after we warned him, he continued his adulterous affair. The Regimental Party Committee has decided to revoke his party membership and impose disciplinary sanctions. This will serve as a lesson for him and a warning for anyone with similar reprehensible ideas."

Deputy Commissar Liu concluded his report with a reminder: "Corps soldiers may not be romantically involved for a three-year period. You are to cultivate lofty aspirations and great ideals. Late marriages are the order."

AFTER COMBING his hair and shaving, Jiang looked years younger. "To underscore their praise for our work detail, the company rewarded us with a basket of apples," he said, his face glowing with health.

Once the others had their pick, the Mongol herdowners and I were left with a few tiny green apples. Daoerji leaned up against his bedroll and lamented the fact that he had no Oceans cigarettes to celebrate the new year. "I'd trade all my apples for a pack of Oceans," he sighed.

Jiang surprised me by handing me a letter. Postmarked Beijing. From Xu Zuo. I grabbed it like a wolf pouncing on a lamb, opened it with a shaky hand, and devoured its contents. It was, I think, the first letter I'd received since my arrest, and I couldn't stop reading it, poring over every word and phrase for hidden meanings.

The first person to come to my aid when the shit really hit the fan was neither my father or mother, nor one of my so-called "loyal friends." No, it was Xu Zuo, who had broken with me a year earlier.

In bed that night I savored the pleasant residue of the day for as long as possible, until shame, gratitude, and sadness took over. A strong wind blew, which portended a precipitous drop in temperature. The fire in the yurt was out and my nose and ears were nearly frozen. I grew feverish.

"Rise and shine!" Jiang's shout ripped through the darkness. My head was throbbing. I shivered as I put on every piece of clothing I owned. It didn't help much. Then I tried to stand up straight, but I couldn't keep my head steady. I was so weak, all I wanted to do was lie down again.

Jiang could see I was really sick. "Stay in bed today. You probably caught a cold last night. I never saw anybody get so excited over a letter. Must have been good news." He was treating me better now, after I had lent him the money.

Liu Fulai glared at me enviously when he heard I was staying in bed, since everyone but the cook was supposed to be out working. But even with my coat wrapped tightly around me I was cold, and I couldn't carry the weight of my own head.

I tried eating a small flatcake, but my temples throbbed with each bite. So I dunked it in warm tea to soften it up, then chewed gently to keep my brain from exploding. When I'd finished, I struggled to my feet, cinched up my pants, and staggered outside. Every step was sheer hell; the sledgehammer in my head was back at it again. My legs felt like lead, and it took forever to get to the work site.

Daoerji held the drill so I could hammer a dynamite hole in a huge boulder, but I could barely lift the hammer. Each swing was accompanied by a pounding in my head louder than the hammer against the rock. Every few minutes we stopped so he could scoop the rock dust out of the hole, allowing me to rest for ten or fifteen seconds. I'd lean against a rock and let my body relax for every one of those seconds.

I was terrified of slipping and smashing his hand, but somehow I managed to finish the job. Daoerji sat on a rock, cross-legged, and lit up a cigarette. His boots and coat were dusted with rock powder. He told me to go back, since I could barely hold my head up, but I figured I might as well stay put. Who knew what they would accuse me of?

After a short rest I began lugging rocks. The pain was excruciating. Why didn't that fucking sun hurry up and set?

One trip after another. I must have been crazy to come out in my condition when I didn't even have to. I'd happily have eaten a cowchip if that would have transported me back to my dark, filthy yurt.

Finally the sun reached the horizon, and Jiang gave the order to knock off for the day. Before the echo of his shout died out, Liu Fulai let out a whoop and scooted down the mountain as fast as his legs would carry him. But I stayed where I was for the moment, staring at the setting sun as it turned into a red ball and bathed the sky with scarlet rays, like a vibrant heart sending its lifeblood onto the steppe below.

The wind was like a dagger. Frost gathered in the corners of my mouth and on my cap, and for some reason I began to weep. The image of that blood red sunset was still with me years later, for I felt that I had proved my devotion to Chairman Mao.

ONE MARCH DAY Jiang was notified that he was to assume the duties of First Platoon leader. Lei Xia would take his place on the mountain. The news put a broad smile on Jiang's scowling face as he gleefully packed his belongings. He gave me an affectionate nod as he was leaving, his way of saying good-bye.

Off he went, delighted to become platoon leader.

Meanwhile, my supervised labor reform had barely begun.

28

MOTHER

DISOWNS ME

"I WANT TO talk to you," I said to Lei Xia when we were alone.

"Weren't you listening at the denunciation meeting?" he asked calmly, his eyes clear and deep. "I said it all there. You and I have nothing to talk about." No compromise or conciliation. Maybe he felt that since he'd offended me already he might as well go all out. You learn more about life at one denunciation meeting than in ten years of school. The One-Smash and Three-Oppose campaign had been a maturation process for him, and he was now a practiced advocate of social Darwinism. Circumstances had compelled him to learn servility before his superiors and duplicity with his peers. But I was willing to bet it made him uneasy.

Lei Xia was an impassioned speaker whose words could make you fidget and sweat. This gift had gotten him out of all sorts of tight scrapes. Over time his relationship with the PI underwent a subtle change, until it was hard to tell who was manipulating whom. Around me he showed no signs of remorse, convinced, I suppose, that he had done nothing wrong by exposing me. In fact, he'd have seen his activities as fair and reasonable, given the different standards of evaluation our backgrounds called for.

Anyone from a reactionary background could complain from now till next month and never get satisfaction; but if you're the offspring of a revolutionary cadre, everything's fine. The worse your background, the more you're expected to bear up under pressure. So for him to deflect some of his pressure onto me was just. At least I assume that's how he viewed it.

Unlike his predecessor, he refrained from jerking the covers off his sleeping charges to get them up and going. He pretty much ignored the tendencies of Liu Fulai and Dumbbell to show up late and goof off, unless he thought they were overdoing it.

Liu Fulai, tall and thin, with an innocent, even immature face, was given to ostentatiously flipping his long hair. No matter how cold it got, vanity, not comfort or health, dictated his attire. His favorite pastime was arguing and hurling insults. Like a rat that gnaws to keep its teeth sharp, he never let a day pass without bickering with someone. He was the company's prince of insults: He had the vocabulary, technique, speed, and response time.

He never tried to hide his randy nature, lusting after every pretty girl in the company. When Li Xiaohua, pretty in her own way, received a suggestive letter from him, she turned it over to the PI, who forced Liu to make a public self-criticism and work up on the mountain as punishment. From then on he referred to the despised Li Xiaohua as the "soldier's whore." But this didn't stop him from falling for all the other pretty faces in view: local or urban, Mongol or Han, married or unmarried, young or old.

After lunch one April day Lei Xia found an uneaten sliver of steamed bun in the stove ashes. "Who threw this away?" he asked, obviously displeased. "Who would do something like that?"

Liu Fulai glanced my way, and as soon as Lei Xia walked outside, he fished the filthy thing out of the ashes and tossed it into my bowl. "Eat it!" he commanded.

I was slurping the soupy rice in my bowl and was so stunned that it took me a moment to react. Then the adrenaline kicked in, and without a second thought, I scooped it out and threw it at him. "Fuck your old lady!" He ducked, picked it up off the floor, and flung it back. By now it was dusted with cowchip residue and goat hairs.

"Fuck *your* old lady!" By the time I picked it up, he was running outside. "Fuck your little old lady!" he screamed. "Have you forgotten what we can do to you? Counterrevolutionary!"

"Fuck off!" I hurled the food at him with all my might.

He stood with his hands on his hips, flicked his hair back with a toss of the head, and said again, "Fuck your old lady, Yang Mo!"

I was on him before the sound died out, sending him thudding to the ground with a flying kick.

His face was ashen as he picked himself up, but he didn't back down: "Fuck your old lady, Yang Mo!" Flat on his back again. The little punk was a sucker for those flying kicks.

Lei Xia ran up and wrapped his arms around me. "What's going on here?"

"He's calling my mother names."

"He threw good food away!" Liu Fulai screamed.

"Did you?"

"Hell no!"

"Well, I don't care who it was. The corps has begun a food-conservation campaign, and the company thinks we're too wasteful up here."

From then on our food intake was strictly controlled. Lei Xia told the cook to prepare our rations in accordance with a head count—two flatcakes per person per meal, and no more. For the others, who did only light work, two was probably adequate. But for me, the one who had to lug all those rocks out of the quarry, it wasn't nearly enough. I was hungry all the time and reduced to thievery to keep myself going. I'd swipe an extra flatcake when no one was looking, then eat it under the covers at night. Luckily I was a fast eater and could gobble one down in thirty seconds. I was never caught.

Lei Xia refused to talk to me most of the time. But one day, maybe on a whim, he called a meeting of the work detail—to help me make some ideological progress, he said. He would read some passages from Chairman Mao's pronouncements on class struggle, then get my comments, followed by "helpful" critiques from the others. I quickly discovered that I was in for a tough time: My comment on the first passage elicited complaints of dishonesty and intransigence. Liu Fulai, the asshole from Tianjin who thought he was a model revolutionary, really laid into me.

After everyone had had his say, Lei Xia launched into a lecture on the importance and arduous nature of ideological reform. He managed to hold forth for half an hour on the significance to class struggle of a cast-off slice of bun. Did he really think I'd forgotten how he'd stolen an army overcoat in Changdu? Or how he'd said to me once, "No matter how much I study the works of Chairman Mao, I never get much out of them."

This so-called "helpful" gathering was a phony excuse to further oppress me under the banner of class struggle. I was Lei Xia's captive, a handy target for his invective.

He was the perfect man to break me, since he knew me like a brother. At work, if I slowed down, frowned, and got a little glassy-eyed, he knew I was hungry and would keep me working an extra quarter of an hour or so; if I went to bed earlier than usual, he'd be sure to keep the lamp lit, since he knew I couldn't sleep with it on. Once I told him I was grossed out by the sound of someone blowing his nose. It was the beginning of frequent and energetic nose-clearing marathons. It sometimes nearly drove me nuts, and it was all I could do to keep from flattening that cute little nose of his.

At one point a work detail from Company Three joined us, and what first caught my attention was the way they openly abused a fellow named Liu Yi, who had been in charge of their grain silo. In 1968 he was taken into custody by a rival faction (a bunch of ignorant slobs) for slandering the great Chairman Mao by saying that Mao had once served as propaganda minister for the Nationalists. Soon afterward, he was labeled an active counterrevolutionary, and his wife divorced him.

One evening, Platoon Leader Qiao, a demobilized soldier attached to Company Three, noted gleefully to Lei Xia, "Having Liu Yi around is great for morale. I get the little shit out working every morning at four o'clock and don't let him come in for breakfast till ten. After I work his ass off all day, at night I make him kneel in front of Chairman Mao's picture to report on his activities. He's no dummy. He brags about how good a worker he is, and when he's finished, we make him shout, 'Down with Liu Yi!' We laugh our fucking heads off every time."

"How about food?" Lei Xia asked. "Do you give him enough?"

"More than enough. He eats so much, he pisses off the cook. I gave him five huge pieces of hardtack and half a pot of gruel one time and told him I'd kick his ass if he didn't finish it. Shit, he sat there taking his own sweet time, until he'd finished off every last crumb. We were worried he might stuff himself until he dropped dead. A cow did that the · other day. But the next morning he dragged himself up the mountain and went to work the same as always."

"Does he do what he's told?" Lei Xia's interest was growing.

"You're damned right he does," Qiao said smugly. "Zhang Qingli coughed up a wad of phlegm once and spit it into Liu's bowl, then told him to drink it. He closed his eyes and gulped it down. I was there, I saw it with my own eyes. They'd have kicked the shit out of him if he hadn't."

"Watch out you don't go overboard," Lei Xia warned.

"Don't worry about that."

I overheard every word and wondered how Liu survived it.

The next night, when I was taking a cow past the Company Three yurt, I heard an angry voice inside: "What's the idea of hitting the sack so early?"

"I've got a splitting headache," came the weak reply.

"How'd you do today?"

"Pretty good."

"You brought up all the rocks?"

"Just about."

"You call that pretty good?"

"I put in a good day's work, honest."

"Honest, your old lady's ass!" That was followed by the crisp sound of a slap across the face.

"How dare you say you did a good job when you didn't even finish! On your knees. Ask Chairman Mao's forgiveness."

Silence.

"Out with it! Down with the active counterrevolutionary Liu Yi! Say it three times."

A murmur.

"Louder!"

Almost audible.

"Didn't you say you had a headache? Must be a cold. You need to sweat it out. Run in place! Left, right, left, right, let's hear it!"

As I passed by the open flap I saw that Liu Yi was wearing only a pair of underpants, with a sheepskin coat thrown over his shoulders, as he strained to run in place barefoot, his head drooping as he grunted weakly, "Left, right, left, right . . ." His companions sat around playing poker, smoking, and having a grand old time, as if he weren't there.

Compared to him I lived a charmed life. Even at his meanest, Lei Xia never treated me that badly.

A few days later, while they were dynamiting, I took cover in the Company Three quarry just as Liu came up lugging a heavy rock on his back. He was bent nearly double, his blackened face was streaked with sweat, and the veins on his forehead were popping out. Gripping the rock tightly with his rough, callused hands, he stumbled forward, one tortured step at a time.

We didn't dare say anything, since we weren't alone. Two active counterrevolutionaries deep in a rock quarry acknowledging one another's presence with only a brief glance.

I'll never forget the look of melancholy in his eyes.

One day in early April, when Company Commander Wang was up on the mountain to inspect our progress, he took me aside after giving us a rundown on what had transpired at the expanded meeting of the Regimental Party Committee.

"What the hell's going on here?"

I told him what had happened in the company after he left to attend the "Support the Left" meeting in Baochang. I knew there was bad blood between him and the PI.

"What do you think of Lei Xia now?"

"Quick mind, smooth tongue. A good mixer and a good worker, but he's always bragging and blowing things out of proportion. He's undependable and lacks the will to knuckle down and get things done."

He sighed sadly. "How about you, any problems?"

I shook my head.

"Follow their lead," he said. "Work when they work and rest when they rest. Keep focused on the goal of clearing your name as quickly as possible. Your work record's been pretty good lately."

I screwed up the courage to say, "Company Commander Wang, please don't think I'm a glutton, but sometimes I don't get enough to eat. Everybody gets the same amount, no matter how big or small their appetite is . . . two flatcakes . . ."

"Okay," he said sympathetically. "I'll see what I can do."

I felt like grasping his hand but didn't dare.

"Hey! Who's letting you go hungry?" Lei Xia demanded angrily after Company Commander Wang left.

"I don't get enough to eat."

"How much do you want? You exceed your quota at every meal."

My complaint had cost him some face.

Liu Fulai gave me a scornful look and muttered, "Pig!"

TOWARD THE END of April 1971, the letter I'd been expecting from Mother finally arrived.

Ma Bo:

What happened to you was inevitable. You let the party and us down. We support the decision by the corps and after considerable soul-searching have decided to sever relations with you so you can concentrate on reforming yourself.

In the past no bad deed was beyond you, and now it's time to pay for your transgressions. But still you insist you're being treated unjustly. I'm not trying to scare you when I say you'll seal your doom if you keep this up.

You claim that in subjective terms you're neither antiparty nor anti–Chairman Mao. Then how do you explain your actions, since most are in opposition to Chairman Mao and Mao Zedong Thought? We tried to get you to spend more time studying the works of Chairman Mao instead of those rotten novels, which clouded your mind with feudal, fascist, corrupt thoughts. The party chose not to put you in jail because of your age, and you've repaid their leniency by sending accusatory letters all over the place.

Put an end to these pleas and humbly admit your crimes to the party and to the people. That's the only way out. I repeat: We staunchly support the Corps Party Committee's handling of your case and hereby disown you. You must obediently accept reform.

Yang Mo

That made it complete. Now even my own mother and father had me pegged as a bad person. Biting down on my lip, I tore up the letter and scattered it over the mountain.

29

WOODCUTTING

IN 1971, THE INNER MONGOLIAN Production Corps thrived as never before. Construction reached unprecedented levels. Large brick buildings with tile roofs were built for Regimental Headquarters, the Political and Logistic sections, the regimental commander's office, and more—an impressive row of buildings alongside the adobe huts of Injgan Sum. Since there was no available lumber on the steppe itself, an agreement was struck between us and the tree farm in Wula Sitai, some 120 li distant, to which we sent a team of woodcutters. Each company was responsible for cutting its own lumber, under the direction of Staff Officer He.

MY FOUR HORSES pulled the wagon proudly down the road, leaving a trail of dust in our wake. We reached the foot of the mountains in the afternoon, after traveling the winding road for ten or twenty li without seeing another soul. The mountains rose suddenly and independently out of the plain, no two of them touching. In the valleys peonies, chrysanthemums, and Chinese roses grew in profusion, and the stillness was unimaginable; the absence of any sign of human activity accentuated a feel of the ancient. Every once in a while a cuckoo flew past, flapping its wings loud and hard. Even at a distance, the sound of its wings fanning the air came through with amazing clarity.

Situated in the southwestern corner of the Great Xing'an Mountain Range, the Wula Sitai tree farm was home to so many serpents that people usually referred to it as Snake Pit Tree Farm. Dense, billowing fog enshrouded the valleys between the mountains, whose lower halves were densely forested, while the towering, craggy peaks were bare.

We made camp in a gully luxuriant with trees and undergrowth. The soil was so damp that water gurgled wherever the ground was poked. Every time it rained, mushrooms sprouted inside our yurts.

Lei Xia walked up on the first day and said somberly, "I expect you to work hard. No goofing off!"

"When did I ever goof off?"

"You know damned well." His nose twitched.

I didn't reply. He scrutinized my every move to see if he could detect any latent disrespect. I avoided provoking him.

After hiking a couple of li up the mountain, we cut down some trees and dragged them back to the wagon. It was back-breaking work. Over the first couple of days Lei Xia watched me like a hawk, just waiting for me to screw up. I started work early each morning and returned late at night so as not to give him the excuse he was looking for. I put in one exhausting day after another, rain or shine. When others harvested fifty trees, I cut down a hundred or more. How was I to know that the harder I worked, the more he despised me?

On one of his inspection tours, Staff Officer He spent the night in our yurt. Lei Xia jumped out of bed at the crack of dawn and bellowed, "Okay, up and at 'em!" I ignored him and lay around a while longer, until he walked up and nudged me with his foot. "Get up." He kicked me. "I said, Get up!"

"Don't kick me," I said.

He kicked me harder. "Who said you could stay in bed?" I jumped up, fists clenched; he froze. "Well, well," he said with a sneer, "quite a temper we've got. Come on, let's see what a counterrevolutionary can do."

Staff Officer He ran up and stopped us.

That night, after Staff Officer He had left, Lei Xia pointed at me and said, "Don't you ever pop off like that again! The PI and Staff Officer Zhao said you're in for another session if you don't behave yourself."

I glared at him, barely able to believe that this was the same proud, loyal person who had once been my sworn brother, though everyone knows that if you have a falling-out with your best friend, he often turns into your worst enemy.

I assumed that his enmity toward me had complex origins. Maybe he thought that all those denunciation sessions had failed to change me and that I was still the same Ma Bo, whereas he had undergone profound changes. If he couldn't make me look bad, he'd look bad; if he couldn't flatten me, he could never stand tall; if he couldn't make my life miserable, he'd never rid himself of his own anguish.

The Tianjin students Liu Fulai, Dumbbell, and the others spent most of their time scheming against one another. A good 70 percent of what they said was pure bullshit. For them it was an endless round of contests to see who could out-curse, out-deceive, or out-boast the other. Liu Fulai once tied a string around Dumbbell's dick while he was asleep, stripped him naked, then woke him up and led him around the outside of the yurt until he was squealing like a stuck pig, afraid of losing the family jewels.

Lei Xia had no use for this bunch, refusing to pal around with them or get involved in their antics. And I wasn't about to hang out with a bunch of pricks like that.

With my anxieties mounting, I wrote Mother another letter:

Dear Mother:

You haven't answered my letters, so I can only hope that everything is okay. I'm cutting trees deep in the mountains, at least a hundred li from company headquarters. Lots of major construction is planned for this year.

I'm stuck with a bunch of rotten kids who spend all their time goofing off. I have nothing in common with them, so I work all the time. I went back to the company once and kept my mouth shut the whole time. What did I get in return? Sarcasm mainly. They joked about my thick lips and pointy head. I can't stand it any longer. Thinking about having to stay up here for a whole month really depresses me.

Mother, you have to help me. You're the only one who can save me from this hell. I'm *not* a counterrevolutionary, Mother, dear dear Mother, and I'm begging you. I'm your own flesh and blood, so I think I deserve some kindness.

Your son is here waiting and hoping, day and night.

Bo

July

Thunder rumbled in the morning as dark clouds gathered. The mist filling the valleys was a sure sign that a heavy rain was on the way. As soon as I finished breakfast I swung my ax over my shoulder and went up the mountain, taking some hardtack with me. As I passed by the Company Nine yurts a student I didn't know hailed me: "You're not going out in this weather, are you?" I nodded. I'd rather be out working, even in the rain, than hanging out in the yurt.

When I reached my destination, I attacked the trees with a vengeance, the sounds of my ax shattering the stillness for miles. Meanwhile the sky turned dark and the clouds opened up. The forest was quickly alive with the sound of pelting water. I was drenched in no time, my clothes plastered against my skin.

I stopped working long enough to wipe my face; then the sound of my ax filled the air again. Poplars as big around as a bowl came down with one swing; birches, which were a little harder, usually took two. By then the chopping sounds were swallowed up by the rain thudding against the leaves, and I was refreshed by the cool water.

A mist spread through the valley; low-hanging clouds sucked the peaks up into them. As it drove off the summer heat, the rain turned the forest gloomy and cold. My ax sliced through the wall of rain around me until noon, when I knocked off and sat on the wet roots of a tall birch, startling a couple of toads.

I marveled over the beauty of the forest as I ate the water-soaked hardtack, swallowing the doughy cakes along with rainwater that sluiced down my face; it turned the skin of my arms pallid and wrinkly. It ran down my pantlegs, so pleasant and so stimulating. Rain-soaked thoughts began to drift in all sorts of crazy ways, and before long my head was filled with thoughts of women.

Liu Fulai, Dumbbell, and the others talked all the time about doing *it*. No detail was spared, and they sounded very experienced. Their graphic descriptions made my lustful juices flow in abundance, the dictatorship of the proletariat be damned!

To love and be loved, including the physical variety, seemed to me the sweetest of all possible dreams. Youth is still youth, even if you're a counterrevolutionary; passions and the biological imperative know no political boundaries. People who are shunned and discriminated against need warmth and love as much as anyone else—more, probably.

Sitting in that downpour, I fantasized a lithe girl in a white shawl emerging from the forest: beautiful and elegant, she was like the girl in the *Moonlit Night* painting that hung on Mother's wall. Any girl willing to give her favors to a counterrevolutionary huddling beneath a tree like a drenched chicken would have received his undying love even if she had six fingers on each hand and a cratered face.

Then my thoughts turned to Wei Xiaoli. What was she doing? Was she still a solitary swineherd out on the steppe? Or was she out gathering cowchips?

I remember reading somewhere about a Tibetan serf who had never tasted candy. Once, as she was sweeping her master's yard, she picked up a sweet that had fallen to the ground and hid it away. Unwilling to eat it and be done with it, she sucked on it for a while, then spit it out and wrapped it up again. It lasted her a whole year that way. Wei Xiaoli's image was the candy that sustained me through those trying times. When life was so difficult that I wasn't sure I could endure it any longer, I would think of her, and those sweet thoughts brought me joy.

The forest whistled softly. Sounds of wind, rain, and rustling leaves were joined by a lone wolf's howl.

When the Decembrists in czarist Russia were exiled to Siberia, noblewomen gave up their lives of luxury to search for their men in the frozen wastelands. But who would come searching for me in the desolate steppes of Inner Mongolia? Even my own mother had disowned me. Forget your dreams of marriage, I reminded myself. Where's your sense of shame?

Thud thud. I went back to chopping down trees. Rainwater cascaded down my nose, my chin; cold rivers slid down my spine, my buttocks, and my legs.

When I returned to the yurt I gobbled down some hardtack.

"You sure get your money's worth for the fifteen-sixty you pay for food."

"Why shouldn't I? I'd be a damned idiot not to."

"I'm fucking glad we've only got one like you. If there were any more, the poor cook would be in the soup!"

I kept my head lowered as I gobbled down the food, not saying a word. There was no other way to avoid a nasty scene.

That night Liu Fulai gave an animated account of how he had secretly watched a Mongol woman give birth. Everyone listened greedily, afraid to miss a single word. Except for Lei Xia, who scowled in disgust and ignored them.

They finally slid under their covers much later that night, then started trading lewd remarks. "Hey," Dumbbell said with a laugh, "look at Liu Fulai's comforter. It's a little tent."

"Who's the lucky girl this time?"

"Guess."

"Big Swan, I bet."

"Shit!"

"Wang Yingying?"

"Horseshit! I'm thinking about Wei—Xiao—li!"

My heart nearly stopped, as though struck by lightning.

"Big fucking deal! With that short neck of hers, her chin bounces against her tits, and she's got the face of a dead fish."

"Well, I think she's kind of cute."

I ignored them, pretending to be asleep.

"She's not so fucking pretty."

"Heh heh. I'd let her be my girlfriend if she was crippled and blind in one eye." There was hidden meaning in Liu Fulai's comment. I had written that very line in my diary once. Maybe the PI had read it aloud, and Fulai had memorized it.

"I wouldn't want her if you turned her upside down," Dumbbell giggled.

"Hell, I guess I shouldn't be wanting her either," Liu Fulai said. "Some people are just jealous. Who wants prick-teaser Wei, anyway?"

The words *Wei Xiaoli* were sacred to me, which was why my companions were dragging her name through the mud. I buried my head under my coat to keep from losing my temper.

"How about you, Ma Bo, you want her? You'd be even better looking if you had a little pointier head, thicker lips, and smellier feet. She'd really jump your bones then."

"Fuck you, fuck all of you!" I thundered.

They nearly choked with laughter.

I finally managed to fall asleep.

Before sunup the next morning I was startled out of my dreams by Lei Xia's shouts of "Up and at 'em!" No one else made a move as I crawled out of bed, nearly in tears as I thought about what lay ahead of me that day.

What a transformation: Red Guard to counterrevolutionary to laborer deep in the mountains.

The darkness of the yurt was broken by a sliver of murky light seeping in through a crack in the doorway. Lei Xia would wake one of the sleeping men, only to have another go back to sleep; after breakfast I swung my ax over my shoulder and went up the mountain again. Working alone was fine with me. On this particular day I crossed a bridge and went to a different gully, where the grass was shoulder-high and there were wild-boar tracks. Plus piles of grayish dung, real gritty stuff. I wondered what kind of animal had left it.

The soft, springy ground was covered by a blanket of dead branches and rotting leaves a foot thick. Clumps of beautiful azaleas and peonies stood among the tall grass.

The forest was denser here than in other places and much gloomier, since sunlight barely penetrated the tree cover. I started felling trees right away. When I began to tire I had only to think of Liu Fulai, and my strength was renewed—I pretended that the trees were my companions' skinny legs.

The call of a nearby wolf drifted over on the wind. It couldn't have been more than half a li away. Normally I would have stopped to listen to the sound, so melodic yet so mournful. But today I was too busy to pay any attention. This particular gully was among the most remote in the tree farm and so overgrown with wild grass that few people ever ventured into it. I grew nervous, sensing that a pair of wolf eyes was watching me from somewhere in the dense foliage. I sure didn't want to become wolf bait. As the only person within a radius of five or six li, I'd be easy pickings. So I took a whetstone out of my pocket and began honing my ax blade, constantly looking up to see if there was any movement around me and planning how to use my weapon if an animal charged me. One would be easy to deal with; what worried me was the possibility of a whole pack.

After a while things settled down again, and I decided to stop at three hundred trees and head back. But after cutting down another dozen or so, I was on tenterhooks, afraid that a wolf would pounce on me from behind and bury its fangs in my neck, even though I knew that the wolves around there were timid. I headed back down the mountain before reaching my self-imposed quota.

Wild grass rustled as I threaded my way through the trees, and just as I was emerging from the forest, I heard movement in the shrubs directly ahead. Scared shitless, I gripped my ax tightly . . . Two wolves emerged, heading for the trees. I shouted, took a couple of menacing steps toward them, and watched them vanish into the forest.

Dumbbell was waiting for me at the yurt with a letter. It was from Mother.

Bo,

After your letter arrived, Xu Zuo told me how things are with you. I can see that everyone is still beneath your contempt. It's a mistake to keep your comrades at arm's length. The only way to get out of your predicament is to work hard at changing your outlook.

No one else can save you—you must do it yourself. I'll say this one more time, and I hope it doesn't go in one ear and out the other. If you don't take my advice, things will only get worse for you. Any more fighting, and I'll have nothing more to do with you. You'll be no son of mine.

Yang Mo

Obviously, Xu Zuo had gotten to her. But she was still my mother, and I knew she'd come around sooner or later. Then, just as I was beginning to feel better, Liu Fulai returned from the women's clinic reeking of face powder.

"Who said you could knock off early?" he asked.

"None of your business."

"Lei Xia went to buy boots and left me in charge."

Shit, in charge of the nurses is more like it. "What gives you the right to lord it over me?" I asked with disgust.

"You're a fucking counterrevolutionary under supervised reform, that's what!"

"Fuck you!"

"You haven't forgotten the airplane position, have you? Fuck your old lady!"

"Fuck *your* old lady!"

"Fuck your old lady, Yang Mo!"

I advanced with clenched fists. Dumbbell blocked my way.

My beloved mother, who had been received by Premier Zhou himself, was being reviled by some shitty little thug.

"Get out of my way, you ass-kissing piece of shit!" I trembled as I held Mother's letter in my hand.

"You'd better watch your step, you little pussy!" Liu Fulai said, pointing his finger at me.

What had I done that was so bad? I had knocked off early after meeting up with a couple of wolves, that's all.

30

THIS IS WHAT
HARD WORK GOT ME

THE NEXT MORNING, June 30, 1971, broke clean and clear.
Right after breakfast I went up the mountain alone. The valley was lush
and green, with tall, pristine peonies creating an explosion of color
amid the shrubbery. Chirping birds raised a din I didn't think would
ever end. Golden rays of morning sun filtering through the leafy um-
brella mottled the ground below. I loved this gorgeous valley, where the
melodic chatting of birds floated on air redolent with nature's perfume.
It was free of the arrogance of the civilized world. Violence existed only
as a by-product of the law of the jungle, but all creatures received equal
treatment; there were no class distinctions here.

July 1, the fiftieth anniversary of the Chinese Communist Party, was
just around the corner, so I worked extra hard, cutting down three hundred trees a day, and still I wasn't satisfied. I wanted to celebrate the occasion by increasing my production to four hundred. What better way
to show my devotion to Chairman Mao?

My ax left a trail of toppled trees in its wake. By three that afternoon
I'd reached my quota of four hundred, each a magnificent specimen of
poplar. After mopping my sweaty face, I lay down in the grass to gaze
contentedly into the blue sky. Although poplars are easier to harvest

than birches, four hundred in one day was nothing to scoff at. My companions—as a team—would have killed themselves cutting down that many.

Following a well-deserved rest, I strolled back to the yurt. It was deserted, and I wondered where the others had gone off to. After guzzling a bellyful of water straight from the teapot, I took off my shoes and lay down. In no time I was fast asleep.

"Kind of early to be in bed, isn't it?" Lei Xia was standing over me. I woke up.

"Get up."

"Why?"

"Because I said so." He nudged me with his foot, his new boots glimmering in the murky lamplight.

"Don't kick me."

"I said, Get up!"

"I'm tired. What's wrong?"

"What time did you return to camp?" His foot was so close to my face, I could smell the boot polish.

"I didn't look," I said softly. "When my work was finished."

"Bullshit. You waited till I was gone, then came back around noon. You ought to be ashamed of yourself for loafing like that."

I don't know what he thought made me so tired, but anger began to build inside me, and I was rapidly approaching the boiling point. I pulled my coat up over my head so as not to do or say anything I might regret.

"Who do you think you are? You're heading for a fall, I can tell you that."

My anger blinded me to the realization that I was being disrespectful by lying in bed and ignoring my own squad leader.

"I said, Get up!" he snarled, yanking away my sheepskin coat and grabbing me by the collar. He reeked of alcohol.

That's when my anger let go, like a tire that's blown its valve stem. I jammed my hand up against his throat and warned him in a shaky voice, "Don't you touch me."

I was already on my feet.

"How dare you hit me, you fucking counterrevolutionary!" He came at me like a madman, his fist thudding into my jaw. I stumbled backwards, but quickly assumed a fighting stance, my right fist cocked and ready to strike. Then I recalled Mother's words: "Any more fighting, and I'll have nothing more to do with you. You'll be no son of mine." It wasn't easy, but I held back and glared at him like an animal about to pounce. "Son of a bitch. Faggot. Bastard. Turncoat." I called him every name in the book. My temples throbbed.

He stood there open-mouthed, white with anger. "Shut your arrogant mouth." His fist connected again. *Pow!* Loud and crisp. He put everything he had into it. I saw stars.

Still I didn't hit back. I was afraid, not of him, but of being dragged off to another denunciation session by Staff Officer Zhao, of being disowned by my mother, and of cheapening my devotion to Chairman Mao. It wasn't worth it.

We squared off in the murky lamplight like mortal enemies.

He hated being called a son of a bitch.

"Son of a bitch."

Pow!

"Fuck you, you son of a bitch."

Pow!

His eyes, big as saucers, glared in the murky light as he swung again and again. I stood there taking one punch after another.

Liu Fulai, Dumbbell, and the others came in, bringing the stench of more alcohol with them. They joined in on the fun, fists and feet flying. Kicking the shit out of a counterrevolutionary was the sort of free entertainment that couldn't get them into any trouble.

Realizing that this was no time to worry about appearances, I curled up into a ball and wrapped my arms around my head. Then when I tried to get to my feet, they knocked me down again.

"Kick him in the belly."

"Harder, beat some humility into him."

"Let him up."

"No, keep him on the floor. Tie the mangy dog up."

I jumped to my feet.

"Go for his eyes!" Lei Xia shouted.

Someone connected with my left eye, temporarily blinding me. The ceiling began to spin and the floor started moving. Dark images danced around me . . . Something salty and sticky pooled in the corners of my mouth.

Lucky for me the lamp went out in the confusion, turning the yurt dark. The sounds of heavy breathing were punctuated by a clattering of utensils.

"Block the door."

"The lamp, hurry!"

"Hold him down!"

"Get something to tie him up with."

"Flashlight."

The moment of truth had arrived. I broke for the door under the protection of darkness and chaos. Someone grabbed me as I reached it, but I broke his grip with a downward chop; Lei Xia wrapped his arms around me from behind, planted his feet, and wouldn't let go. "Grab his legs," he shouted, "and hurry!"

Confident that they couldn't tell who was who in the dark, I wrenched free and ran outside as fast as my legs would carry me, followed by Lei Xia's shouts of "Catch him!" and "Don't let him get away!"

I ran barefoot into the darkness with the determination of an infant at the breast, jumped off a ledge, and made my getaway into the woods, tumbling and crawling most of the way. I tried to open my left eye, but it was no use. For someone as nearsighted as me, getting by with one eye was murder, and I fell more times than I could count. I was afraid to stop, even when I reached the relative safety of a dark gully.

Lei Xia wouldn't stop until he caught me, I figured, so I staggered on, gasping for breath, until I was too exhausted to run another step. Finally I collapsed beneath a large outcropping and tried desperately to force gulps of air into my lungs.

Stillness all around. They hadn't followed me, after all.

I sat there massaging my bloody, battered face, trying to soften the hardest knots.

Now what? It was so late and so dark.

I heard a wolf nearby, but I didn't care. I just closed my eyes and lay back. I was cold, and my feet and legs hurt, all scratched by brambles. After crawling into a clump of dry shrubs, I curled into a ball to get some sleep, and that's when the fear hit me. I was lucky I hadn't broken a leg or something.

It must have been two o'clock, but I was still wide awake. My teeth were chattering, my stomach growled. I sat up, buried my head between my knees, and wrapped my arms around my legs to conserve heat, as scenes from my life flashed before my eyes: Mother washing me before bedtime; Father taking me to the Great Hall of the People over Lunar New Year's; my teacher giving me a fancy diary for being admitted into the Young Pioneers; having our picture taken in Tiananmen Square before leaving for Inner Mongolia . . . It all seemed so real, whereas the present was just a bad dream.

I couldn't believe that the "human punching bag" could have pounded me like that. My most loyal friend ever was now hounding me to death. I had just had my ass kicked for the first time in my life. How would I ever live it down?

At dawn I limped over to the Company Nine yurt. "Where are you from?" one of the students asked guardedly. His companions eyed me warily, probably taking me for an escapee.

"Company Seven."

They gathered round to get a better look. "Ah," one of them blurted out in surprise, "you're Ma Bo, aren't you?"

I nodded.

"What happened to you? Your eye's all bloody and swollen."

They knew what had happened just by looking at me: barefoot, a torn pantleg flapping in the wind, calves scratched bloody by brambles, left eye swollen shut. I didn't have to tell them I'd been thrashed.

After inviting me inside, they brought me some water to wash up, and a bowl of noodles. I nearly wept with gratitude but held back. People look down on you if you're too emotional. As dispassionately as possible I told them what had happened, and they agreed that Lei Xia had gone too far.

"If you broke the law, the authorities will handle things. He had no cause to beat you like that."

"We know you go out to work early in the morning and don't come back till late, rain or shine, because we've seen you."

"Report this to Staff Officer He. Don't let it fester."

I'd never had any use for Tianjin students up till then. But that all changed after meeting this group from Company Nine.

Staff Officer He rode up after I'd eaten and washed up, and when he heard my story he said sympathetically, "I'll talk to them, then we'll get you patched up. Okay?"

That sounded fine to me. Noticing that I was barefoot, he let me ride behind him all the way to the yurt, where a smiling Lei Xia greeted us as if nothing had happened.

"What were you thinking? You had no right to beat him like that!"

Lei Xia launched into a litany of complaints: I was dishonest, I goofed off when I should have been working, I chopped down seedlings instead of adult trees, I stole food, I put wet clothes on top of grain sacks. I knocked off and came home early when he wasn't around.

I felt like running up and slapping that pious look off his face. He had no right to be that handsome.

"Well, our intrepid warrior has returned," Liu Fulai said when he saw me. "The way you scurried out of here last night would put a rat to shame."

Ignoring his sarcasm, I turned to Lei Xia and said, "If you ever lay a hand on me again, you'll get what's coming to you. My patience has its limits."

"Where does a one-eyed counterrevolutionary get off being so cocky?"

"Watch your mouth, you son of a bitch."

"God damn it." He blanched. "You watch what *you're* saying." He shoved me.

"See, Staff Officer He, there he goes again," I said as I reached out and slapped Lei Xia. The crisp sound was music to my ears. Too bad I hadn't slapped him harder.

"You're asking for it, you little pussy." Liu Fulai picked up a stick,

Dumbbell grabbed a cleaver, and Lei Xia snatched up a rolling pin. All three of them came at me, and when Staff Officer He blocked their way, I turned, ran out of the yurt, and scooped a stick up off the ground. But something hit me on the shoulder before I could turn around. I turned in time to see Liu Fulai's stick slicing through the air. Cocking my head to absorb the blow on the side of the neck, I leapt at him. But he nimbly jumped behind Staff Officer He. "You and your pubic pigtail," he cursed, brandishing his stick. "You cocksucker!"

That did it. I went after him, but Staff Officer He wrapped his arms around me. "Ma Bo, stop right there!" Just then a wagon pulled up with a load of harvested trees, and he managed to wrestle me onto it. Old Chang, the driver, picked up my bedroll and tossed it onto the wagon.

Once we were rolling, Lei Xia came out with my beat-up cloth shoes, holding them disgustedly between his thumb and forefinger, and flung them at me. He made some sort of wisecrack. I didn't hear what he said, but everyone else cracked up.

You can imagine my surprise when I glanced down at the bed of the slow-moving wagon and saw the poplars I'd cut down a couple of days ago, all neatly stacked. It was filled with them. My gift for the party's fiftieth anniversary, for which I'd been thanked with a lumpy face and a puffy black eye.

I wrote to Mother, telling her what had happened and begging for her help. So long as I remained a counterrevolutionary I'd keep getting my ass kicked, and I could do nothing about it.

That night I tossed and turned, unable to sleep, and as I lay there aching all over, I wondered what I had done to make Lei Xia want to annihilate me. The only thing that made any sense was that he had lost his self-esteem. He was a mediocre, docile person blessed with his share of qualities, talents, and character traits. But his family background had shattered his confidence; the only path open to him was getting obsessively involved in politics—exhibiting as much courage, combativeness, and loyalty as possible. And after all that effort to create a heroic image, he had come to grief at the hands of yours truly; no wonder I was on his shit list.

On my third day back at the company, the potbellied Political Instructor Shen looked me up right after breakfast.

"Ma Bo, they want you at a meeting at the regiment. You can take the day off."

That sounded like ominous news to me.

I was not in a particularly good mood as I sat on the tractor later that morning, accompanied by Li Xiaohua and some other girls dressed in new army overcoats and caps, perky as can be. They chattered away or sang the whole time; for them a meeting meant a good time or, at the very least, a day off.

Just as I had feared, Staff Officer Zhao took me aside when we arrived at the regimental reception hall. One look at my companions — Liu Yi, Gonggele, and all the rest — told me all I needed to know: Every "bad egg" in the regiment was there. Another damned denunciation session. We were told to stand on the right edge of the stage as secondary targets.

This time Director Li was running the show. "We're here today to criticize the counterrevolutionary arsonist so-and-so from the Sixty-third Regiment and would-be murderers so-and-so from the Sixty-second Regiment."

The prisoners were led up onto the stage in the customary fashion but couldn't be forced into the airplane position, since they were handcuffed.

"Never forget class struggle!"

"Strengthen the dictatorship of the proletariat!"

Shouts from thousands of throats reverberated through the hall, but there was less tension in the air this time. After all, these miscreants were from other units.

After all the pertinent facts relating to the prisoners had been stated, company representatives launched their attacks. The outpouring of venom suddenly made it all very real.

Finally, Director Li pointed to our pitiful little band. "There you see people belonging to the four bad categories from our own regiment." His voice took on a menacing tone: "Raise your heads and let everyone get a good look at you."

He introduced us one by one: "Here we have so-and-so, a thief from Cattle Ranch Three; here you have Liu Yi from Company Three, a counterrevolutionary who refuses to stop trying to have his verdict overturned; here you have Gonggele of Company Seven, a herdowner and misfit who sabotaged a reaper during the busy season; and here you have Ma Bo, a counterrevolutionary from Company Seven who was caught fighting only a couple of days ago and who still refuses to accept labor reform."

Staff Officer Zhao reached out from behind and jerked my chin up to show my face to the mob packing the hall. My left eye was still swollen shut, not to mention black and blue, and my face was as dark as a cowchip.

"Long live the dictatorship of the proletariat!"

On our return trip I sat in the back of the tractor, letting the wind cool my feverish face. My young female companions, meanwhile, were excitedly comparing the scarves and silk stockings they had bought at the regiment co-op. They didn't shut up once during the entire trip.

Released from custody, I swore I wouldn't give the PI an excuse to make things harder on me than they already were. But it's not easy to get people to like you when you're as ugly as I am. And I can never find the words to put people at ease. About all I have going for me is my strength. You do what you do best, and for me that was to work hard.

I was so exhausted at the end of the day that the simple act of walking made me grimace; squatting in the crapper was life's greatest pleasure, since it was about the only place I could rest. Sometimes I couldn't even hold my rice bowl without resting my arms on my knees. For months I worked like a man possessed, just to show I wasn't a counterrevolutionary and to prove my devotion to Chairman Mao.

The autumn harvest meant I had to work at night as well. I was given the job of feeding millet into one of the winnowers, making sure it never went hungry. Its roar didn't let up as the night deepened, but my worn-out body was finding it hard to keep up the pace, and the arching stream of grain began thinning out.

"Faster! If we don't meet our quota, we'll come looking for you," Shen screamed hoarsely.

Then one drizzly day, as I was tossing mud into a newly built toilet, someone handed me a letter. It was from Mother.

I scooted into the crapper, sat on a pile of dirt, and read.

Bo,

You say you don't oppose Chairman Mao, but everything you do runs counter to Chairman Mao's teachings. Even now you have no sense of the crimes you've committed. You hide behind the insistence that you've never set out to oppose the party or Chairman Mao. You fight, you say crazy things, and you steal from your own parents. What have you ever done to make yourself a useful citizen of the new China? You won't confess your crimes and you keep fighting. Don't you know how disappointed you make me?

I won't write you again, not until you show me you've changed your ways. Don't you write to me either.

Mother
July

I sat there rubbing one foot against the other, sending flecks of dried mud flying. Not a single word of encouragement. That was my total return on an investment of sweat and toil. Was I really as insignificant to them as the flecks of mud lying at my feet?

31

A WORLD OF

ICE AND SNOW

As soon as the busy harvest season was over, I was sent back up the mountain to make little rocks out of big ones. Jin Gang and Dumbbell, who were being punished for fighting, went with me.

The herdowner Gonggele, who had been guarding our rocks from the small tent he called home, had been summoned to mow the steppes, only to be sent back after damaging a reaper in a careless moment. Daoerji, in failing health, was allowed to return.

The gently undulating skyline was as solemn as ever. Last winter's quarries were a sorry sight, overrun with dead grass, dirt, and cast-off stones.

We were lonely up there—three men crowded into a rundown yurt—but since we were all targets of criticism, we managed to put aside our distrust of one another.

Dumbbell was a beefy, dark-skinned fellow with sparkling teeth and closely cropped hair who took after his father, a pedicab driver. He talked like a guttersnipe. "I'll kick your fucking ass!" was his favorite expression, and he hated anything to do with studying. You didn't have to look far for the source of his nickname.

Jin Gang, as I have indicated, was a skinny runt with a pointy chin, a beak of a nose, and thin eyebrows. His eyes were in a perpetual squint, like those of a fox; his lips were pencil thin; and his hair was soft and fine. He looked and acted like a rodent: jittery, cautious.

When he first arrived, he refused to ride horses, unable to bear the thought of tiring one of them out. And while you might catch him talking about slaughtering a goat, you'd never see him actually do it. A bad background and frail health had turned him into a melancholic soul who liked to be alone with his fantasies. Urbane in speech and manners, as a worker he left considerable room for improvement, and his prestige suffered because of it. For a while he followed my lead in infrequent baths and frequent cursing, regular workouts and irregular dress—in order to remove his "sissy" image—until people began calling him my disciple.

He had been sent up the mountain as a "disciplinary warning" for slugging Little Sichuan during a heated argument. Being denounced made him more cautious than ever, and though he treated me well enough while we were working, he avoided everything that might put him at risk. Since there was bad blood between him and Dumbbell, whose gluttony drove him nuts, he treated me with courtesy that bordered on friendliness.

In late november 1971, Dumbbell and Jin Gang were summoned back to the company for a meeting, leaving me alone up there with Gonggele, who looked like an apparition with eyeholes burned into a leathery face. He didn't say two words all day, limiting himself to grunts in response to my comments. He had all the spunk of an inchworm.

Deprived of any worthwhile activity and virtually all sound, I went to bed earlier than usual. But I had too much on my mind to sleep. What was the meeting about? Why them and not me? Envy and humiliation gripped me.

Three days later they returned, and Dumbbell hadn't taken two steps into the yurt before he was crowing about how he had pinched a chunk of pork from the kitchen. During one of our work breaks I asked Jin Gang, "What sort of meeting was it?"

"Don't ask," he replied somberly yet with no rancor as he lay on the kang. "We're not supposed to tell you."

That really pissed me off. What was he afraid of? That I'd blow the whistle on him or something?

Desperate to know what it was they weren't allowed to tell me, I went over all the possibilities and kept my ears open. From snatches of a conversation between him and Dumbbell I sensed that something important had happened. But I never dreamed that Vice Chairman Lin Biao, once Chairman Mao's anointed successor, would attempt a coup, then flee Beijing when it failed. The Lin Biao Incident, which became headline news around the world, was not to be shared with members of the four bad categories, which is why I was being kept in the dark.

In December, Squad Two returned from Injgan Sum, where they had been sent to dig a tunnel—a failed project that exhausted enormous amounts of dynamite. They joined us on the mountain, as did Xu Zuo, who had talked his mother into letting him return to the steppe. His request for rock-quarry duty had been approved by an astonished Company Commander Wang.

Skinny and frail as ever, but looking rested, he fished out a pack of Peony cigarettes from Beijing and treated us all—even me. It was only a butt, yet the simple gesture created a model of friendliness toward me that the young students from Tianjin emulated.

Our duties were heavy, but there were enough of us to spread the work around. Xu Zuo waited until he and I were alone to inform me that "a certain high-placed traitor named Lin had failed in an attempt to overthrow Chairman Mao and had crashed in an airplane during his escape." As a rash of new party policies was being set into motion following the attempted coup, Xu Zuo went to convince my mother to help me. She sent word for me to work hard, make a good impression on people, and wait to see what happened. I was to be patient, since her own problems weren't resolved yet.

News of this reconciliation opened my heart like a flower, the same heart she had savaged with her rigid orthodoxy.

THE COMPANY ASSIGNED us a quota of fifteen hundred cubic yards of stone to meet the following year's construction plans. The pace of work, even with a detail of fifteen men, was fierce.

Xu Zuo was our foreman, but he didn't act like one, for he worked as hard as the rest of us and said little, even helping out in the kitchen from time to time. The Tianjin students respected him, in part because of rumors of bad blood between him and Director Li.

The clang of sledgehammers and crack of dynamite filled the air over our remote mountain. As the quarries deepened, the rocks were harder to get to, but still the piles grew.

Toward the end of 1971, we received a company directive that the New Year holiday was to be celebrated as a revolutionary affair in accordance with the "Learn from Dazhai" campaign. In other words, we would get no time off.

The first thing we did was send word that our provisions were running low. But the weather, bad and getting worse, sealed the roads and made resupply impossible for the moment. We were in a pickle, and we knew it. By the thirtieth we were down to one day's supply of millet, and all we could do was stand around the stove shivering as we watched some of the last of our food cooking. Dumbbell, his coat draped over his shoulders, sighed and grumbled, but Xu Zuo inveighed against Big-Belly Shen for neglecting his comrades up on the mountain. Jin Gang went even further, calling all officials cold-blooded ass-kissers.

After breakfast Jin Gang volunteered to ride back to camp for provisions. We lent him the warmest clothes we had to protect him from the treacherous elements, and by the time he was wrapped in his army overcoat and fur cap he could barely raise his arms.

"All the clothes in the world won't protect you if you don't cinch up around the waist," I said, getting down on one knee and cinching his waist as tightly as I could. He'd be heading into the freezing wind on his way down, so I wrapped his head with an old bedsheet until only his eyes showed.

Icy winds howled and tore at our faces like the claws of a wild animal. As Jin Gang prepared to set out, his camel brayed unhappily and balked at leaving the warmth of the yurt, spraying the area with its slobber. Since it refused to kneel down, poor Jin Gang had to start out on foot, leading the hulking animal behind him as it brayed piteously. They were quickly swallowed up by the murky sky.

As soon as Jin Gang was out of sight we rushed back to the yurt to change into "battle gear" that consisted of torn, filthy quilted jackets, leather gloves in shreds, grimy mufflers, and electrical wires cinched to our waists. Then we fell in silently behind Xu Zuo and emerged from the yurt in single file, straight into a gale that forced us to keep our eyes shut and walk doubled over as we strained to reach the mountain peak.

Our work day had begun.

Dumbbell sat on a freezing rock holding a drill in a dynamite hole for Xu Zuo's fourteen-pound hammer. Li Guoqiang was red in the face as he strained against a crowbar, trying to pry loose a rock that simply wouldn't budge. Sun Gui tramped slowly up the slope with a two-hundred-pound boulder on his back, his eyes nearly popping out of his head.

When the dynamite hole was finished, Xu Zuo flopped down on his belly, slipped an arm out of his jacket sleeve—an agonizing task—and stuck his hand into the three-foot hole to scoop out the frozen mud. The raging gale forced him to thrust his numbed fingers under his clothes every few seconds to keep them from getting frostbitten. His teeth were chattering.

Meanwhile, Li Guoqiang, failing at his frontal assault on the boulder, wedged himself beneath it and pried with all his might. Sparks flew as steel scraped rock.

The others went into a six-foot dugout in the quarry, got down on their knees, and began digging out the accumulated dirt and gravel, a substantial part of which came back at them on the wind. Stopping to rest was too dangerous in that weather. Our lips were blue, our brows frosty as we fought the elements. The gale continued unabated, sending the temperature plummeting.

"Your nose, it's white!" I yelled to Xu Zuo.

He couldn't hear me. "What—did—you—say?"

"Your nose—freezing! Go—back—camp!"

"No—problem!"

Each swing of his sledge sent the drill leaping into the air with a loud clang. Tears streamed down his frozen cheeks as he waved us back to camp; but now that the battle against the elements and the rocks had been joined, we scowling young men refused to admit defeat. Eyes red from anger and the cold, we ignored Xu Zuo and threw ourselves into our work, grunting loudly to undermine the power of the cold. Our spit was solid ice before it hit the ground, but the elements weren't going to beat us, no matter how cold it got, not us. *Clang! Clang! Clang!* The sounds of life merged in the swirling wind and were carried off—a song of metal on stone.

Quitting time.

We cupped our hands over our ears, tossed our heads in the direction of home, and ran like hell to the protection of the yurt, trailing shouts of celebration and defiance.

A sticky fluid oozed from Sun Gui's ears. Xu Zuo's nose was frostbitten. Li Guoqiang's feet were red and swollen. No one had escaped unscathed. But we were proud of our unprecedented New Year's celebration and spent the rest of the afternoon planning the holiday meal. Counting on the timely arrival of supplies from the company, we had finished off the last of the meat, which left us only a little flour, some lard, and a few green onions. That was it. Which meant that we would have to usher in the new year with a pot of bland noodles. But that was better than nothing, and we slurped it down until we were happily full.

After dinner we occupied ourselves with glove-mending, a little chess, some tunes on a harmonica. Dumbbell sat alone, staring gloomily into the kerosene lantern.

"Wishing you were home, Dumbbell?" Li Guoqiang asked as he sewed a hole in one of his gloves.

"Yeah, I miss my mother."

"You'll just make yourself feel worse. Get some shut-eye."

"You don't know what I mean to her."

"Bullshit. My mother loves me too, but I don't sit around moping about it."

"Dog humper!" Dumbbell grinned proudly over his choice of words.

Maybe we were too young to grasp the implications of New Year's Eve, or maybe the freezing air had numbed our feelings, but there was no festive air in the yurt on the eve of our most important holiday. Sun Gui and Li Guoqiang were engaged in a lively debate over who had the hardest job; Xu Zuo sat beneath the lamp poring over a copy of *Selected Works of Lenin*; and Dumbbell lay in bed with his coat drawn up over his head. Then, once we began to thaw out, our "personal livestock" started to squirm. I climbed out of my pants and underwear and slipped naked into bed to put an end to the activities of the lice inhabiting various parts of my body. Having grown fat and lazy, they popped like beans over a fire as they expired between my thumbnails, which were soon dotted with my own blood.

"Get away from me," Dumbbell complained when he saw what I was doing. "I feel sorry for anyone who has to be next to you."

Our only source of water up there, both for cooking and hygiene, was snow. Bathing was out of the question (washing your face was bad enough), as was changing clothes, and with nine people squeezed into a single yurt, it was the rare individual who didn't play host to a substantial brood of lice. Li Guoqiang once counted his harvest from a single pair of pants: over 130, a new record. But instead of disposing of them he put them into a tin can, some dead, others alive and kicking, to take back to Tianjin and show his family, just so he could watch their eyes pop out of their sockets.

A storm raged outside, forcing cold air in through seams ripped open by whistling, howling winds. Dumbbell's head was an inch from the stove, half of Xu Zuo's covers were on top of dying cinders, and Sun Gui was encircled by buckets, bowls, chopsticks, and cooking pots. I slept on a pile of cowchips near the door flap.

The storm didn't let up all that night, and when we awoke the next morning we couldn't believe our eyes. Everything—our clothes, the felt rug, cooking utensils, the floor in front of the stove—lay under a blanket of snow. During the night the *toono* had blown open, inviting the storm in on top of us. Having slept with our heads under the covers in order to escape the cold, we now formed nine snow-capped mounds. "Only in Inner Mongolia can you sleep under snow blankets," Xu Zuo exclaimed gleefully. That got the rest of us stirring, for we had to figure out what to do about breakfast; a bare cupboard on New Year's morning was a new experience for us. All we found was some corn, which we used as horse feed back in the wagon squad.

So we stayed in bed to curse, sing, hurl insults, boast, anything to keep from having to get up. It was as cold inside the yurt as it was outside. At long last Xu Zuo and Li Guoqiang climbed out of bed, shivering and shouting as they threw on their clothes and lit a fire.

"Get up. When the snow melts the bedding will get wet."

Reluctantly we climbed out of bed, got dressed, and swept the snow off our bedding. We scooped melted snow out of the pot to brush our teeth, then filled a basin halfway and took turns running a wash rag over our faces.

After dumping the last of the corn into the pot, we put it on the stove. It took forever to cook the stuff to an edible consistency, and we couldn't keep a fire going with damp cowchips. Finally Xu Zuo soaked a worn-out cloth shoe in cooking oil, lit it, and tossed it in. *Whoosh!* Then in went its mate. By the time the corn was good and mushy, the stove had consumed all our goat chips, four shoes, and half a bucketful of diesel oil. We sat around slurping up watery corn, hoping to see Jin Gang pretty soon, so we wouldn't go hungry on the first day of the new year.

When he hadn't shown up by noon, we began to worry, and Xu Zuo decided to go borrow food from Company One. But just as he was dressed and ready to set out we heard the braying of a camel. We ran outside, whooping with delight, as Jin Gang rode up, a pair of filthy trousers wrapped around his head, with only his eyes showing. He was groaning pitifully.

We quickly carried the grain, vegetables, mutton, and pork inside the yurt, while Jin Gang removed his battle gear. His face was frozen numb and horribly distorted: shriveled nose, twisted mouth, and watery eyes. Like a death mask. As he limbered up painfully he forced a weak smile onto his face. "In case you guys are interested, the Western Ujimqin Banner meteorological office reported that the temperature fell to forty-four below yesterday, the coldest in over thirty years." He massaged his misshapen face. "Ouch, I'm frozen stiff! The damned camel wouldn't obey me, and I didn't think I'd ever make it to Company Three."

He blinked with difficulty; a large blister—now broken and oozing something yellow—rose above his cheekbone. He tried to smile, but that just made him even uglier and more uncomfortable. "Shit," he grumbled, "a fur cap doesn't cut it in weather like this. You have to wrap your face real good. And not with a bedsheet, either. I managed to find some old leather pants in a storeroom." He stopped massaging his face long enough to fish out a pack of cigarettes, which he passed around. "I ran into Lei Xia at Company Three. He said he damned near lost his nose on a trip to the regiment and would have if he hadn't had the sense to wrap it in a bag he'd brought along."

"It's a good thing you came back when you did," Dumbbell said, "or we'd have gone hungry on New Year's Day."

"The company commander's on home leave, and the PI got stinking drunk with some 'visiting firemen' from the regiment. If I hadn't gone, we'd have had to feed ourselves on the wind."

That night we made wontons. Jin Gang had even lifted two sacks of cowchips from the mess hall, so we didn't have to cook over a fire fueled by plastic sandals. Our yurt may have been damp, dirty, and chaotic, but it became warm and toasty with a roaring fire in the stove. The wontons were ready in no time, and so was Dumbbell, who scooped out a bowlful before anyone else made a move and gobbled them down contentedly, sweat dripping from the tip of his nose. We were right behind him, but before we had finished half a bowlful, he was back for more. Jin Gang gave him a contemptuous look and commented loudly, "The sign of the petty bourgeoisie—gluttony."

That was our New Year's Day, 1971.

Two days later the storm died out and we went back to work, slogging through half a foot of snow to get there, only to discover that the quarries were filled in. So the first order of business was to dig out, and that took all day. The deeper we dug the harder the going, as the airborne snow came flying back at us, slipping under collars, sticking to our heads, making our hands slippery, and slithering down our boots, where it turned our socks cold and brittle. By the time we'd reached the bottom, we were lugging the stuff out by the sackful. By then our clothes looked like armor plating.

We didn't eat very well over that stretch of time, mainly corn mush and corn cakes with frozen cabbage. The mutton was parceled out a little at a time to make it last as long as possible. We drank melted snow and a yellow tea that tasted like horse piss. The yurt offered little protection against the cold, but our spirits were high. Except for Dumbbell, that is.

On the second he lay in bed, weeping softly. New Year's without all the hustle and bustle—not even a plate of melon seeds to nibble on— was more than he could bear. Creature comforts were important to him (despite the fact that his father was a pedicab driver): If the rug he slept on was lumpy, he carefully smoothed it out; if a blade of straw was stuck to his bedding, he carefully picked it off. He couldn't sleep otherwise. Jin Gang, on the other hand, could sleep on his sledgehammer if necessary.

On the third, Dumbbell complained to Xu Zuo, "My back's killing me. I'm going back to the company to see a doctor. They don't give us decent boots or lined pants or gloves and won't be happy till we're a bunch of stiffs. I'd like to see them spend a day or two up here." He grumbled all the way down the mountain.

On the fourth, Jin Gang, Xu Zuo, and I went to borrow some dynamite. It was dark by the time we reached Company Four Headquarters, where we spotted someone walking toward us with a flashlight. "Who's there?" We didn't answer. We must have looked like a band of scruffy bandits in that little bit of light.

"Who's there?" He stopped, but we kept coming without making a sound. When the light hit our faces he jumped back in alarm. "Wh—where are you from?"

"Company Seven!" we bellowed in unison.

"Oh, students. You scared me. I thought you were robbers." He was off like a shot.

That little prank was a real morale booster.

We were proud. To us, split skin that oozed pus and clothing held together by patches and electric cords were a form of beauty—the scars of a bitter struggle. There was nothing bogus about our enthusiasm. It wasn't generated to get ahead (that was a concept we universally scorned), nor was it for financial benefit, since our wages stayed at thirty-two a month no matter how much or how little we did. And it certainly wasn't intended to impress girls, since there were no girls to impress up there.

And what were our leaders doing as we struggled against the cold and the snow, the rocks that wouldn't budge, and the frozen ground? How did they pass the time while we went hungry, stained the rocks with our blood, and hobbled around on swollen feet? They played cards in heated offices, made corrupt deals and hoarded foodstuffs, engaged in lurid sexual conduct, filled their homes with public property, and raised a hue and cry over job transfers.

Even our own Political Instructor Shen, who never passed up an opportunity to talk about the hard life he'd lived, finally brought shame on himself.

32

I MUST
SURVIVE

THE COMPANY WAS buzzing over the scandal involving Political Instructor Shen, the same man who had purged Dr. Wang and his girlfriend.

It was New Year's. He was sloppy drunk in the women's dorm, so Li Xiaohua and another girl helped him home. In the darkness he kissed Xiaohua, who burst into tears. She promptly reported him to the regiment. Naturally he called her a liar, but that didn't squelch the talk, which sent him to bed for a couple of days. Lust, however, is more tenacious than a deflated spirit, and he was not about to quit until he had sampled all the citified feminine pulchritude—sixty or more grape-sweet faces—in Company Seven.

Which brings us to Qi Shuzhen, whose dream of joining the party never allowed her to stray far from the organization. She worked hard, spoke passionately at meetings, volunteered to clean the toilets nearly every week, and spent most of her free time visiting the PI, who knew instinctively that she would do anything to gain admission to the party. His chance came when Company Commander Wang went on home leave, abandoning the headquarters to Shen, who spiffed himself up with his wife's knitted vest, invited Shuzhen over, greeted her with a smile and an earnest look, then claimed her on the Company Commander's bed.

If you ever need a shadow, just set up a pole. Shen not only handed her a membership application the next day, he even went to the regiment on the pretext of resolving organizational problems with progressive stereotypes just so he could grease the skids for her. Having finally realized the dream of a lifetime, Squad Leader Qi was catapulted to the top of the company list of students.

All the time Shen was diddling Qi, he was the same old PI at work—if anything, more so. At the end of each day, no matter how cold it was, he inspected every platoon's work, hands clasped behind him, belly thrust out in front. Then back to headquarters to analyze the results of his inspection with his superiors and to discuss ideological attitudes. At the nightly company meetings he would stand up front, eyes glaring, and lash out at the corps soldiers assembled before him: The next time you go on sick call, Zhang Baofeng, I'll garnish your wages. Any more hanky-panky with the girls, Liu Fulai, and it's up the mountain for you. And so on. Just because he was sleeping with one of the students didn't mean he had to give up his cherished work ethic.

Eventually they were caught—by Li Xiaohua, of all people. She was still steaming over his behavior and couldn't stomach Qi Shuzhen's obsession over party membership. Now she had them where she wanted them; an avenging woman was more than the PI could handle.

She blew the whistle on them when Company Commander Wang returned a couple of months later. Having been squeezed by the PI for so long, he gleefully struck without warning, sending for Qi Shuzhen while Shen was off at a meeting and forcing a confession out of her. He forwarded the particulars to the newly arrived commissar, a man named Kang, who blasted Shen with both barrels at a standing-committee meeting: "You shameless fucking animal! Is this the sort of example we deserve from one of our political officers?"

When the PI's wife got wind of what was up she was fit to be tied. "You shameless, horny ass!" she was heard to wail. For days he didn't poke his head out the door. Placed on probation, he was reassigned as an assistant in the Regimental Logistics Section.

Then, as if that weren't enough, Deputy Commissar Liu made a special trip to the company to call a public meeting and read us the riot act: "There's been funny business of one sort or another in Company Seven ever since it was formed." He waved his arms in exasperation. "We're going to clear the air around here, do you hear me? We're here to reclaim land, not see how many scalps we can hang on our belts. We'll suck the poison out of this company, you can count on it." He then reiterated corps policy: "You may not become romantically involved for at least three years."

We were given the day off to discuss Liu's comments and criticize Shen's actions, the goal being to purge the company of evil immorality. All in all, it was the best news I'd heard in a long time. I hadn't seen the PI since he'd chewed me out the previous summer, and I knew that my verdict would never be overturned as long as Big-Belly Shen was in Company Seven. Now he was gone.

The time had obviously come to send off my appeal, so I went to Regimental Headquarters, where I heard that Daoerji was in the hospital—in pretty bad shape, I was told. I went to see him. "Where can I find a man named Daoerji?" I asked a young nurse.

"Which company?" she asked indifferently.

"Seven."

"An old Mongol with a chunk of his nose missing?"

"That's the one."

"He's dead."

"He's what?" I was stunned.

"He's dead." She turned and walked off.

Dumbbell came up just then, grumbling in his native dialect, "They ought to take those motherfucking dogshit doctors out and shoot 'em!" They had probably denied his request for sick leave.

"Hey, Dumbbell, did Daoerji really die?"

He nodded and, with undisguised fury, told me what had happened. After the old Mongol's camel fell on him he was taken to the regimental hospital with possible internal injuries. The doctors said it was nothing serious and prescribed bed rest.

Then one day he slipped into a coma. His anxious wife hitched up their oxcart and rushed him to the hospital, where she spread a rug in the corridor and propped him against the wall while she tried to get him admitted. Told there were no empty beds, she carried him piggyback out to the oxcart and took him to the nearby guest house.

He died that night in a cheap, smoky room reserved for laborers, drivers, and Mongols, on a bed with a thin blanket that probably had never been washed.

"All that bullshit about serving the workers, peasants, and soldiers!" Dumbbell exploded. "For officials, they supply not only beds, but the girls to go with them. In their eyes Mongols are no better than dogs. The doctors here are all pricks. Xie Chunhua had appendicitis, so they cut her open like they were castrating a pig. Old Chang's three-year-old kid went in with a slight fever, so they hooked him up to an IV and pumped him so full of something, he croaked. You'd have to be crazy to come here. If they don't kill you with their quack medicine, you'll die of fury."

How could a big, hulking man like Daoerji up and die like that? This was the same man who weaved back and forth in the saddle as he sang a Mongol folk song, a sorrowful, moving lament for the whole tenacious Mongol race. Mean and ugly, he had no use for friends, and would turn on you in a minute, like the time he accused me of attempted murder when he wanted to kill my dog. But put him out in a pasture with a herd of sheep, and he'd stick to them like glue, regardless of the season or the weather. Nothing could make him leave, not a downpour, not the blazing sun, not even a force-eleven storm. He had lost a chunk of his nose to frostbite, for which he had received no compensation. Hard work was what he did, twelve months a year, until his face was as weatherbeaten as bark. Whatever he turned his hand to he was good at. When he wasn't working, he slept, drank tea, bragged about his wife and kids, mended a rug. His greatest extravagance was an Oceans cigarette at New Year's.

I returned despondent to my mountain.

A few days later I learned that Daoerji's wife had dumped his body on an East River sandbank. The man with whom I had fought, whose yurt I had shared, and whose food I had eaten now lay quietly in the wilderness feeding buzzards and wild dogs.

AN ARCTIC FRONT moved in without warning, and the bottom dropped out of the thermometer. Study replaced work throughout the company. Jiang Baofu came up to report on the latest Central Committee directive and to organize a discussion group. So we crowded into the yurt to soak up heat from the stove as winds howled outside. The yurt may have been an eyesore, but in weather like this it was our best friend. It was too cold to go outside even to pee; the pile of cinders served just fine in that regard.

"Let's get started," Xu Zuo said to Jiang.

He nodded, then looked at me. Something was up.

"Outside, Ma Bo."

"What for?"

"The directive is confidential. Members of the four bad categories aren't allowed to participate in the discussion."

A dozen pairs of eyes were filled with curiosity, smugness, and sympathy. For a moment I had forgotten that I was a counterrevolutionary, a subhuman. But they hadn't. My face burned as I walked outside. How could a directive regarding Lin Biao be so sensitive that they would let me freeze rather than hear a single word of it?

Winds whipped in from the north, driving the snow ahead of them. Where was I supposed to go? More by habit than by design I headed toward the peak, the wind hitting my face like daggers. Protecting my face with my arms, I walked to the rock quarry, where I scooped out some snow, burrowed in, and sat in a carrying basket.

It was as still as a tomb down there, and as I sat looking at the frozen dirt, rocks, and dead grass, I reflected on the relatively cordial relations I'd had with the others lately. It was as if no barriers existed between us. When smokes were passed around I got one, and when someone returned from home leave, a piece of candy wound up in my hand, too. Such signs of friendship were like healing scabs on the open wounds of my face. Being driven out again was the same as ripping them off, and my face felt lacerated and bloody. I'd noticed the smug look on Li Guoqiang's face as I walked past him: It was the look of a child riding in a car who sees a pedestrian heading down a country road, one that embraces both innocence and cruelty.

There are people who would die over a slight like that, but I was determined to live on. And not because I was afraid of dying ignominiously, like some mangy dog. What's there to be afraid of? Everyone is born under a death sentence.

I shook with rage, dreaming about what it would be like to dynamite Regimental Headquarters. Then I'd be avenged for all the humiliation I'd suffered.

My little cave kept getting darker. The cold crept up from my fingers and toes, so I curled into a ball, wrapping my arms around my legs and burying my face between my knees.

Before my act of revenge, I would write to my folks and to the Corps Party Committee to tell them why . . . bury my diary . . . Our gunpowder was of such poor quality, I'd have to process it first, then buy half a dozen new batteries; Political Instructor Shen's office would be the best spot.

I was so absorbed in my fantasy, I didn't realize that the falling snow had sealed the opening of my cave, throwing it into complete darkness. The walls, the frozen dirt, the scattered rocks, and the tufts of dead grass were sucking up the last remaining warmth of my body.

Was this really happening? Was a lone counterrevolutionary really being buried alive beneath a blanket of snow? Yes, it really was happening. I wanted to cry, but couldn't. Cold, so cold. If only I had a box of matches . . .

Movement out there. Somebody was digging through the snow.

"Ma Bo! Ma Bo!" It was Xu Zuo. He dug through in record time. His clothing was coated with snow. Like a lost child spotting his mother, I grasped his hand tightly but said nothing.

"Everything's okay now; let's go. I figured you'd be here."
Silence.
"Let's go. I should have warned you, it's my fault."

More silence.

"What's wrong? Say something."

"I can't take it anymore," I muttered. "I can't go on."

"All we did was send you outside. What's the big deal? With Lin Biao out of the picture, you should be examining your problem from a new perspective. You mean you can't go on, now that your struggle is just beginning?"

"I was thinking about dynamiting Regimental Headquarters and blowing old Shen and myself to smithereens. I can deal with the hard work, but not the loss of face."

"No more of that kind of talk. I mean it. You'd be a counterrevolutionary for all eternity if you did anything that stupid," he said somberly. "A wild goose lives only three days after being driven from the flock. But you were driven from the ranks of corps troopers, assaulted by three thousand scowling, cursing, raging members of the regiment, and you're still hanging in there, refusing to acknowledge any criminal activity. You can be proud of that. I mean it, you've got balls!"

I shook my head despondently.

"Only the strong survive in a place like this. A sheep that leaves the flock dies. But a wolf, he's different. Use your head, and don't be so thin-skinned."

It was seven o'clock at night when I returned to the yurt. Xu Zuo handed me a piece of hardtack. "Eat up, it's still warm."

I crawled into bed when I'd finished the hardtack; I couldn't sleep. To insult someone from my generation all you had to do was accuse him of being scared of dying. But I'd have been a fool to die on some quixotic impulse, since I had to survive to fight the bastards. I knew I had to hang in there for as long as it took to stop being a counterrevolutionary. Those bastards weren't going to be entertained at my expense if I had anything to say about it.

Sure, I was scared of dying, and I didn't care who knew it. Shen and his crowd couldn't wait for the people they purged to die off. That way they'd never run the risk of a payback. But was I going to die and let my story be buried with me? Let their insults live on forever? Not a chance.

They could dump me in the crapper and cover me with shit, maggots, and mucus, or they could humiliate me, laugh at me, and treat me like a dung beetle, but I'd hold out until the tables were turned.

Several days later I walked into Regimental Headquarters to see Staff Officer Zhao. He had put on weight in the year since I'd last seen him. His Adam's apple now was hidden beneath a roll of fat; his face looked like a ripe melon. He was cleaning his camera when I entered. Laying it down gently, he leaned back in his chair and glared at me.

"What's on your mind?" Noncommittal, neither hot nor cold.

"I want to talk to you about something." I stood at attention to appear respectful. "Staff Officer Zhao," I said glumly, "I want to participate in the anti–Lin Biao campaign and be educated in the proletarian revolutionary line. All right?"

"Where did you hear about that?" He had a guarded look.

"I overheard the others talking about it one night in bed. They thought I was asleep."

"And maybe you heard something from your mother?"

"She mentioned it in one of her letters."

His face darkened. "That directive was not meant for your eyes. You're not allowed to participate in the study sessions."

"Why not? I wasn't formally labeled a counterrevolutionary."

"A technicality. Being called an active counterrevolutionary by the corps is a de facto label." His eyes were wide; the soft skin on his face emitted a menacing glow.

"I can't participate even to be educated?"

"Not this kind of education."

I dragged myself back to Stone Mountain, my spirit broken. That night I didn't sleep a wink. There was no getting through to him. Did he really have the right to treat a counterrevolutionary like a lowly animal?

The fall of Lin Biao weakened their case against me. During the interrogation, Zhao had confronted me repeatedly with directives issued by "Vice Chairman Lin." And all that bullshit about vilifying Vice

Chairman Lin. My ass! My only regret was that I had been too timid to vilify him as I should have.

A letter from Mother came a couple of weeks later. She approved of my plan to appeal to the corps. Her support would make all the difference, so after work each day I sat under my kerosene lamp and wrote the letter, too excited to feel tired.

33

I APPEAL

THE VERDICT

SPRING WAS JUST around the corner. Finally.

Warm, moist southern winds were the first sign. Then the snow began to melt, creating thousands of fingers of runoff, over which a new thin layer of ice formed after the sun went down each night.

The earth, having languished in a frozen limbo for months, was reborn, and life that had lain dormant beneath the ice and snow was revived in the warm air. A layer of green emerged on the ground, and above was the constant din of tiny larks that limbered up their wings to release a winter's accumulation of energy. Gaunt oxen lazily cleaned accumulated filth from their hides with long lapping tongues. The sun's rays forced the thin morning mist higher and higher into the air.

We stood near the peak to soak up the springlike breezes. Bareheaded for the first time in months, we breathed deeply, welcoming the fresh air with smiles and contented shouts. The true beauty of spring is revealed only to those who have struggled through a bitter winter.

What beggars we had become. Xu Zuo's leather pants, ripped at the knees, oozed padding; Jin Gang's pants were held up by black electrical wire, and wadding was slowly being liberated through holes in the sleeves of his padded jacket; Li Guoqiang was covered from head to toe with a fine layer of rock dust and had worn a hole in the seat of his pants. We presented a perfect picture of China's students of the early 1970s.

A MONTH HAD gone by since I'd sent in my request for a review of the case, and it was time to follow up. So I washed, changed into clean clothes, and took off for Regimental Headquarters, trying to map out what I'd say on the way. I went straight to the newly constructed, as yet unoccupied bathhouse to rest for a while and cool off. There I used a hand mirror to practice the expression I thought was most likely to get their sympathy. Was it natural? Was it off-putting? Then I went over my little speech one more time, took a deep breath, and walked outside. I was as fearful and anxious as a subject summoned for an imperial audience.

No one answered my cautious knock, so I opened the door a crack to peek inside. The room was deserted except for someone sleeping on the kang. Big, fat, and noisy.

"Commander," I called out anxiously.

He didn't stir.

"Commander." I turned up the volume.

The mound of flesh quivered as a chubby face turned toward me. Two sleepy eyes opened a crack. "What?"

"It's me, Ma Bo of Company Seven. I'm here to get my case reviewed." After managing to spit it out, I forced a smile. I must have looked ridiculous.

He sat up, yawned heroically, and squeezed his eyes shut until he was fully awake. "Go see the commissar," he demanded once his blood-shot eyes were open again.

The smile froze on my face. Should I wipe it off or let it stay there?

"Go on, go see the commissar."

"Where is he?"

"The eastern end of those buildings in front." Another impressive yawn.

I made a snappy about-face and walked out with my head bowed. I was more relaxed once the smile was gone. After giving myself a few minutes to get composed, I knocked on the commissar's door. The former occupant, Commissar Chen, had been reassigned—a sex scandal, it was rumored—and Xu Zuo told me that his replacement was a straight shooter not known as a womanizer, a man who stood on line at the mess hall like everyone else and washed his own clothes.

"Enter."

The light bouncing off his sleek scalp was nearly blinding.

"What do you want?" Hawklike eyes set in a thin face watched me from the bed where he was sitting.

"My name is Ma Bo, Commissar. I'm from Company Seven. The corps says I'm an active counterrevolutionary, and I'd like to talk to you about the verdict." Another ingratiating smile.

"Oh, I've heard. I wondered when you'd show up. The verdict was correct, and I advise you not to go off half-cocked."

"But it was unfounded," I replied anxiously.

"We're living under the dictatorship of the proletariat, do you understand that? Lawbreakers must be punished, including capital punishment for the most serious crimes. Trying to get your verdict overturned will only buy you more grief."

I nodded vigorously, giving him my undivided attention.

He looked at his watch. "Now you'll have to excuse me, since I've got a meeting." The interview was over.

Outside I mopped my brow and took several deep breaths. I hated myself for acting like a supplicant in his presence. Like some chickenshit thief.

It was time to swallow my pride and go see Staff Officer Zhao.

He was polishing his shoes when I walked in, and the room stank of shoe polish. He had that stern look common to all law enforcement officers.

"Staff Officer Zhao, with the Lin Biao Incident out in the open, I'd like to have my case reviewed."

He rolled his eyes and said firmly, "I can't comment on your specific case, but a recent directive from the Central Committee states that no one convicted under the Regulations on Public Security will be considered for rehabilitation until further notice. You must examine your case in light of the current climate, your background, and their influence on you. Don't think that with Lin Biao out of the picture you're home free. He was Chairman Mao's handpicked successor, so anyone who opposed him at the time opposed Mao. You must take the historical view."

Strike two. But I still had one left, Deputy Commissar Liu. I only hoped that officials weren't all cut from the same cloth.

As a regimental leader responsible for the One-Smash and Three-Oppose campaign, Deputy Commissar Liu had a reputation for being an honest, unpretentious man who knew how to get things done. It was he who had stopped the demobilized soldier from kicking the bejeezus out of me while I was in custody.

He was talking to a woman from the corps when I walked in. A thick stack of documents sat in a pile on his desk. "What can I do for you?" he greeted me warmly.

I told him who I was and why I was there.

The gray-haired, wrinkled old man slipped his glasses on and looked me over. "You're within your rights to dispute the disposition of a case. If we made a mistake, we'll correct it. If the mistake was yours, we'll do what we can to help you. In short, we welcome your opinion. But put it in writing."

"I already did. I sent it to the regiment a long time ago."

"You did? I never saw it." He was genuinely surprised.

"I have a carbon copy."

"That'll do. Leave it with me."

I handed it to him. "Commissar Liu," I said plaintively, "I really need your help."

He nodded agreeably. "I'll see what I can do at the next meeting of the standing committee."

He saw me out the door like a regular guest, smiling and nodding.

Nothing touched the heart of a counterrevolutionary more deeply than a smile from a deputy commissar. I sighed and mopped my sweaty brow.

———

JULY ROLLED AROUND and still no news, so I decided to go see Commissar Kang one more time.

"How about my case, Commissar?"

His once-shiny scalp now sported a growth of hair. He was poring over a copy of *Red Flag* when I entered. He looked up over the top of his glasses. "Didn't I say the original verdict was correct and would not be overturned?"

"But I'm not a counterrevolutionary, Commissar, honest, I'm not." One more minute and I'd have been blubbering.

"Do you hear Soviet revisionists admitting that they are counterrevolutionaries? How about Liu Shaoqi, did he admit he's one? Counterrevolutionaries *never* admit it, Ma Bo. People are complaining about how you've been running around trying to have your verdict overturned. Are you forgetting who you are?"

Not wanting to beg, and realizing the futility of arguing with him, I just stood there feeling shitty.

"Sit down," he said, pointing to a chair.

I did, and tried to smile.

"There's still a way out, you know. All you have to do is reform yourself. There's certainly no future in raising a stink."

Just then I heard a girl's voice outside: "Deputy Commissar Liu, are you in there?" Before Commissar Kang could answer, the door swung open and a girl's head poked in through the crack. She looked at Commissar Kang, then at me.

My heart skipped a beat. It was Wei Xiaoli.

She smiled apologetically and closed the door. Her delicate features, a radiant gathering of pearls and fresh flowers, sent an extraordinary burst of vitality coursing through me. I raised my eyes, looked straight at the commissar, and said, "No future, you say? Tell me what future I have as a counterrevolutionary."

His hawklike eyes bored into me. "Who told you to commit all those crimes?"

Director Li walked in just then, stinking of alcohol as usual. He took his cue from the commissar as he eased into a chair. "Ma Bo," he barked, "keep trying to have your verdict overturned, and they'll slap a label on you, sure as hell. Don't tell me that fat ass of yours hasn't been whipped enough?"

"But I don't oppose the party or Chairman Mao."

Seeing me refuse to knuckle under really set him off. "What? You don't oppose the party? Your head is chock-full of fascist militaristic ideas. Feudalism, capitalism, and revisionism are what make you tick. What stance were you taking when you attacked Comrade Jiang Qing? What class were you serving then?"

I was too scared to speak. A chill ran down my spine.

He flung his hat down on the kang and poured a glass of water. After gulping it down, he glared at me. "What you need is some more hand-cuff time."

In a milder tone Commissar Kang said, "Stop thinking you're too good to heed the advice of your superiors."

"Go on, get out of here," Director Li said with a wave of his hand.

I walked outside shuddering and twisting my neck to work the kinks out. I had to clear my head of all that thunder.

There wasn't a soul in sight on the steppe as I dragged myself home on legs that had turned to lead. I had nearly reached Stone Mountain when I heard hoofbeats behind me. It was Wei Xiaoli galloping down the road on a sorrel pony. I hid by the side of the road, not wanting her to see the hangdog look on my face.

She flew past, like a woman warrior, eyes straight ahead.

After she passed, I continued walking, following her with my eyes until she had ridden out of sight. Was that what I could look forward to, watching her draw farther and farther away from me?

A few days later I mailed another letter to the corps, then decided to try the genial Deputy Commissar Liu one more time. He was lying on the kang staring at the ceiling. "Deputy Commissar Liu," I said tentatively, "any news?" I was smiling.

He sat up. "Who sent you here?"

"Nobody." I was immediately on the defensive.

"From now on, use the chain of command if you have something to report."

"I have to talk to you, Deputy Commissar." I screwed my face into the gentlest look I could manage.

"I haven't got the time." He turned away, bringing our little chat to an end. The smile stuck on my face as if it were baked there. "But Deputy Commissar . . ." I muttered anxiously. Where were the tears when I needed them?

"Get out of here!" he roared, scaring the hell out of me.

"Are you there, Commissar?" The sweet bell of a feminine voice.

I was amazed by the transformation. His face softened, lit up, was ten years younger. "Ah," he sighed as a smile spread across his face. "It's you, little Zhang. Have you finished the copying?"

The girl nodded as she floated into the room, giggling coyly. I just glared at her, consumed by jealousy, and stormed out.

The door slammed shut behind me.

Just my fucking luck to be born a male.

34

ANYTHING TO GET
BACK TO BEIJING

IN LATE JULY Squad Two met its quota of fifteen hundred cubic yards of rocks; as soon as Company Commander Wang inspected our work, we could return to the company. His companion, Staff Officer Zhao, asked for the draft of my appeal letter to the corps. I handed it to him.

All told, we had dug a dozen or so quarries, each holding a number of boulders that were too big and too heavy to excavate, probably a total of 150 cubic yards or more. Commander Wang thought it would be a good idea for me to stay up there and find a way to get those rocks out.

"You're better off here than back at the company."

"Will you let me go on home leave when I'm finished?"

"If you can do it in two months, we'll recommend it."

"Okay. I expect you to keep your word."

He smiled and nodded. "What do you say, old Zhao?"

Staff Officer Zhao rolled his fishy eyes. "It's okay with me," he said. He was waiting impatiently for the work detail to pack up so he could get back to headquarters.

As the tractor chugged off with a final blast of smoke, Jin Gang nodded to me by way of saying good-bye.

Once again it was just Gonggele and me on the mountain: a tent near the peak for him, a yurt lower down for me. Two of us, a counter-revolutionary and a herdowner, both representatives of the reactionary classes; yet there was no contact between us. When he saw me he just smiled obsequiously.

In the summertime yurts are a haven for flies, which swarm around pots on the stove so thickly, you can snatch them out of midair. In surroundings like that, anyone who didn't get sick was lucky, and my luck didn't hold. A few days after the others left, I had diarrhea something awful. I tried to tough it out, figuring it would get better on its own; but it got worse, until I was up five or six times a night. The stomach pains were joined by a soreness in my lower back and a case of hemorrhoids from all the water I splashed on myself. It was sheer agony.

To top it all off, the rains came, and I didn't think they'd ever stop. I had no choice but to relieve myself inside the yurt, next to the stove, which was just fine with the flies—the gooey mess was like heaven on earth. As time passed, sticky, bloody stains began to show up on my pillow, coat, and bedding, yet I could only lie there in a semiwakeful state and try to console myself: Don't worry, it won't kill you. The sun will be out in a day or two, and you can go to the Company One clinic for some medicine.

At some point, I have no idea when, I heard a sound at the door. Gonggele drifted in. "What the hell is he doing here?" I mumbled as he stood over me. I grew suddenly alert. Even in my weakened state he was no match for me.

"Uh-oh," he exclaimed when he saw the shit all over the place. "Got to get you to Company One."

In this rain? I doubt it. I nodded weakly as he left with the bottle of oil he'd come to borrow, then pulled the covers up over my head to keep the little dive-bombers away.

Footsteps. Couldn't tell if they were real or if I was just dreaming. They were real, all right. The old shepherd was back. He'd been out hitching up his rig. I lay in the wagon, sandwiched between two halves of a large felt rug under a cowhide to keep me dry. He sealed the yurt with wire, tied a burlap bag over his head, and set out for Company One, leading the ox by its tether.

The old Mongol's boots squished as the wagon rumbled slowly across rain-drenched hills. I gazed out through the seams of the rug at the watery vista—glistening green grass, tender white mushrooms. Suddenly a thought penetrated the void of my mind: Even as a counter-revolutionary I was blessed to know someone who allowed me to lie in his wagon. We weren't related, I wasn't even a Mongol, was in fact a student who had once given him "love taps" with a stick and a halter. A decent old man, no getting around it. If it had been my wife, ailing mother, and kids who had been forced out into the snow like his, I wouldn't have rested until I'd gotten even with the person responsible.

AFTER RETURNING FROM Company One, Gonggele cleaned the stove and the area around it with a spade, then lit a fire and made some tea. He even gave me a small pat of butter; it was so small, I don't think I even tasted it, but he had never done anything like that before, and I was deeply touched.

Instead of being buried after they die, Mongols are left out in the open to be devoured by wolves and wild dogs. Possibly because of their inhospitable environment, they have developed a ruthless, truculent façade. It took Gonggele's coming to my aid for me to realize that they can be as gentle as anyone else.

It was dark outside. Gonggele, whose coat was drying by the stove, wasn't even wearing a shirt. I could scarcely believe my eyes when I saw his dark, sunken chest, his rail-thin arms, and the row of ribs showing beneath the skin. How had he stood up to the beating we gave him with a scrawny frame like that?

A single dose of medicine cured my diarrhea. Gonggele had saved my life. Why, then, was I in such a foul mood? I guess I was feeling like a louse because he had repaid my brutality with kindness. So I took off my sweater and handed it to him—tattered or not, it was my most valued possession, for it was stained with my own blood. At least he'd have something to wear under his coat. He accepted it with no pretense of modesty, although a hint of an ingratiating smile played on his face.

Several times after that I tried to talk to him, but he just waved me off with a curt *gwai* (no). The episode had done nothing to change our relationship.

He hardly ever spoke, and if it hadn't been for his frequent coughs, I'd probably have forgotten he was even there. And what a spartan existence he lived: a sack of fried millet, a brick of tea wrapped in a dirty rag, some dried, slightly mildewed yoghurt in a kidskin bag, and a small sack of salt. That, for him, was the staff of life, day in and day out, year after year.

ONCE I'D REGAINED my strength, I went back to work making little rocks out of big ones, then lugging them under the blazing sun. I had to keep at it, since the wagon masters who came to fetch the rocks always reported back to the company commander. Whenever I felt like throwing in the towel, the thought of "back to Beijing" got me going again. I always had something left inside, and that brought it out.

I worked in the heat, the rain, and the moonlight. The piles grew: big rocks, little rocks, rocks of all shapes and colors, neatly stacked. I kept at it for two solid months, until my fingers were rubbed raw, my feet swollen, and my clothes tattered and buttonless. But I accomplished what I'd set out to do. A hundred fifty cubic yards of stone now lay on, not under, the ground. What a feeling it was to carry out the last rock and heave it onto the tallest pile, where it landed with a resounding thud. I lay in the dry grass and gazed up at the autumn sky, just luxuriating.

I had moved a couple dozen cubic yards a day, probably in excess of ten tons, or a hundred stones weighing two hundred pounds each. For each one I'd had to squat down, bend over, scoop out the dirt around it, pick it up in both arms. No wonder it felt so good to lie down and do nothing. I dozed off surrounded by the wilderness and the quiet.

Company Commander Wang was pleased to hear I had finished the job. All the food I'd put away during those two months hadn't been wasted, after all, he said. Back in 1970 it had taken five men all winter to produce 150 cubic yards of rock. He had his clerk send a home-leave request to Regiment Headquarters and told me to work out the details with Staff Officer Zhao.

"Did I say that?" Zhao asked when I confronted him.

"You sure did," I said. "When you came up to get that letter from me." He'd forgotten all about it.

"Okay," he said with a watchful eye. "I'll check with my superiors and get back to you."

Two months later I still hadn't heard anything.

35

FIREFIGHTING

As AUTUMN DEEPENED, the windblown steppes turned tinder-box dry. Thickets of grass became undulating waves of yellow when winds whipped across the grassland as far as the eye could see. Dried cowchips the size of platters turned light and airy. A single spark could turn the vast steppe into a raging inferno.

A fire, the most disastrous in the history of the area, occurred in the autumn of 1972 at Wula Sitai where I had once cut wood. Even standing on Stone Mountain, over a hundred li away, I could see the red rim of the night sky.

Fear showed on the faces of wagon masters who came up the mountain to fetch rocks. Their stories about this long-raging fire were confused and contradictory, but I got the gist of what had happened.

COMPANY COMMANDER WANG received an urgent predawn phone call from Regimental Headquarters. After hanging up, he hastily organized firefighting teams, which set out with brooms and hoes. Deputy Commissar Liu stood solemnly on the dusty regiment road, an army overcoat draped over his shoulders. Trucks carrying members from the various companies raced toward the Sixty-third Regiment district.

"How many are going from Company Seven, old Wang?"

"Forty."

The tractor screeched to a halt, diesel engine sputtering.

Deputy Commissar Liu walked up and said to the faces arrayed in front of him, "Comrades, if we don't put this fire out fast, it could spread to the Great Khingan Range forest. It's all up to you." He waved his hand, and the tractor headed noisily down the road.

"Wait up!" A skinny trooper from Corps Headquarters ran up, climbed aboard, and squeezed in beside Liu Yinghong. Commissar Liu looked at her anxiously. "You're not dressed warmly enough. It's cold up there." He tossed her his overcoat. As the tractor picked up speed, cool predawn breezes struck the faces of the defiant, fearless youngsters. The faint voice of Deputy Commissar Liu drifted up from behind: "Be careful."

The winding dirt road ended a little over three miles from the fire, so they jumped down and moved forward on foot. Alternately running and walking behind Company Commander Wang, they quickly negotiated four ridges on their way to the fire. Some had worked up such a sweat, they shed their padded jackets on the run. The girls, finding no place to relieve themselves, peed in their pants.

The frail Company Commander Wang had to stop when his stomach began acting up. Jin Gang stumbled and fell. His ashen face was lathered in sweat as he lay on the ground mumbling between breaths, "I can't make it, can't run anymore, not if you paid me by the step. No more for me, I'm going back. They can do what they want to me." He was gasping for breath.

The girls were so far behind, they were nowhere in sight, except for Liu Yinghong, who was right on the heels of a group of boys. The stubborn streak we'd noticed when she harvested wheat had reappeared; she didn't stop even when she lost a shoe. Damned if I know what made her so different from the other girls, but she even left some of the boys in her dust.

"Here, wear this!" A shoe came flying over.

She scooped it up and put it on as she looked back to see who had thrown it: a girl from another company who was leaning weakly against a rock to catch her breath.

"Thanks!" Yinghong shouted as she took off again, a plastic sandal on one foot, a cloth shoe on the other. Columns of shepherds, students, and soldiers charged up the mountain toward the fire. The slopes and thickets were littered with jackets, trousers, and overcoats. A sense of sacred mission for the motherland surged in everyone's heart.

Most members of Company Seven were sprawled on the ground, exhausted, before they reached the fire. Hungry and thirsty, they screamed for their fathers and cursed their mothers, now that the initial rush of adrenaline was spent. A few kept surging toward the billowing black clouds, Yinghong among them.

Mounting an assault against a wall of fire was so much more interesting, dangerous, and exciting than making adobe blocks. Armed with the faith of young people everywhere, they knew they would be spared; the fire was no match for their strong, healthy limbs and their cleverness.

But at a critical moment, Company Commander Niu of the Sixty-third Regiment's Company Four made a fatal error in judgment. His was the first company to reach the fire, which had spread to the area behind Hill 1054. Ordering his firefighters to take up positions on the hill, he assumed that the fire would be less intense where the undergrowth was sparse, making it an ideal vantage point to launch an assault. He also sent a tractor with twenty people or so on a flanking maneuver to the top of the hill.

Since they were on a ridge, they had to negotiate a broad ravine covered by waist-high grass to get to Hill 1054. The swirling pall of smoke blotting out the sky and bearing down on the mountain was so thick and hot, it burned the noses and stung the tongues of people over a mile from the fire; it also struck fear in their hearts.

A local peasant cautioned Company Commander Niu, "You can't fight a fire into the wind." But his warning fell on deaf ears.

"The flames are our orders," he declared. "The fire is our battleground. Charge, comrades!"

The troopers charged up the mountain without a murmur of dissent, quickly reaching the grassy ravine, the faster boys even gaining the ground near Hill 1054. Dense black smoke hugged the ground like a sinister beast closing in on them, step by menacing step. The fire was to the northwest, the direction from which the wind was blowing and the direction of the corps assault.

Liu Yinghong was caught up in Company Four's charge, led by a student named Du Hengchang, the deputy political instructor. Suddenly Hill 1054 was engulfed by an enormous, terrifying cloud of smoke that rolled down the mountain toward them. For a second or two, their morale peaked, but their bravado quickly turned to terror as the temperature shot up; they broke ranks and retreated in panic. An occasional ball of blood red fire catapulted through the cloud of smoke and soared into the air, igniting a sea of flames. There was no shelter. Dense smoke encircled the startled firefighters, who fled in all directions. The blinding smoke distorted their sense of direction and made breathing nearly impossible. Many swooned.

Then came the fire itself, and its fearful sound, like the roar of a thousand automobiles, an avalanche, a tidal wave. Huge balls of fire, like gas explosions, billowed skyward, fueled by the dense growth of dry grass in the ravine, the flames searing everything in their path as they tore through the black smoke.

Gale-force winds howled, blasts of superheated air howled, incinerated grass howled. Most of the students were caught in this tinder-dry brush. Fighting the fire was the furthest thing from their minds at that moment. Their only thought was to escape. But it was too late—they were trapped by a ring of fire.

Du Hengchang, the student from Beijing, was more experienced than the others; instead of running from the fire, he took a deep breath and ran straight ahead, managing somehow to get behind it. But then he heard the screams of others and ran back to save them. He brought one out, then another, but when he ran back for a third, he disappeared, never to be seen again. Aroused by his heroic actions and infused with his self-sacrificing spirit, the two students he had saved rushed back into the fire, only to meet a similar fate.

THE MERCILESS FLAMES scorched her calves and arms. Utterly exhausted, she struggled in desperation. Flames above her, flames at her feet, flames clawing her body, flames everywhere, and heat that would melt iron. She lost her bearings in the roar of the fire. The sound of cowchips crackling in ten thousand yurt stoves. A million chimneys turning red from the heat.

"Li Ding!"

"Zhang Fuchun!"

"Liu Yinghong!"

Great gasping coughs, pitiful screams.

She should have heard the screams, calmed herself, and charged through the wall of killing heat to safety. But no. The poor girl instinctively headed away from the intense heat, following the wind, not realizing that the fire would be sucked in that direction. The flames followed her, seared her, never left her. Finally she fell, and the greedy flames swarmed over her body.

Her hair was smoldering, her clothes burning, her shoes smoking. Fair skin roasted by the merciless heat. Nasal passages, lips, eyes—all incinerated. Breasts, arms, and legs oozing grease, like meat over a spit. Her seared, cracked lips curled upward when they kissed the ground. Scorched earth was a cool refuge from the superheated air. Her mouth opened involuntarily and began gnawing at the ground.

Dry grass crackled when it ignited. Her lips, reduced to crusty scabs, continued to kiss the dancing flames, the red and black cinders. She embraced the smoking grass and dug with such force that her nails broke off. Her living body and pure soul underwent the suffering of a roasted lamb; her innocent, unsullied heart was fused to the blackened earth. Her name was Liu Yinghong. She had rescued no one, had performed no heroic deeds, before breathing her last.

Lots of students died as abruptly as she, contrary to the report published in *Corps Comrades-in-Arms*: "Everyone fought furiously, charging the fire and shouting slogans while saving one another." In fact, most simply fled for their lives; the Du Hengchangs were the exception, not the rule.

The tractor sent on a flanking maneuver by Commander Niu was trapped in a ring of fire on its way up the mountain, and when the gas tank blew, the driver was killed outright. Only Liu Xiaowen of Xilinhot survived; all the others perished. The tires were burned to a crisp, the angle iron in the cab melted. Twenty or more scorched bodies were found in and around the vehicle.

It was Wang Lianfu, the man in charge of Company Three's wagons, who dragged Wei Xiaoli safely out of the fire. With a war whoop, he charged into the flames, a urine-soaked jacket over his head. He wrapped his arms around a girl and carried her out. A rash of unintelligible jabbering, another war whoop, and back into the flames he went. He had an unerring sense of smell, invariably heading straight for the nearest female. Badly singed, his face black with soot, his legs scarred and crippled, he railed, "Motherfucking cunts, what are a bunch of stupid skirts doing up here? Burning to death is too good for them!" He single-handedly rescued three of the "stupid skirts."

Females only. He ignored the males.

The fire moved like the wind on a southeastern course. Then cracks appeared in the cloud of black smoke, letting in slivers of blue sky. As the remaining smoke dissipated, the scorched earth of Wula Sitai was exposed, and one by one the dead were located. Each white dot in the black pall was a corpse, stark naked except for an occasional strip of cloth under the arm. A piece of melted plastic shoe was stuck to the sole of Du Hengchang's foot. He lay quietly on his belly, his head seared bald.

Contorted by the fire into all sorts of weird shapes, some were curled up until their buttocks touched their shoulders; others were twisted like pretzels, their thighs curled up under their ribs.

The scene would have made an executioner tremble.

The foul stench of burned flesh, hair, cotton, and plastic sandals floated on the air. The surviving students looked like black demons who had crawled naked out of the cinders, their faces grimy with soot. Dazed and weakened, they held their hands in front of their chests like prisoners of war. Death all around them. Stunned, stupefied, idiotic, they lacked the strength to cry.

Rescue vehicles didn't start arriving for about half an hour, in the company of Commissar Kang and other VIPs. He wept when he saw the carnage.

There was no need for anyone to take charge. People did what had to be done. Forming up in groups of four, the students grabbed arms or legs to heave the bodies up onto the vehicles, dumping them in a pile like so many gunnysacks, with no concern for the niceties of gender. Some of the bodies had been baked so long, the skin peeled off at the slightest touch and left a greasy film.

They found Liu Yinghong, her face buried in dirt that filled her mouth. Her body, naked but for a sanitary napkin still in place, was so bloated, it was almost perfectly round. Nearby lay another corpse, the girl who had jumped onto the tractor that morning. Deputy Commissar Liu's overcoat had been reduced to ashes and carried off in the wind. Tragically, they had been only a few yards from safety when they died. Sometimes that's all that separates life and death.

Deputy Commander Liu of the Fifth Division and other VIPs arrived in their cars, having set out on the thirty-mile trip as soon as they heard that people had died in the fire. After surveying the gloomy death scene, they rushed over to the headquarters of the Sixty-third Regiment's Company Four, which had lost the most people, and when Deputy Commander Liu spotted Company Commander Niu, he exploded: "You son of a bitch! We're not even at war, and you've lost half your company!" Commander Niu was so shaken, his face turned the color of clay. Bereft of common sense, he had ordered his students to fight a fire with the wind in their faces.

The corpses were brought back and stacked in the tractor shed, the last ones arriving after dusk. A shifting jumble of bodies—heads, arms, and legs intertwined—formed a reddish mass that was swallowed up in the dying rays of the sun as it slid behind the mountain.

The final tally of students killed in the fire was sixty-six. Three more died of their injuries afterwards. One, a Moslem student from Ulanhad, complained constantly of a need to urinate, but he couldn't do it. His penis had been fried, and when the doctors were forced to snip off the tip, the seared flesh popped. The boy stopped breathing soon afterward.

Deputy Commander Liu blew up again when he saw more than five dozen corpses in a heap in the tractor shed: "Those troopers died protecting our national treasures! What's the idea of just dumping them like that? What are they, sheep?"

So they were wrapped individually in comforters and laid out neatly. Two students, assigned to make sure the bodies weren't disturbed by hungry pigs or cattle, spent a terrifying night in the shed, as the tomblike silence was interrupted by internal rumblings and other sounds of recent death.

More than two hundred square miles of grassland were blackened in the fire, the news of which even reached Premier Zhou, who dispatched six helicopters and three transport planes for aid purposes.

Following the incident, the Revolutionary Committee of the Inner Mongolian Autonomous Region appointed an investigative team headed by a member of the party's Standing Committee. They were lavishly received by the Fifth Division, everything local conditions would allow—including two banquets a day, with eight to ten courses; a carton of Peony cigarettes; and half a dozen bowls of canned fruit, all served by beautiful young waitresses attached to the regiment's propaganda team.

For some reason, the corps leadership was reluctant to acknowledge responsibility for the gross incompetence. Perhaps, given the number of deaths, the onus was too great. So not only did the commander of Company Four go unpunished for his reckless use of personnel, he was even nominated for a commendation. Only violent opposition from the victims' families squelched the citation. One of the relatives said it best: "The actions of our children are certainly worthy of being honored. People like Du Hengchang, who ran back into the fire to save others, were heroes. But why were there no comparable acts by responsible cadres? Why did only students die and not a single active-duty soldier? Where's the glory in the fact that half a company was lost? How can you commend someone for that? We won't tolerate it!"

Official magnanimity characterized the aftermath: Families of the dead firefighters were given a pension of 180 yuan—230 for squad leaders—and the victims were honored as "revolutionary martyrs." Those who had applied to the Communist Party or the Communist League were granted posthumous membership. And in order to enhance regiment morale, the movie *Heroic Sons and Daughters* was shown five or six times, until the students grew so sick of seeing it, they stopped showing up.

The fire had badly scarred the mountain slopes, where patches of black were interspersed with yellow. The few remaining clumps of dry grass in hollows shivered and rustled in the autumn breezes, as though weeping or pointing the finger of blame.

Scorched earth as far as the eye could see, vast in its blackness. Not a bird to be heard. Next year's grass would surely grow in great profusion.

CONSTRUCTION CAME TO a halt in the regiment so that crude coffins could be built, with three shifts working day and night for two days, tears in their eyes the whole time. The authorities were determined to get the dead into the ground before their families showed up. Under no circumstances would they be given a chance to view the bodies of their loved ones.

Apparently, in the confusion, the gravediggers dug seventy graves, one more than necessary. For this they were severely reprimanded, but those responsible for the deaths of sixty-nine students were subjected to no criticism. What happened to the reckless Company Commander Niu? He was promoted. It was even suggested that the fighting of this fire was another triumph of Mao Zedong Thought. As if the larger the number of deaths, the greater the revolutionary victory.

36

RUNNING

AWAY

FAREWELL, Liu Yinghong, I'll never forget you. I will always remember how you attacked me at the denunciation sessions, how you turned your back on your friends, and how you demonstrated your conformity. You helped me understand how a wonderful girl could be so defiant and fearless in her work, yet cringe before the dictatorship of the proletariat.

IN TIME, the fire faded from memory, and things returned to normal. Now that I'd accomplished what I'd set out to do, I could relax. My days revolved around sleeping and eating, interrupted from time to time by a little work. My hair grew long and matted, my fingernails began to look like talons. The wagon masters ragged me constantly: "You could grow grass in your ears," they'd say.

One day led to another, and soon it would be winter again, time to put on my leather pants. After Gonggele's departure I seldom saw anyone except for a wagon master every week or so. It was as if the world had written me off, except for the kitchen help, who sent rations for one up the mountain each month.

Man has an innate need to be noticed. I knew I couldn't bear staying all alone on my mountain, forgotten by my superiors, comrades, and friends. All those letters I'd written to regiment, division, and corps leaders had gone unanswered. So to reaffirm my existence, to be noticed, I decided to sneak off to Beijing over the New Year's holiday. Even if I didn't make it, I'd sure as hell shake things up. People would not have to be reminded that someone named Ma Bo was undergoing labor reform up on Stone Mountain. Once the planning began, I was on such a constant high, I could hardly sleep.

Injgan Sum is twelve hundred miles from the nearest train station at Ulanhad, and there is only one way to get there — via Western Ujimqin and the city of Linxi. You take the overland route at your own peril, for one wrong turn can mean freezing or starving to death. The drivers in the transportation company all knew me as the target of denunciation sessions and the regimental street-sweeper, so there'd be no help from them. I'd have to make it to Western Ujimqin on my own, then take a bus. Without a letter of introduction, buying a ticket would be tough enough, and I didn't even want to think about the problem of lodging.

Running away is a skill requiring specialized knowledge and some acting ability. Just my luck to be an idiot who can't tell a lie without setting his heart thumping a mile a minute. Being dirt poor wasn't going to help, either.

My problems were many and formidable. Under the best of circumstances running away would be a tricky proposition. For an active counterrevolutionary it bordered on the impossible. But it was either that or stay on my mountain, alone and lonely, until I joined the walking dead.

Early winter, 1972. I fired off some more letters to the corps and division, begging them to listen to the plea rising from the ranks and to send someone to review the verdict. I vowed to take my case to Beijing if I heard nothing within two months. Then I continued to plan, for I expected to be ignored.

Anything I didn't need — suitcase, felt throw rugs, boots, a case for my glasses — I sold to shepherds for the grand sum of sixty yuan. Then I bought a pair of padded cloth shoes, since I'd be walking a lot, and buried my documents and diary under a pile of rocks. I studied a map until I had committed all the stops and the distances between them to memory.

As New Year's approached I put together the stuff I'd need on the trip: towel, flashlight, compass, map, Mongol dagger, ration book, matches, cigarettes, hand mirror, stuff like that.

Predictably, the two months passed without any news. So after frying enough fruit to fill my backpack, I cooked ten or fifteen pounds of mutton and wrapped the necessary documents and letters in plastic. I planned to set out on February 2, 1973, the day before Lunar New Year's, at the crack of dawn. To keep from being discovered I would first walk a hundred miles or so across the sparsely populated, snow-covered grassland to Ulanhad, where I would board the bus. (I'd have taken a camel if the company had seen fit to supply me with one.)

The man upstairs smiled down on me. For two days before my departure he loosed a storm that sent the thermometer plummeting, just what I had hoped for. My chances improved with every degree the temperature fell.

I went to bed early the night before. Only some scurrying rats disturbed the silence. This would be the third time in my life I'd run away: once to Vietnam in a group of ten; once to Inner Mongolia with three other people; and now to Beijing alone. On the eve of my momentous trial I was too excited to sleep. So I got up, lit the lantern, and made a final entry in my diary.

FEBRUARY 1, 1973, late

A storm raging outside. At dawn I'll trudge my way to Beijing. They're making me do it, those people in charge who close their ears to cries from below. They leave me no choice but to take my case to the Central Committee.

My water bucket, cookpot, and flour sacks were hidden in shadows cast by the pale lamplight. I finally drifted off, fully clothed, but I was awake before sunrise. I made a fire in the stove and boiled some tea, in which I steeped a piece of hardtack. Breakfast. The time had come to gather my essentials, walk outside, and wire the door flap shut.

Nothing but gray. The northern winds shrieked around the yurt. My face immediately began to ache from the cold, so I wrapped it in a towel, cinched up my coat with a rope, and set out onto the darkened grassland. Snow crunched beneath my feet. Stone Mountain, standing in the darkness, observed my shrinking figure in silence.

It was light when I reached Regimental Headquarters, somehow convinced that the public-security folks knew what I was up to and were waiting to nab me. With my heart in my mouth, I gave the headquarters compound a wide berth and took a leak in the still-vacant tractor-repair garage, writing the word *onward* in the virgin snow.

Once I was on the road, I headed southwest as fast as my feet would carry me. Icy winds cut like daggers; my misty breath turned to ice around my mouth, my nose, my brows, and the edges of my cap. I forged onward.

Hunger pangs hit on the twisting road at about noon, so I took out some fried fruit and ate it as I walked. Snow took care of my thirst. My legs never stopped pumping, whether I was eating or drinking, perpetual-motion machines. I walked all that day, not stopping for a single minute.

Darkness settled over the land as the wind whistled. I was so sleepy, I couldn't keep my eyes open, and could kick myself for having let excitement keep me awake the night before. Exhausted after sixteen hours of walking, I had to rest. But the cold took over as soon as I stopped moving, so I struggled to my feet and started out again, weaving back and forth as I pushed myself along.

I'm beat. I need sleep. My mind's turning to mush, don't know what's keeping me awake. Keep those legs churning and that head up. Finally I made it to the first stop, a commune. It had a tiny, windowless room, which was where I'd spend the night. But halfway there I tripped and fell in a snow-filled gutter. After scrambling to my feet, scared witless, I gripped my dagger and walked cautiously into the little room. Empty. At least there were no wolves waiting to rip out my throat.

Perched on a rammed-earth stove in the middle of the room, I scraped the snow off the soles of my shoes, then took out some of the meat I'd brought. It was hard as a rock. I stuffed it under my coat and against my chest to thaw it out.

My teeth were chattering, my ass was frozen numb. In Beijing at that very moment people were finishing their holiday dinner and sitting around visiting, or watching TV, or setting off firecrackers with the kids. I removed the mutton, which had thawed out nicely, and ate it, vowing to write this all down someday.

After a short catnap, I ate some more fruit and munched on snow. I couldn't keep sitting there—it was much too cold—so I got back on the road and hobbled through the swirling snow. The brief rest made it painfully clear how spent I was. My body seemed to be coming apart at the seams. I could barely lift my legs, and pains shot up from the balls of my feet. Every step was sheer agony. My pace fell off dramatically, since I had to stop so often to scrape snow off the soles of my cloth shoes, which made walking far more difficult and painful than it should have been. Finally unable to take another step, I lay down in the snow and looked up at the sky.

In no time, I was nearly frozen stiff, but I didn't feel like getting up, so I lay atop snow packed hard by passing trucks. Was this highway from the Forty-first Regiment to Western Ujimqin Banner going to be my final resting place? Was this to be my last day on earth?

Wei Xiaoli's angelic features floated in the distance, surrounded by a garland of cold stars and swirling snow. Her sparkling eyes were fixed on me. It was Mother seeing me off all over again, white strands of her hair suspended in the cold air.

Dying here would have been a travesty, so I struggled to my feet, gripped the dagger tightly, and lumbered forward.

That night I reached my second stop, though I nearly had to crawl to make it. I felt my way to a cowshed and stumbled in. A dozen or so supine calves looked at me with no fear in their eyes. The tented enclosure, which stank of dung and straw, was perfectly still. I warmed up by sticking my feet under the belly of a piebald calf and resting my head against another. The placid animals stared at me with benign curiosity.

In thirty-below weather, they were furnaces that lowed from time to time.

No more fear of freezing to death, not with roommates like this. I laid my face against a downy hide, which had a warm, dry smell. I was thawing out and feeling better. I slept like a log that night and was ready to hit the road before sunrise to avoid being discovered. But before I had taken a step I fell in a heap with excruciating pain. My foot felt broken, but it was just a tendon that had frozen up. I had to hobble to my third stop, which I reached at four that afternoon. Now I was only thirty-some miles from my goal. I walked into the commune café, bought some meat pies, and gobbled them down like a ravenous beast. Then I swigged down four or five bowls of boiled water, a refreshing treat after subsisting for two days on melted snow.

That was it, I couldn't walk another step. My legs were like lead weights, and my joints creaked painfully. If I tried to keep going in that weather, I'd probably freeze to death. So I decided to put up there for some well-deserved rest. I could start out again the next morning.

I hobbled into the stable and dug through the snow covering a bale of straw that would serve as my bed. All that walking after months of doing hardly any work had taken its toll on my stamina. Now it was time to curl up and enjoy the luxury of doing nothing. But just as I was nodding off, a voice asked, "Who's there?"

I scrambled to my feet, brushed the straw off my clothes, and stood facing a man in his thirties holding a pitchfork.

"Where are you from?"

"The Forty-first Regiment. I've got business in Western Ujimqin. I'm just taking a break."

He looked me over guardedly. "There's a wagoners' inn for the Forty-first Regiment here. Why not go there?"

"I'm going there to take care of a personal problem, not business," I explained.

"Well, you can't spend the night here. How would it look if you froze to death so close to New Year's?"

I didn't know what to say.

"Go on over to your regiment's inn. If old Bao won't put you up, you can stay at my place."

To avoid arousing his suspicions I decided to do as he said.

"So you're ma bo," the innkeeper greeted me warmly. "Your reputation precedes you. Have a seat." His wife and daughter came out to see what a notorious counterrevolutionary looked like. In the suffusing warmth of the room I told them what had happened to me and had them nodding sympathetically. Old Bao's wife and daughter even brought me tea with milk and some yoghurt, fruit, candy, and melon seeds. He couldn't take his eyes off my dagger, so I gave it to him as a gesture of friendship.

"You've got spunk," he said with an admiring sigh, "making it this far like you have. You must be dead on your feet. Stay here tonight, and I'll get you to Western Ujimqin tomorrow."

"I'd be mighty grateful," I said with an appreciative nod.

He led me to a small room. "I'm afraid this is the best I can offer," he said apologetically. "At least it's warm."

The unpredictability of fate weighed heavily on me. As I lay on the kang I massaged my legs. They had earned me a victory over Wang Lianfu and had allowed me to carry rocks weighing hundreds of pounds; but they had failed me this time. Everything else was holding up, but my legs hurt so much, I could barely move them. It looked as if I were fated to fall thirty miles short of my goal. I must have walked too fast at the beginning, and the ill-advised cloth shoes had made the going tougher, with the constant buildup of snow.

Sometime in the middle of the night I heard the door creak and a flurry of footsteps.

"Get up, Ma Bo!" a low, raspy voice ordered. A flashlight shone in my eyes. All I saw were some shadowy figures. I rubbed my eyes and slid slowly off the kang. I was immediately taken into Bao's room. He grew fidgety when he saw me. What a fool to have given him my dagger. Just so he could turn me in.

After a quick frisk, Staff Officer Zhao stood in front of me in his army overcoat with a deadpan look on his face. The lamp cast his shadow on the wall; it seemed to take up half the room.

"Where do you think you're going?"

"Division Headquarters at Western Ujimqin Banner."

"Heh heh." He sneered and removed his gloves. *Snap.* My hands were cuffed behind me before I knew it.

"Let's go."

Two men grabbed me by the arms and dragged me outside to a waiting Jeep. Zhao and another man sat me between them in the backseat. The third man sat up front. In spite of the cold, the Bao family was lined up outside to see us off. As we set out across the snowy steppe, the ground rose up to meet us in our headlights and was gone, just like that. It had taken me two days and two nights to get that far, one agonizing step at a time, and our four wheels just gobbled the miles up. Telephone poles whizzed by, hills took but a minute to negotiate, and in no time the commune was behind me. I caught a fleeting glimpse of the rundown stable.

All that planning, all that torment, all those miles, all for nothing. I tried to control my emotions but couldn't. "Why are you doing this?" I shouted, straining to reach the door and feeling the blood rush to my head.

"Sit still!" Zhao grabbed me around the throat with gloved hands.

The inside light clicked on, and the man up front unsnapped his holster, drew his revolver, and waved it in my face. "Ma Bo, if you try that again, whatever happens is on your head. Now cut it out!"

The Jeep had me back in the Forty-first Regiment two hours later. It was three in the morning, and I was in Staff Officer Zhao's office. My possessions were piled on his desk. He was inspecting them one at a time, enjoying himself immensely.

"Why all this fruit? Expecting to go to Outer Mongolia?"

"Where'd you steal this compass?"

"Why five boxes of matches? Planning on a little arson?"

"Speak up, where were you heading?"

"Western Ujimqin."

He sneered. "Bullshit. You squat, and I know what you'll shit! You were going home to plead your case. No more funny business."

"I was told I could go home if I finished my job in two months. Did you think I'd wait forever?"

"You shameless piece of shit, you wanted to go home to lodge a complaint, didn't you? You thought you'd make some political capital out of your experience. Well, you can stop dreaming. Anyone who opposed Lin Biao before his fall from power is a counterrevolutionary, and that's the name of that game!"

I was too sore and too tired to worry about what he said.

"Don't you mess with Mr. CCP! This is the dictatorship of the proletariat, which is why you can't spout your bullshit or carry on like you do."

I said nothing. His round baby face seemed softer and paler than ever under the hundred-watt bulb. Turning grave, he said, "I arrest you in the name of the Regimental Party Committee."

Who did he think he was? No one below division level had that authority. Still I held my tongue. Why give him the satisfaction of knowing I was scared shitless?

"Take him away."

The guard looked at me and muttered, "Do you realize you forced us out of a warm bed on New Year's Day?"

"That's how he planned it," Zhao said.

Shortly after that, a regiment-wide denunciation meeting was called. Armed guards arranged us by criminal categories. I was up front, just ahead of Old Gigolo, who had also fallen afoul of the law. People out on the street, adults and children alike, eyed us with curiosity. "Get a move on." Someone jabbed me in the ribs with a rifle. Pains shot up from the balls of my feet. Damn those fucking cloth shoes! At the meeting site a white tablecloth had been draped over a table. Deputy Commissar Liu, Director Li, and some other VIPs sat behind it; a line of despondent men stood in front, me among them.

"Never forget class struggle!"

. . .

The slogans hit us like crashing waves. One by one the young people flung their venom at us, but it was aimed at grafters, thieves, and profiteers, not at me. I secretly rejoiced.

"Let's not forget Ma Bo," Director Li said toward the end, "a man who needs no introduction. He tried to run away, but we caught him and brought him back."

Staff Officer Zhao snatched my cap off my head, exposing the matted hair on my pointy head, then cupped his hand under my chin and raised my head to give the masses a good look at a reactionary. Their eyes were glued to my face, which was held firmly by Zhao's pincerlike fingers. I stared back, emboldened by the fact that I'd cleaned up before the meeting.

A girl in the front row said softly, "He looks mean."

"He's scary."

They tossed me in the regiment lockup, where I spent the day handcuffed. My cellmate was Old Gigolo, who had been arrested by Company Commander Wang for food profiteering. He nodded and bent slightly at the waist when he saw me, like a real kiss-ass, if you know what I mean.

Three weeks later I was taken back to see Zhao, who said, "Division forwarded a directive from the corps. They've agreed to review your case. But until we get word to the contrary we're to treat you in accordance with the original verdict."

"Starting when?"

"How should I know? That's their business. Now go back and work hard. They'll send someone soon enough."

After removing the handcuffs, he returned my letters and the other stuff they had confiscated. "No one ate any," he said, pointing to the fruit piled on his desk, "not a bite." He picked up a piece with the tips of his fingers, as if it were a dead rat, and studied it carefully before tossing it back. More or less the same way he'd handled my chin in front of the masses.

———

I WAS BACK in Company Seven.

Jin Gang, who grew nervous when he heard I'd been publicly denounced at the regiment, handed me a letter, then slinked away.

Mother had written to say she had asked someone to report my predicament to the Political Department of the Beijing Military District, which had ordered the Inner Mongolian Production Corps to review my case.

Leave it to a mother to forgive a son for stealing her stuff, destroying her property, and cursing her to her face. Thank you, Mother. I know how it must have felt to take an unfilial, fascist son back under your wing.

37

QUILTS

ON THE ROOF

THE WEATHER TURNED hot and muggy, dark clouds gathered, and thunder began to rumble. Immediately after dinner, all platoons were mobilized to move the grain inside and cover it with tarpaulins. Company Commander Wang was there to take note of absentees.

Suddenly the skies opened up and the rain fell in buckets. It had been so long since we'd enjoyed some time off that we greeted the downpour with whoops of delight. Now the heavens had come to our rescue, and we could turn in for some well-deserved rest without having to beg the company commander. Good going, you up there, keep it coming. Three days would be nice. After all our back-breaking work we needed a good long respite.

It was still raining the next morning, and by the looks of the dark sky and heavy rainclouds, it wouldn't let up for at least another day. Acting like the lucky stiffs we had temporarily become, we lolled around, chatted, played poker, and smoked up a storm. It was about three in the afternoon when we heard shouts from outside, "Company Commander says the grain silo has sprung a leak. He wants everyone out in the square with plastic covers, on the double!"

Anyone who had a plastic cover grabbed it up and was out of there like a shot. The rest of us picked up rugs, rush mats, and burlap bags, then ran into the rain with a series of loud whoops. Xu Zuo, who couldn't find anything else, grabbed his quilt (he knew he had to have something) and lit out for the square. When he reached the silo he flung it onto the roof. "Are you crazy?" the men up there shouted.

"Use it," he said, "it's okay."

Might as well, since by then it was all wet and muddy.

Seeing Xu Zuo sacrifice his bedding thrilled Li Guoqiang, who ran to the dorm, snatched up his own quilt, and was back in a flash. Jin Gang and Sun Gui followed suit, adding their bed mats and overcoats to the mix. Onto the roof it all went.

The girls in Second Platoon were green with envy. Kicking themselves for stumbling on the road to progressive behavior, they turned and headed back for their own bedding, but were stopped by the company commander. His blockade proved less effective, however, since some of them managed to sneak their nice, clean bedding over to the silo without getting caught. They whooped and hollered as if an admiring world were watching.

When the old farmers saw the colorful new silo roof—quilts, rugs, plastic covers, overcoats, goatskins—they shook their heads and muttered, "The whole bunch of them's gone crazy." But the youngsters were proud of themselves for sacrificing their own bedding. They were sitting on top of the world that day.

Xu Zuo tilted back his head and let the rain hit him in the face. "Try this, Jin Gang!" he shouted. "It's like swimming through a school of minnows. It cools you off."

"Why don't you take off your pants and let the wind blow up your asshole if you want to cool off?" Li Guoqiang said snidely.

"Eat shit, you little prick!"

A quick count revealed over sixty cotton quilts soaking up the rain or channeling it into rivulets that puddled on the ground. The boys in First Platoon, looking like a bunch of drenched chickens, ran back to their rooms to wring out their hair and change into dry clothing.

Our quilts stayed on the roof, peacefully and proudly, for several days after the rain stopped and the sun reappeared. Then they were taken down to be washed by girls in Second Platoon.

Xu Zuo had developed a low-grade fever that hung on despite his rainwater bath. It made him edgy, grouchy, sleepy, and flatulent as hell. So he went to the regimental hospital, where they discovered he had an elevated amino-enzyme count; that could only mean hepatitis, and he was hospitalized. We felt sorry for him, of course, but no one except Li Guoqiang dared touch anything he had handled, not even the chess pieces.

FOLLOWING THE TRANSFER of Political Instructor Shen, it was a case of "Monkeys scatter when the tree is felled." Demobilized soldiers stopped lording it over us, and those with connections wangled transfers to Regimental Headquarters, realizing that because they were the losers in the battle between Company Commander Wang and Political Instructor Shen, Company Seven was no place for them. Old Jiang, with his reputation as a thief, was transferred to Company Nine to drive a wagon, and his place was taken by Xu Zuo. Qi Shuzhen was formally removed as leader of Second Platoon and replaced by Li Xiaohua. Jin Gang was promoted to squad leader; Wei Xiaoli was made the company's branch secretary. In other words, all the important positions were now filled with the PI's former victims.

Company Commander Wang had shown what he was made of.

Now it was Lei Xia's turn to be on the outside looking in, and the more isolated he became, the more time Qi Shuzhen spent with him, for reasons no one could explain. Misery loves company, I guess. She complained to him about Company Commander Wang's power trip, and she even washed his clothes for him. She had her qualities, a sort of appealing innocence, but Lei Xia would have none of it. On one occasion he screamed at her over the loss of a bridle: "You lost it, so you pay for it! If you don't, I'll cut off that pigtail of yours and use *it* for a bridle!"

"You make me sick!" she snarled in return.

"Get the hell out of here!" he growled. "You smelly turd!"

In the fall a herdsman broke his leg in a wagon accident and had to be taken to the hospital in Ulanhad. Lei Xia volunteered for the job. But once he'd dropped off his patient, he lit out instead for Beijing, where he stayed for over six months. Meanwhile the herdsman, who could barely speak Chinese and was away from home for the first time in his life, left the hospital after days of ridicule and neglect, returning to the company on his own. His leg healed wrong as a result, which so angered the company commander that when Lei Xia returned he was relieved of his duties and fined six months' pay.

But Lei Xia was unruffled. He knew how to get out of this predicament, for back in Beijing he had spent some of his time learning magic from a member of an acrobatics troupe. After his return, he performed for anyone who would watch, doing everything from getting a Ping-Pong ball to pop out of his ear to making a steamed bun disappear in front of our eyes. "When there are no tigers on the mountain, the monkey is king." His performances breathed new life into Company Seven, whose members, young and old, mobbed him wherever he went to watch him perform magic; no one ever left disappointed.

In no time at all he was every family's most welcome guest, and he soon made the broken-leg incident disappear like magic. Even Company Commander Wang mellowed and reinstated his wages.

With the planting season upon us, the fat regimental commander visited Company Seven, where the first order of business was a command performance by Lei Xia, who quickly wowed the commander with one trick after another. He knew what he was doing. Winning over the regimental commander was a real coup, and from there it was just a matter of getting into the rotund leader's good graces, which he managed to do by fetching water for him, sweeping out his room, and airing his bedding, all in full view of everyone. Let them laugh, he didn't care. At night, when the commander was relaxing, Lei Xia dropped by to show him more tricks and chat with him.

It took all of two weeks to achieve his objective. The fat commander placed a phone call to Director Li of the Political Section to recommend Lei Xia for the Regimental Propaganda Team.

IN AUGUST 1973, the long-awaited Tenth Congress of the Chinese Communist Party was held in Beijing. I listened raptly to the radio broadcasts, paying particular attention to the makeup of the Standing Committee of the Politburo, China's top ruling body, and hoping to get a fix on future party policies and trends by identifying the major players. Having Jiang Qing out of the political limelight would lessen the nature of my "crime." But things didn't go my way, since her leadership of the Cultural Revolution was strengthened at the congress.

Still, I took hope from a speech by Wang Hongwen, the newest member of the Politburo, who gave his stamp of approval to the trend of bucking the tide.

38

WRITING

POSTERS

FOR DAYS ON end I expected to have my case reviewed. I sent letters to Director Fang but heard nothing. Slowly my youth was slipping away, in spite of the presence of Wei Xiaoli; my counterrevolutionary label stuck, and I burned with impatience. How could anyone with a mug like mine get close to a girl like her?

Then something in a report from the Tenth Party Congress brought me inspiration. I'd take the offensive by putting up a poster. I had nothing to fear, since I'd be answering the call of the Party Congress. After all, I'd already hit bottom, so there was nowhere to go but up; it was worth a try. After three years of humiliation, three long years of living like a dog, I was ready to hold my head up again. I wanted the three thousand members of the regiment to know that Ma Bo was a force to be reckoned with.

Drafting the poster was easy, but I didn't want to ruin the effect with my chicken-scrawl handwriting, so I went to see Xu Zuo in the infirmary. We slipped into one of the wards and knocked it out in no time.

A few days later I tiptoed out of my room late at night and headed for Regimental Headquarters. The night swallowed up everything but the occasional hoot of an owl, which was like a baby's cry. Midnight:

The entire regiment slept as a solitary counterrevolutionary shuffled past with a rolled-up poster under his arm and two paste-filled mess tins slung over his shoulder.

When I reached headquarters I looked up and down the street to satisfy myself that it was deserted. The intersection was the ideal spot, since that was where everyone would be sure to see it. My heart raced from nerves and excitement as I slapped on the paste.

Rebellion Must Be Treated Harshly
Mistakes Must Be Corrected

The historic Tenth Party Congress has reached its triumphant conclusion.

At the Congress Premier Zhou admonished us to "always carry out Chairman Mao's proletarian policies."

How have we done on that score? Since being branded a counterrevolutionary in 1970 I have complained often to the leaders that they bungled my case. But to this day they have taken no action. They would be well advised to listen to the call of the people with an open mind, to stop performing their duties perfunctorily, and to quit ignoring what is going on all around them. Their irresponsible attitude toward the students' political lives must cease at once.

Long live the united, triumphant Tenth Congress of the Communist Party!

Ma Bo
Company Seven
9/19/73

It was the first such poster put up in Injgan Sum since the formation of the corps in 1969. I chose a vantage point behind a nearby wall and watched from early morning to nearly sunset as a stream of people walked up to read it. News of my poster made the rounds like a whirlwind, setting the entire regiment buzzing.

"How stupid can you get?" Jin Gang remarked furtively, keeping his voice low. "Writing posters is a waste of time."

"I know that."

"Then why do it?"

"Since being publicly denounced, all I've wanted is to proclaim my innocence in front of the regiment. It's time to vent what's been building up inside me for three long years."

"But this will only get you in deeper."

"The papers keep telling us to buck the tide, so I don't think they'll do anything to me."

"Ma Bo, be careful. There's more to life than getting your kicks."

Jin Gang was forever cautioning me to watch my step.

Xu Zuo, who had spent over a month in the hospital with a dangerously high amino count, was being sent to Beijing for treatment. Before he left, I asked him to help me make a few more posters. We spent the night working.

He cast a huge shadow on the wall for a slight fellow who wasn't much bigger around than a roofbeam and whose skinny shoulders gave him the appearance of a mantis.

"Xu Zuo, you're in bad shape. Don't go belly-up on us."

"Don't worry."

"We never should have fought over Ingush. I'm sorry."

He smiled weakly. "Why bring that up now? That's ancient history. I don't hold grudges."

A WEEK LATER my second poster, "The Truth of the Matter," went up. In it I described the party-rectification campaign in Company Seven, openly denouncing Political Instructor Shen's smear tactics. I filled fifteen sheets of paper with the most intense writing I could manage, in order to raise a small corner of the Red Flag of Communism that had camouflaged the seamy activities of the Inner Mongolian Production Corps.

This one also went up late at night when no one was around. I went out and lay in the grass until daybreak before returning to see if anyone had torn it down.

No, it was still safe and sound.

That afternoon it rained, damaging some of the pages; so I recopied them and sneaked over to paste them up again. I didn't do a lick of work all day.

The next morning I was summoned to Company Headquarters. A Beijing Jeep was parked in front.

"Did you put up another poster last night?" Staff Officer Zhao asked me gravely.

"Yes."

"Have you forgotten how the corps dealt with you the last time?"

"They were wrong."

"The original verdict stands unless and until our superiors change it."

"I'm answering the call of the Tenth Congress."

With a look of loathing he said, "That's enough of your bullshit! You have no right to put up posters."

"Do you mean I don't have the right to make revolution?"

"*Make revolution?*" He froze for a moment, then burst out laughing. "You can say that with a straight face? Since when is clutching at straws making revolution? Why, you're nothing but . . ."

"I'll keep at it even if you people sentence me to death."

"Keep your mouth shut when I'm talking!" he shrieked, his face livid. "Okay, I'll tell you exactly what the Regimental Party Committee directive says: You are forbidden to put up posters, and you'll suffer the consequences if you do."

"I'll take my chances."

"Shit. You shameless pussy. You're the kind who doesn't start crying till he sees the coffin."

"I'm answering the call of the Tenth Congress."

"Keep your trap shut! Don't you mess with Mr. CCP!"

I looked calmly at the pale, slack face and tiny hands of this law enforcement officer and kept my silence.

Instead of denouncing me as the directive ordered, Company Commander Wang sent me up the mountain to work on the rock pile again.

As I was leaving, a frightened Jin Gang ran up with more advice: "Ma Bo, no more posters, period. Staff Officer Zhao went out and took pictures of every page. Be careful."

Old Chang, the driver, put it more succinctly: "Can it. An arm's no match for a leg. They can get you anytime they want."

Their advice and concern saddened me more than anything.

After six months I was returning to the embrace of my gloomy, lonely mountain, where broken ridges gazed skyward and piercing winds howled.

The steppes turn old and sallow at the first sign of autumn: sere, yellow wastelands as far as the eye can see.

Once again I was consigned to a prison without walls.

A WEEK LATER I returned to Regimental Headquarters to mail a letter to the corps. There I bumped into Little Sichuan, who had been reassigned to Company One after snitching on Jiang Baofu for uttering a reactionary slogan. Little Sichuan had been called on the carpet and accused of falling back into his old ways, which he denied adamantly. These days, if he wasn't raising a stink at the Political Office, he was firing off letters accusing the PI of treachery.

Wei Xiaoli strolled into the post office as we were talking, and when our eyes met, it was lightning bolts—at least for me. Hungrily gulping down the air she left in her wake, I turned and walked out, trying hard to look as if I hadn't noticed her.

"How come you turn to wood whenever you see her?" Little Sichuan asked me.

I ignored him. I refused to discuss the girl of my dreams with that little creep.

He giggled. "I've got some news for you. Want to hear it?"

I tried to look uninterested, but probably failed.

"Wei Xiaoli feels sorry for you."

"Really?" I dug my fingers into his arms.

"Ouch, that hurts, you motherfucker. Let go!"

"Really?" My muscles tensed.

"Really. I swear to Chairman Mao. I go see Li Xiaohua all the time, and so does she. They talk about how sorry for you they feel."

My head was feverish, and I felt dizzy. The news rocked me to the depths of my soul. Her image was a bright moon suspended above the dark void of my life.

I couldn't sleep that night.

Wei Xiaoli was my goddess, a ray of hope shining through the misery. A single glance from her invigorated me; now her pity made me reel. I knew I had to put up my final poster, this time in broad daylight.

Early November. I slogged down Stone Mountain to headquarters through the first snowfall of the winter, carrying a poster under my arm. But my way was blocked by the Injgan Sum River, covered by a thin layer of ice. As though the eyes of the goddess were gazing down at me from the enigmatic blue northern sky, I stepped onto the ice. Flowers of joy bloom for the bold warrior. I knew she could never love a sniveling coward.

Crack! The ice protested loudly. I began walking faster. *Hoooong!* Water splashed and ice flew as I fell through. Bone-chilling water engulfed me up to my thighs.

An unearthly scream split my throat as I lit out for the opposite bank. *Crunch, crunch!* Like an icebreaker opening a passage.

When I reached headquarters, Wei Xiaoli's face flashed before my eyes, so I took a deep breath and began pasting up my poster, quickly drawing a small crowd. They looked with astonishment at my wet trousers and muddy shoes—a real eyeful for November.

"I hear the Party Committee is meeting in secret right now," a middle-aged man said softly. "You'd better watch out." My smile belied a sense of alarm. Then I thought again of Wei Xiaoli and my calm was restored.

A Question for Certain Leaders of
the Inner Mongolian Production Corps

WHERE DO YOU STAND?

The Central Committee directive of the 30th told us to attack class enemies whose criminal maneuvers are sabotaging students' opportunities to work on the mountains and in the countryside. We must punish the small band of criminal elements who hound and subjugate students. We must encourage and support students who buck the tide with revolutionary spirit and struggle against misguided tendencies.

I beg to ask certain leaders of the Inner Mongolian Production Corps: Do you care about students who answered Chairman Mao's call to go to the border regions? Or are you turning a blind eye to the willful rape, arrest, detention, and vengeful attacks they are suffering?

Having been branded an active counterrevolutionary, I take this opportunity to shout once more: The Corps Command must adopt the spirit of the Central Committee directive of the 30th and send someone to review my case to implement Chairman Mao's revolutionary policies toward students.

Ma Bo
Company Seven

I decided to give Commissar Kang a handwritten copy, since I'd heard he seldom read posters. Everyone said he was a pretty good guy who had broken down and cried when he saw the charred bodies of all those students after the forest fire. I definitely wanted him on my side.

Outside his door I took a deep breath, envisioned Wei Xiaoli's lovely face once more for courage, and entered.

"Commissar Kang, I've written a poster I'd like you to see," I said insipidly as I handed it to him.

A shiny bald head rose from behind the desk. Commissar Kang removed his glasses and stared at me for a second or two, then looked down and scanned the handwritten copy. "Weren't you told not to write these?"

"I'm answering the call of the Tenth Congress."

He threw down his pencil, which skipped across the table and landed on the floor. "Counterrevolutionaries have no right to put up posters."

"The corps was wrong. I'm no counterrevolutionary."

Thud! He pounded the table. "Don't be so damned cocky!" he roared. "Who do you think you are?"

"I'm not who they say I am."

"You'd better change your tone, you son of a bitch. I won't have you talking and acting like that here."

"Commissar Kang," I said calmly, "that's the wrong attitude to take. Talk sense if you want, but don't call me names."

"I don't need to talk sense to you. The corps decision is irreversible. You are a target of the dictatorship of the proletariat. Do you hear me, a target!" Here was a man who could cry over the burned bodies of a group of students, yet turned into a raging tiger around me because of my counterrevolutionary label.

I glared at him with mounting rage, like a boxer sizing up his opponent's jaw. "I'll fight to have my verdict overturned as long as there's breath in my body."

"Maybe that won't be very long." He jumped to his feet and glared at me wide-eyed as a couple of clerks rushed in and began dragging and pushing me out the door. "I'll fight you people to the death, count on it!" I shouted with mounting hysteria, shaking my fist menacingly.

"Your verdict will never be overturned, Ma Bo, *never!* Do you hear me? Never!" Spittle flew from his mouth; his bald head shimmered with a green light.

ONE DAY IN mid-November I drove my wagon to Company One to fetch water. There I ran into Little Sichuan, who told me that public-security people had come from the corps to review my case, apparently on the orders of You Taizhong, first secretary of the Inner Mongolian Party Committee.

That was the news I'd been waiting for.

My fate was now in their hands. That night I rushed back to Company Headquarters and told Jin Gang. He was as excited as I was. "Ma Bo," he said, "there's hope for you yet."

"Sooner or later they'll want to talk to you, so tell them how Shen made us suffer, okay?"

"Don't worry."

I clenched my teeth as the unhappiness that had filled my heart for years spilled out: "Show some guts this time. I need help. Don't ignore me like you did that time I was in custody."

He was a study in calmness, but his eyes betrayed a complexity of emotions. As he adjusted his glasses, he said emotionally, "Ma Bo, you have no understanding of people. If I was as cold as you think I am, I wouldn't give you the time of day. Who doesn't wish he could have friends who would lay down their lives for him these days? I'm not a strong person, so in a wild place like this I need friends more than you do. You might think that Lei Xia and I are friends, but deep down I have no respect for him. That's something you could never understand."

He put me up and lent me a clean comforter. We stayed up half the night talking and planning, agreeing that he would ride up the mountain in the dark of night if there was any urgent news. I lent him a luminous compass so he could find his way.

As we said good-bye the next day I reminded him, "Of those who were attacked in the past, Liu Yinghong's dead, Xu Zuo's back in Beijing, and Lei Xia and I are no longer friends. That leaves only you. I'm counting on you to tell the truth."

"I have a conscience, you know," he defended himself. "I'm not thrilled about some of the things you do, if you want the truth, but I'll speak up for you."

———

"YOU TAIZHONG ORDERED my case reopened," I announced to everyone I met. This was the chance to increase my worth in their eyes, the only possible way to get them to pay attention to a lowly counterrevolutionary like me.

39

THE PRESSURE IS ON

FIVE DAYS LATER I was summoned to Company Headquarters. More tension. People who had begun to greet me as one of them now shunned me like the plague.

Jin Gang was sitting on the kang with some friends when I walked into his room. They went on with their conversation as if I were invisible.

Later on I learned that when the corps team arrived, Staff Officer Zhao announced that a review of my case did not imply rehabilitation and that the original verdict stood until it was overturned, *if* it was overturned; in other words, I was still an active counterrevolutionary and was to be treated as such. "Some of you have taken pity on Ma Bo," he said, "including whoever helped him write his posters. That is fraught with danger. Anyone who relays news to him will be dealt with severely."

Then he changed his tone: "You youngsters see things too simply," he said, dripping with sincerity. "The review could very well lead to additional discipline as a show of leniency. Consider your acts very carefully, if you know what's good for you. When the organization criticizes you, it's for your own good. If you commit a youthful political indiscretion, what will you say to your parents? This cauldron is no playground."

I became an outcast.

The blackboard in the company office was now decorated with a large, conspicuous slogan: NEVER FORGET CLASS STRUGGLE! Below it a condemnation by Qi Shuzhen:

Quotation from Chairman Mao

Stop counterrevolutionaries from utilizing freedom of speech to further their counterrevolutionary goals.

The active counterrevolutionary Ma Bo has bounded into public view in order to have his verdict overturned. This is emblematic of class struggle. He has embraced a reactionary ideology for so long that even though he is guilty of all sorts of evils, he refuses to bow his head in contrition. What he calls an attempt to have his verdict overturned is in reality an attack on the dictatorship of the proletariat. To show mercy would be to deal a cruel blow to the people. We must force him to make a clean breast of things and not allow him to go off half-cocked. To those comrades he has duped, a warning: Come to your senses quickly. Renouncing someone who has deceived you is the only way to avoid sliding into a morass of antiparty, antipeople activity.

Finally we must raise our arms and shout: Down with the active counterrevolutionary Ma Bo!

So! This attack from a revolutionary trooper who thought nothing of using her body to gain admission to the party. I copied it down—a keepsake, as it were.

At Company Headquarters I was confronted by a sea of cold faces wherever I went. The fact that a single order could turn more than two hundred people against me was truly disheartening.

Company Commander Wang had been reassigned to pasture duty. I never found out why.

Since I had no place to sleep, after borrowing a sheepskin coat from Wagon Master Chang, I sneaked into the grain silo near the threshing floor to spend the night. Cold winds sliced in through the cracks; squeaking rats scurried back and forth. Outside mules chewed lazily on wheat husks as muffled footsteps moved back and forth across the cement threshing floor.

As a counterrevolutionary I was affected by the dark side of people as never before. The change in my situation was reflected in the faces around me—warm one minute, cold the next—with amazing accuracy, sensitivity, and speed.

Take Jin Gang, for instance. When he heard that You Taizhong had ordered my case reexamined, he enthusiastically volunteered to help, promising to tell exactly what had happened. But when Staff Officer Zhao said I might remain a counterrevolutionary for a long time, he did an about-face. He wouldn't even squat beside me in the crapper.

Staff Officer Zhao's scare tactics had turned all those simple, lively students into a pack of jittery chameleons. But it wasn't Zhao alone, since he was backed up by the monstrous dictatorship of the proletariat, which was enough to scare the shit out of anyone. What difference could a few lives mean to people for whom tens of thousands were expendable?

Security Section Chief Lei of Fifth Division and two officials from the Corps Public Security Department summoned me. Lei, a man from Shandong who seemed like a decent sort, treated me well enough. "Now tell us why you're appealing your verdict," he said genially.

"I was denounced for smearing Chairman Mao and Vice Chairman Lin. But it's a lie."

The other men were scribbling frantically. One had a pistol at his hip, and when he bent over, the barrel poked out of the red satin wrapping.

Section Chief Lei blinked and asked me, "What's behind this appeal? The corps has a stack of letters you've written over the years this thick." He held out his thumb and forefinger to show me. "Who told you to write all those letters?"

In other words, did I have backing?

"Nobody. I did it on my own," I said softly. "You can't imagine how it feels to be called a counterrevolutionary."

That was the first of many sessions, each of which required a written report. I learned that I had been accused of slandering the corps by calling it a "fascist dictatorship" and of writing down the names of everyone who criticized me to get even later.

The key issue in my case, the one that had caused me such mental torment, involved my opposition to Jiang Qing. Xu Zuo urged me to deny the charge and tough it out. But what could I do? I'd already confessed. Since I could no longer deny the charges, yet wasn't prepared to admit to them openly, my only chance was to find out from Lei Xia what evidence he'd given. If our stories were straight, the past would take care of itself.

I sneaked over to the Propaganda Section late at night, so quietly I didn't even disturb the ghosts, looking for Lei Xia.

"A corps team is here to review my case. They say You Taizhong ordered it. I hope you tell them the truth about my comment about Jiang Qing."

"What comment?"

"You know, the Empress Dowager."

"What do you mean, the Empress Dowager?"

"When I said she was like the Empress Dowager."

He thought for a moment. "I never said anything about that."

I stared at him blankly. He looked back aggressively.

"We may be enemies, but I'm telling you here and now that I never reported you for that. Check it out if you don't believe me. If you find I've lied to you, I'll post a public apology." He stormed off.

If that was true, it could only mean that Director Fang had lied to me. His genial Hebei accent, those dashing gray temples, his large head and square jaw. Removing my handcuffs, giving me water, allowing me to buy a towel and soap. The olive-drab uniform and red cap insignia . . . it all floated before my eyes.

I was interrogated for five straight days.

Section Chief Lei removed something from his bag. "This compass is the one you used when you ran away, isn't it?"

"Yes."

"We're taking it with us. We'll return it later."

Jin Gang, how could you? That was to help you find your way. What did you stand to gain by giving it to them? They'd never have known I lent it to you.

From Lei Xia and Liu Yinghong to Yan Shu, old Bao and Jin Gang, with their smiling faces and solemn vows, I learned a valuable lesson: Never trust anyone. It is the height of folly, and that's the truth. Never be misled by oaths or goodwill, because they're all for show. Under an oppressive government all the people are traitors, informers, and renegades who know only how to trim their sails.

On my way out I said to Chief Lei, "I hope you'll consider the suffering of the students and take the side of justice when you report to your superiors. Don't use this review of my case as an excuse to launch a new attack on me."

"You must trust the party and the organization."

"I did that once, and look what it got me."

"Do you think we're out to get you?"

"Hard to say."

He smiled. "Does Xu Zuo write often?"

"Yes."

"I wonder if that rascal's really sick or if he's just got balls. He sure is something!" He sighed.

Once they'd wrapped up their work, the cadres from Corps Command went on a shopping spree. Since they'd come this far, it was only natural they'd want to take some local products back with them. They made their purchases during the day and played cards at night. In ten short days they enriched themselves to the tune of four goats, two felt rugs, and dozens of goatskins.

The team had no sooner left than Commissar Kang singled me out in front of the regimental party representatives:

"Recently the active counterrevolutionary Ma Bo of Company Seven has bounded into public view in order to have his verdict overturned. That is the cutting edge of class struggle. When the active counterrevolutionary Ma Bo surfaced to put up his poster, he raised the banner of 'bucking the tide.' But his activities actually reflect the aspirations of a small band of overthrown gentry, rich peasants, counterrevolutionaries, bad elements, and rightists, representing their unwillingness to admit defeat as they swim against the tide of the dictatorship of the proletariat. Yet there are comrades who defend these individuals' complaints of injustice, aiding them with sympathy and support. These comrades must examine their own political stance."

My name was the only one mentioned in Commissar Kang's report, which was printed in pamphlet form and distributed to all companies for study and discussion. In no time I was the target of attacks by the Forty-first Regiment. Bulletin boards and blackboards were covered with condemnations of my reactionary crimes.

A few days later Commissar Kang singled me out again, launching a flood of denunciations against me at the first Congress of Representatives of the Communist Youth League.

My heart felt weighted down by a stone; I was absolutely bewildered. Lin Biao had fallen from power, yet leftism and despotism were, if anything, stronger than ever. The regiment launched a vigorous campaign against me for writing posters. Ugly rumors flew (the Mongols, habitually slow to jump on the bandwagon, often came to my yurt to pass on the latest gossip), but what really angered me was how Jin Gang went around telling everyone I thought about nothing but my own problems. He also raised doubts about my motives for writing the posters. What he meant was: Instead of belaboring injustices perpetrated against me, I should throw myself into my work and concentrate on developing the grassland. In other words, forget about causing trouble and concentrate on being a good little counterrevolutionary.

Meanwhile those in power carried on as always. As I see it, people would be a lot better off if they were more, rather than less, selfish.

But getting angry wouldn't do any good. Let him talk. Fuck him! I was a counterrevolutionary mirror that reflected the people's true souls. When they looked into it they discovered they weren't as attractive as they'd thought. That made them unhappy, so they blamed the mirror.

40

THE LONELIEST
DAYS

I WENT TO Regimental Headquarters to mail a letter to You Taizhong. Everyone gave me a wide berth. It might have been the ferocity
of the campaign that intimidated them, I don't know, but the place was
like a powder keg. It was worse than during the anti–Lin Biao campaign. Later on I learned that You Taizhong had commented favorably
on my appeal but had been ignored.

The painful sight of herdsmen, students, farmers, and workers coming in to do their Spring Festival shopping made me feel like a stranger
in a strange land. Zola once said, "A man who has lost his mother's love
is to be pitied, a man who has lost his wife's love is miserable. But a man
who has lost friendship is truly alone."

I didn't have a wife, but I lost everything else when my situation
turned bad. Even my own mother disowned me.

Isolation is very effective punishment, in fact if not in name. Living
among people told to ignore me made me feel like walking death. They
treated the animals better than they treated me. I could go for weeks,
even months, without seeing a friendly face. Languishing among three
thousand blocks of ice, I was the prime target of abuse, a dirty rat, a
trained monkey, a stinking counterrevolutionary. Crestfallen, I returned

to Stone Mountain. No more for me; this was where I belonged. Bitterly disappointed by my peers' "revolutionary consciousness," I buried myself in the depths of the mountain, severing all contact with the outside world again. This time it was true solitude. My only companions during those long, lonely nights were characters from books. Whenever I felt empty and frightened, whenever my courage deserted me, I tried to imagine myself in their midst. Too bad it didn't do much good. I even turned to Romain Rolland's *Life of Beethoven* for inspiration, copying memorized passages into my notebook.

The rest of the time I watched the rocks.

My monthly flour allotment was five catties, supplemented by husked sorghum and cornmeal (which other production units fed to their horses). The frozen cabbage I got had a disgustingly sweet taste. Meat was closely rationed; condiments were limited to salt and some five-spice powder. On New Year's I was given five large onion stalks as a "special treat."

But it was a carefree life: I slept when I wanted to, ate when I felt like it, and no one could say a word. No longer did I bother trying to figure things out. My philosophy was: What happens, happens. Day in and day out, like a zombie I ate and like a zombie I slept; it was a muddled but untroubled existence.

On New Year's Day, 1974, I lay in bed until well after noon, then got up and took several deep breaths of the cold air. After wolfing down a bowl of coarse porridge, I walked up the mountain, my stroll serving the dual purposes of digestion and relaxation.

The place was quiet as a graveyard, still as death, and that made me lonelier than ever. I woke up the dreary mountain with several loud screams that tore from my throat. Between me and the horizon where the Huolin Gol met the sky, the silvery Injgan Sum River twisted through the heart of the steppe, cutting off the southwest corner. To the north the yellow soil of frozen fields was dotted by a few solitary ruins. To the west a row of black huts bathed in the dull golden rays of the winter sun.

How could "quiet" be so disquieting? I'm not exaggerating when I say that up on the mountain, when there wasn't a breath of wind, the endless quiet gave me goosebumps, and an outburst of hysterical shouts was the only thing that could calm me down.

Slowly but surely time began to blur, and my perception of it grew muddled. What day was it? How many weeks had I been on the mountain? I had no idea. Sometimes I didn't even know the month. Robinson Crusoe at least had the good sense to keep track of the days on his deserted island by notching a piece of wood.

Slowly but surely my few hygienic habits deserted me. I washed my face once a week (maybe) and gave up brushing my teeth and washing my feet altogether. I no longer folded my bedding, I stopped sweeping the floor, and at night I relieved myself in the yurt, turning the stove into a makeshift urinal. No matter how grimy or greasy my clothes got, I never washed them; my hair was long and matted, my teeth yellow, and my breath a disaster. I was as lousy, as filthy as a pig, and I never cleaned my bowl and chopsticks, even though they were covered with a crusty layer.

After taking a shit I wiped myself with dried grass or a road apple, and that took care of that. If I lost a button, I replaced it with a piece of detonating fuse; instead of making noodles with a rolling pin I used an axe handle. Finally I got so slovenly that at mealtime I quit using a bowl and ate straight from the pot. I walked around with kernels of rice stuck to my nose and chin.

The first victim of total isolation is one's sense of shame. There on my deserted mountain, I was the universe, the universe was me. All society consisted of me alone, so there was no need for modesty. I'd stand atop the mountain, undo my fly, and arch a stream of piss toward the burning sun, or squat on a rock, my bare ass facing the regiment, and let it fly. All that kept me from walking around in my birthday suit was the cold.

Next came the depletion of brain activity. I had no books, no newspapers, no one to talk to, and no intellectual contacts; everything I'd learned in school seemed further and further away. I passed my days in a semiprimitive dream. If I felt like it, I crawled up next to a pile of goat dung and scrutinized the little round turds, studying their shapes, sizes, colors and lusters, their similarities and differences. I could study them forever.

Having no use for speech, I began to forget words.

Isolation brought out the bestial solitude in my nature. I thought of women so fiercely, I could neither sit nor stand still. I masturbated all the time, sometimes three or four times a day, usually while cuddling up to my sheepskin coat or embracing my pillow. If a woman had suddenly appeared on my mountain, I'd have pounced on her like a wild animal and raped the shit out of her.

When I lay down at night and stroked my stiff little brother I thought with sadness and anger, "What the fuck good is one of these to a counterrevolutionary? It only makes things worse."

The longer I lived apart from people, the less comfortable I felt around them. On those rare occasions when I met a herdsman, I experienced only frosty repugnance and guardedness, like a wary marmot that hates having its peace and quiet spoiled by humans.

Feelings of anger and hostility welled up in my heart. I hated the evils of human nature, I hated the snobbishness. People had turned their backs on me when my need was the greatest, and even my own mother feared being contaminated by her son. Burning with hatred, I smashed the hardest rocks with an eighteen-pound sledge; burning with hatred, I opened my throat and howled fiercely at the masses.

Sometimes after struggling to move a heavy boulder, I'd catch a startled rat, which I'd then douse with oil, light on fire, and watch scurry frantically, fur ablaze; or I'd gouge out its eyes with a knife and turn it loose to watch it run around blindly; or I'd hack off one of its tiny legs and watch it hobble and tumble along, leaving a tiny trail of blood.

Killing lice was another of my pleasures. I'd pinch them between my thumbnails until I heard a *pop*, leaving a dry, empty shell on one of my nails. Hunt, grab, pinch, kill. *Kill!* My thumbnail was covered with blood, saliva dribbled down my chin. Wholesale slaughter was my sole entertainment.

That's what you brought on me, solitude. The poets describe you as elegant, lovely, romantic. But they're wrong, you stink!

———

IN THE SPRING of 1974 a campaign against Lin Biao and Confucius was launched with a bang. The *People's Daily* headline read: STAUNCHLY REPEL A RESURGING TIDE TO OVERTURN VERDICTS AGAINST BOURGEOIS RIGHTISTS. Stories in praise of popular heroes began to appear. Herdsmen told me that posters were going up in Beijing, Tianjin, and Hohhot, and the common wisdom was that the second Cultural Revolution had begun.

My long-dormant capacity for reason began to stir.

According to *People's Daily*, criticisms of Lin Biao and Confucius must be linked to the realities of class struggle, and I smelled danger: In the past any mention of class struggle had my name on it. I hadn't heard from Mother for a long time, so I wrote twice in rapid succession, asking her to help me.

Finally, in early summer, a letter arrived. She said that when she'd asked someone to look into my case at Corps Command, she had learned that the Forty-first Regiment Party Committee not only refused to overturn my verdict, but had even sent a demand to the corps that my counterrevolutionary label be formalized. She then lambasted me for putting up the posters and for raising hell with the commissar. She said to prepare for the worst.

Big trouble!

Now I was really depressed.

A few days later Little Sichuan of Company One told me that Director Li had mentioned casually to someone: "Ma Bo's finished now. This time the label's going to stick."

My formal appeal had only made things worse. On top of everything else, the distance between me and Wei Xiaoli widened, and I wouldn't have been surprised to see a denunciation over her signature. More than four years had passed since I'd written her. I'd had no contact with her since, hadn't even spoken to her. Just seeing her was enough, and her image grew in my mind.

A goddess in a spray of redolent peonies. During those lonely days she kept me company in my freezing, squalid yurt; if I was hurt or tired, she came to console me. She was the storehouse of my courage. If not for her, I'd never have dared to put up a poster in broad daylight.

Every imaginable carnal desire swirled through my mind, but none of my promiscuous dreams so much as brushed against her. In her company I tried to enter a higher spiritual realm to improve my image. I couldn't let her think I was a degenerate. A year, two years, three years. The goddess took root in my mind, deep and unyielding. She pushed me forward—seek, write, persevere.

But now I was faced with the very real danger of becoming the focus of rightist-verdict reversals and might never have a chance to talk to her again. I couldn't let that happen. No, I'd write and let her see just who this counterrevolutionary was. It would be my final good-bye to the goddess in my heart on the eve of a desperate struggle. My greatest fear was that she, too, would see me only as an active counterrevolutionary. Since she'd rebuffed me the first time, I decided to write to her sister, Wei Xiaoling, instead. She was in Company Nine.

Dear Wei Xiaoling:

This letter comes to you from a man, very much alive, undergoing labor reform on the mountain. The corps has unfairly pinned a label on him—he is not the reactionary thug rumors make him out to be. Since being taken into custody in February 1970, he's been deserted by everyone, even his friends. But since he can't run around tearfully pleading his case, he's suffered in silence all these years.

Lightning splits the sky, thunder rumbles on earth. A storm of criticism against Lin Biao and Confucius is about to break, and the Forty-first Regiment will make me the target of class struggle. They want me dead, and I can remain quiet no longer. I'm enclosing the so-called indictments against me. This is their entire case. I want you and Wei Xiaoli to have a true picture of this so-called counterrevolutionary, no matter what happens from here on.

For all I know, a tragic end awaits me. But that's okay, since there's something to be said for a life filled with hardships. I console myself with the knowledge that the coming struggle won't be some little family squabble. Bound up in Staff Officer Zhao's manila files are puffs of gunsmoke from the party's tenth internal struggle against the Lin Biao counterrevolutionary line.

I enclose information on my major problems.

Ma Bo

April 1974

Mailing that letter freed me of my worries. They could arrest me now and I wouldn't care.

41

A MEMORABLE

ENCOUNTER

WHILE I WAS alone on the mountain, the Corps Party Committee received a report demanding that I be dealt with harshly (I didn't get my hands on this document until years later):

Opinions on the Case Review of the Active Counterrevolutionary Ma Bo

Ma Bo, male, Han race, owing to his consistent dissatisfaction with practical realities, viciously attacked the headquarters of the proletariat and members of the Central Committee. The Corps Party Committee approved the following: Considered an active counterrevolutionary, without the formal label, he was bound over for labor reform under supervision by the masses. Aforementioned individual appealed the verdict and, following the closing of the Tenth Party Congress, put up posters demanding that his verdict be overturned. In order to implement party policy, the corps, division, and regiment launched thorough investigations of the Ma Bo case from October 19 to November 3, 1973.

Initially, principal individuals of the company in question, members who informed on him, and personnel within the organization charged with dealing with his problems disposed of his case after completing their investigation and responding to his appeal. The case was objectively and conscientiously studied and analyzed in conformance with party policy. There is no evidence of "persecution" or "retaliation." Ma Bo is an active counterrevolutionary, through and through, and the disposition of his case was proper and correct.

For a long time Ma Bo has neglected ideological reform, refusing help and reeducation from the party organization and officials at every level. He engaged in evil pursuits during the Cultural Revolution, including bourgeois thinking and political errors, for which he was criticized. Most significantly, after his parents were turned over to the masses for investigation, he treated the party and the socialist system with loathing, publicly and viciously attacking the headquarters of the dictatorship of the proletariat. Ma Bo has not taken the counterrevolutionary road by accident; rather it is a product of social factors and the ideological roots from which they spring.

After the verdict was announced, the accused remained intransigent; refusing to accept supervision by the masses, he adopted a recalcitrant attitude, taking notes on critical documents submitted by activists, in anticipation of his revenge. He also threatened Lei Xia, the informer, if he refused to change his report.

Following the aborted coup by Lin Biao on September 13, 1971, Ma Bo slandered the corps, calling it a fascist dictatorship. In the winter of 1972, taking advantage of his assignment to supply rocks, he ran off to appeal to higher authorities, but his absence was discovered and he was brought back. Seeing the closing of the Tenth Congress as yet another opportunity, he raised the flag of "bucking the tide" and put up posters on four separate occasions attacking leading corps comrades in a futile attempt to have his verdict overturned. His counterrevolutionary arrogance knows no bounds.

The above facts prove that Ma Bo lacks an understanding of his crimes and stubbornly clings to his reactionary stance. Additionally, his public demand for a reversal of the verdict cannot be separated from his mother, Yang Mo. Following the September 13th Incident, Yang attempted to use her connections to have his verdict reversed and revealed to him important secrets regarding the smashing of the Lin Biao antiparty clique by the Central Committee, writing on several occasions to give him counsel.

Based upon the stated facts of Ma Bo's crimes, the results of the follow-up investigation, and his documented behavior during the period of supervision and reform, the Party Committee has unanimously decreed that Corps Party Committee decision number fifty-three is just and proper. In order to repel sabotage by an enemy of class struggle, the committee requests that the label of active counterrevolutionary be formally applied to Ma Bo, and that his labor reform under supervision by the masses be continued. We further recommend that a letter be sent to the work unit of Ma Bo's mother, Yang Mo, informing her that supporting the reversal of her son's verdict is incorrect and recommending that she be turned over for re-education by the organization.

(signed) Party Committee of the Fifty-first Regiment,
Fifth Division, Inner Mongolian Production
Corps of the Chinese Communist Party

The anti–Lin Biao, anti-Confucius campaign was heating up at the regimental and company levels, but even with the smell of gunpowder thick in the air, no one came up the mountain to involve me in the struggle. Maybe I was being oversensitive; maybe I had become a bird frightened by the bow and arrow of class struggle.

I lived like a pig up there. My wilderness captivity was more primitive, and far more absolute, than prison life. Shackles and fetters can restrict your physical movements, but the wilderness deprives you of your soul. Strong-willed people might be able to live in isolation for long stretches of time, but it devastated me.

The process of deterioration was relentless: My sense of touch was dulled to the point where I could sleep like a baby on a bed of jagged rocks, while my ears grew so sharp, I could hear the shouts of grooms several li away. My digestive system was so sound, I could eat three pieces of leathery hardtack at one sitting or go for days on nothing but millet gruel and tea. I ate anything—spoiled meat, mildewed sorghum, snow soiled by my own excrement—without getting sick. I grew as strong as a leopard, without the leopard's mental acumen.

I don't remember the date (and probably didn't know it even then), but at about ten one morning, when I was curled up under my coat like a denizen of the zoo, snoring away, I heard the rumble of a wagon that stopped outside my yurt. After climbing indignantly out of bed, I ran a comb through my hair and dusted some of the goat hairs off my clothes. Who the hell needed company at this hour?

A squat man in his forties walked in, smiling broadly.

"I'm from the commune, on my way to your regiment to pick up some stuff. I need directions."

"Down the mountain, take the road west."

He smiled, nodded, and sat down. I refused his offer of a cigarette. He looked wily to me. What did he want? A meal, maybe?

He lit up, looked around, and asked, "You alone here?"

"Yeah."

"What do you do?"

"Smash rocks."

"Not a bad living, if it wasn't such hard work."

I nodded. He must have taken me as a contract laborer.

"How long you been at it?"

"Almost three years."

"Wow! Got any kids?"

"No, I'm a bachelor."

He smiled sympathetically. "Where you from?"

"Beijing."

"Beijing?" He looked at me suspiciously. "You one of those Beijing students?"

I nodded testily. His questions were getting on my nerves.

"I wouldn't have guessed it. You sure don't look like a city boy."

My shirtsleeves were torn and ragged, my leather pants black with grime and covered with patches of all colors; black hairs stuck out through the holes. Jin Gang once said that my pants deserved to be in a museum to show student fashions of the seventies.

Something suddenly occurred to him. He leaned over and said in a low, conspiratorial voice, "You know a student named Ma Bo?"

"Yeah, we're in the same company."

"How's he doing? I hear he put up posters attacking the regiment bigshots."

"Yeah."

"Where is he now?"

"At a reed pond in Eastern Ujimqin Banner. All the 'four bad elements' from our company were sent there to gather reeds."

"The Beijing students at our commune talk about him a lot," he said sympathetically. "They say he got a raw deal. When they heard I was going to the Forty-first Regiment, they asked me to pass on their regards. Tell him for me, would you? It's the Wuleji Brigade at Baiyinhua Commune."

"Sure, sure, I'll tell him." I suddenly tingled all over.

I tossed some cowchips into the stove, poured out the old tea, and brewed a fresh pot for him. When he'd finished his tea, I accompanied him as far as the road to the regiment, for which he thanked me profusely.

If you live alone for a long time, a single kind word can move you to the depths of your soul.

I gazed to the southeast, where the great mountain slept silently in an ocean of mist. A line of green mountains was visible on the horizon—that was where the forest fire had raged, and where Baiyinhua Commune was located. I stared into the distance for a long time, gentle rays emerging from my wolfishly cruel eyes.

ONE DAY IN July, a wagon came up the mountain with a letter.

A letter, the one item that could bring heavenly and earthly happiness to the saddest of living creatures. I didn't care who it was from or what it said. I was beside myself with excitement: Someone somewhere hadn't forgotten me.

I was shocked when I opened it and read:

Ma Bo,

Your letter to the section chief has been received, and your request forwarded to our superiors. No new decision has been reached, which means you are to respect the original decision of the Corps Party Committee, obey the arrangements made by the regiment and company, and wait patiently. Rest assured that the Corps Party Committee will dispose of the matter in accordance with party policy.

Sincerely,

Security Section
Political Department

I felt hot all over, and my head reeled. The tone made it clear that division wasn't going to deal harshly with me. Director Li's judgment had been premature.

By MID-JULY 1974, there were no more rocks to be taken from the mountain, so I was reassigned as a wagon driver. I had spent a total of three years up there, a drop in the bucket compared to the twenty-four years Robinson Crusoe was on his island, but long enough to have suffered devastating effects, the worst of which was a deterioration in my ability to engage in conversation. My vocabulary had shrunk dramatically, to probably no more than fifteen hundred words, which made it nearly impossible to express myself clearly. And my memory had grown so bad, I'd forget what I was saying in midsentence. Even the simplest train of thought was barely sustainable, and years of silence had so softened my tongue, it petered out after a few sentences, drowning in saliva.

The protracted isolation had also changed my appearance. My face looked like a punching bag, its elasticity gone and frozen in a single expression. The forced smile created by my atrophied cheek muscles led to frequent misunderstandings. Dumbbell said people were horrified when they saw me speak, and Li Guoqiang said it looked like the devil's grin. Jin Gang called it sinister. Girls took pains to avoid me.

Driving a wagon was viewed as the lowest of jobs, but I loved it. I had five new friends, all mutes, and if I took it into my head to run away again, this time I wouldn't have to walk.

My new quarters were dank and dirty, a single room in the wagon shed. One morning, as I was hitching up the team to fetch rocks from the mountain, a girl in a worn military uniform and faded army cap walked up.

"Are you passing by Company Three?"

"Yes." I glanced at her and nodded. Her skin was fair and radiant as the morning sun.

"Can I hop a ride?"

"Sure."

"You're Ma Bo, aren't you?"

I nodded, prepared for the worst.

"I'm Wei Xiaoling."

The girl I'd written to in desperation months before! I was so flustered by this chance encounter, I didn't know what to do except stare at her in wide-eyed surprise. She said she was on temporary assignment to the news section of the Regimental Political Section and had been sent to Company Seven to do a story on enclosed grazing land.

During the trip she asked a lot of questions, which was fine with me, since that spared me from having to make small talk. All I had to do was answer her questions.

"Any developments in your case?"

I told her about the directive, the investigative team that had been sent to the company, and the response to my letter from the Regimental Security Section. I said I was optimistic.

"What about the future?"

My mind went blank. I didn't know what to say.

"Don't you have any plans?" she asked gently from behind me.

I tried to frame a response as I stared at the horses' rumps. "Someday, maybe," I said after a moment of silence, "I'll follow in my mother's footsteps. Writers used to disgust me, since I respected only brute strength. But now I know the power they hold. The pen really is mightier than the sword. During all my years of struggle down here I've thought of nothing but writing about my experiences. Maybe what I have to say will benefit society in some way."

She listened quietly.

The horses plodded along like cattle, the reins so slack, they nearly scraped the ground.

When we reached Regimental Headquarters (she'd changed her mind about going to Company Three), I drove to the post office. "Come see me if you ever feel a need to get away," I said, before walking inside to mail a letter.

She was still standing by the wagon when I came out.

My heart skipped a beat.

She had fair skin and a pretty oval face, and there was a glint of goodness in her eyes. She glowed under the blazing sun.

"Ma Bo, I received your letter. I wanted to write back but was afraid it might fall into the wrong hands." Her voice had the same pleasant timbre as Wei Xiaoli's.

"During the anti–Lin Biao, anti-Confucius campaign, I heard they were going to deal with me harshly, and I was nervous as a cat. I hated to think that someone I respected might assume they were telling the truth about me. That's why I wrote. I just wanted you two to know the truth."

"We knew you weren't a counterrevolutionary," she said calmly, "and we felt sorry for you. But we couldn't . . ."

As we gazed at each other, I completely forgot what I wanted to say. Nothing came, nothing at all.

"Well, good luck in your struggle. Come see me if there's anything I can do. I'm in Company Nine's kitchen squad." She turned and walked off without a backward glance.

I watched her retreating back until she turned the corner and disappeared. The smells of horse and wagon were subdued by the feminine fragrance she had left behind; I breathed it in deeply.

"We felt sorry for you." "We!" That meant Wei Xiaoli felt sorry for me. Little Sichuan was right.

"Hooray!" I shouted as I jumped onto the wagon and twirled my whip in the air. The wagon shot out of the regiment compound, the horses galloping toward the mountain. I could barely prevent myself from jumping down and turning somersaults on the grassland, which had never been so green or so lovely.

42

RAINY

AUTUMN

I HANDED THE letter from the Division Security Section to Company Commander Wang, who smiled and said, "Be patient and work hard." Loyalty was important to Company Commander Wang. If he liked you, he'd back you no matter how serious your errors. After boycotting my interrogation by the team from the corps, he had spoken up for me in private and even written a decent appraisal of me on behalf of the Branch Committee.

To garner support, I launched a diplomatic blitzkrieg, pleading my case wherever I went. The latest letter was my strongest evidence to date, and I showed it to anyone who would read it. The results were encouraging, for people quickly became less guarded around me.

I handed the letter to Jin Gang, who pored over it for the longest time, reading between the lines to see if I would wind up as friend or foe. Yet, as time passed even he warmed up to me and stopped hiding when I was around. Naturally, he kept his distance, not wanting to be implicated if I wound up in prison or anything; but that distance was shortened, and if my case was overturned, I could count him among my loyal friends again.

I pointed out how disappointed I'd been in him during the review process. His billy-goat face betrayed no emotion as he pushed his glasses up on his nose and said placidly, "Fear is absolute, but courage is relative. A coward's always alert to danger. He has to see it coming so he can get out of its way. Fear is the greatest weapon in the coward's arsenal."

He paused and looked at me for a moment before continuing: "I admit I gave you the cold shoulder during your interrogation. I was scared. But what about Liu Yinghong? She criticized you in front of the whole regiment. Why'd she do that? How about Xu Zuo? Why did he insist on hiding in a classroom as a condition to helping you write the posters? Take my word for it, Ma Bo, the person hasn't been born who fears nothing. Psychopaths are probably the only true atheists. Are you really afraid of nothing? Think about it."

He was right, of course. During eight interrogations that nearly drove the soul out of my body, fear was what had saved me. If I'd been truly intractable, members of the regiment would have beaten the shit out of me.

Jin Gang took my silence as a signal to go on. "Survival is man's most basic right. You should try to understand why others avoid you. Napoléon said that society is driven by two levers: personal interests and fear. Fear is the indispensable guarantor of social order. Anarchy would reign if no one were afraid. You have no cause and no right to reproach anyone for avoiding you."

"Courage doesn't mean being fearless," I said. "It means being able to overcome your fears. Only fascist dictators and people who thumb their noses at law and order want people to be scared of their own shadows. The more courageous young people are, the better."

He looked deeply into my eyes. Light glared off his glasses. "No. Fear is a sign of life. It exists in everything, from a mouse to a tiger, from a foot soldier to a field marshal. Life depends on fear, and the higher the life form, the greater the degree of fear. It's not an issue of conquering fear. Fear is at the heart of struggle. Farmers tend fields out of a fear of going hungry, and you, Ma Bo, you knocked yourself out chopping down trees out of a fear of being criticized."

"Hah! Some people even become turncoats out of fear."

He bit his lip and said deliberately, "Strictly speaking, there's a bit of turncoat in all of us, so what's there to be ashamed of? That just points up the frailty of human nature."

"All of us, you say?"

"At least ninety-nine percent of us," he said with growing passion. "Anyone who doesn't know fear is crazy. I'm afraid of the dictatorship of the proletariat, which Lin Biao called a meat grinder. He was right, and that's why you'll never catch me provoking it."

I kept my mouth shut but couldn't accept his assessment of fear. Humans should be more advanced than animals. Experience told me that Jin Gang's sympathy for me was tied to his own interests. If I were drowning, he would be the last person to come to my rescue. But I also knew that if I made my way back to shore, his outstretched hand would be there for me.

In late August 1974, a campaign to recruit students for colleges and universities was launched. Jin Gang told me that Qi Shuzhen, Li Guoqiang, Li Xiaohua, and Wei Xiaoli applied.

"Wei Xiaoli?" I blurted out anxiously. "Has her father's problem been resolved?"

"Not yet. But this time there are slots for so-called salvageable offspring."

I lowered my head in confusion.

"Don't tell me you still have feelings for her!" he exclaimed with uncharacteristic interest.

I didn't say anything.

"Ma Bo, I don't understand you. The way things are now, how can you still . . ."

"Dictatorship over a person's body is one thing, but his feelings belong to him alone," I said gloomily.

"Don't get me wrong," he said. "Wei Xiaoli's not bad. She isn't spoiled, and she doesn't put on airs. Even after becoming company clerk, she went out to slop the pigs. Most children of high-ranking cadres wouldn't do that. Her only problem is she weeps so much."

Xiaoli was so fine, so lovely. And me? I was an active counterrevolutionary, a grimy wagon driver, a stupid, ugly oaf. Surely not good enough for her. I could understand why she wanted to go to college;

who wouldn't want to leave? There was no reason to feel sad. I should have shown her how happy I was for her. I didn't think it would hurt to talk to her one last time, since her sister said they had both felt sorry for me. Finally in mid-September the opportunity presented itself when the company commander told me to fetch a load of straw. Xiaoli and someone named Cao Debao came to help. On the way back, Cao ran ahead, leaving Xiaoli and me alone.

I spread the felt blanket out on the bench for her. But she stayed where she was, at the rear of the wagon, her back to me. Her aloofness disheartened me, but only momentarily. My temples throbbed from the tension of trying to articulate the way I felt.

The sky was overcast—it had just stopped raining—and the air above the steppe reeked of wet grass, the same primitive, fresh, ordinary odor I'd smelled for the first time in the summer of 1969.

The hazy outline of company buildings appeared on the horizon. Knowing I couldn't put it off any longer, I steeled myself and said, "I've got something to say to you." There was a pounding in my ears.

Silence.

"Corps was wrong to call me an active counterrevolutionary. I sent the facts to your sister. You can look at them."

Silence.

"Over the past four years the dictatorship has stripped me of my right to speak. But my silence doesn't mean I've knuckled under. There isn't a word of truth in all those horrible things they say about me." I waited for some consoling words, but there were none. With mounting excitement, blood rushing to my head, I nearly shouted, "I swear my problems will be resolved. Division Security sent a letter telling me to be patient. But even if they aren't resolved, so what?"

Silence.

"The military commissioner of the Paris Commune was right when he said that man lives to engage in action and struggle, and that even failure triumphs over vulgar peace and tranquility."

Even this inspirational outburst failed to spark a reaction.

"Go on, go to college. You're not responsible for my current predicament."

Silence.

I was utterly confused; the pounding in my ears was like crashing waves that washed away everything I'd wanted to say. I never expected her to clam up like that. What was she frightened of? There was no one around for miles. Hadn't she once felt sorry for me?

The horses grazed as they plodded along.

"Why are we slowing down? Let's get moving." The sound of her voice, so calm and even, drifted up from behind me. One terse sentence, that was all.

My whip sang out, and the horses took off at a gallop. She sat there peacefully. Not a speck of dust was raised on the rain-soaked ground. Our wagon burst into the company compound like a scream. I jerked it to a screeching halt.

She jumped down, and out of the corner of my eye I watched her walk off with her head lowered.

NOT LONG AFTERWARDS, the college selections were announced. Wei Xiaoli's name wasn't on the list. Good! That made me happy. I wouldn't care if she never spoke to me, so long as she stayed in Company Seven.

Emotions cannot be turned on and off like a faucet, so even though I stopped entertaining any illusions about Wei Xiaoli, I couldn't get her out of my mind. And as a ploy to see her more often, I subscribed to *People's Daily*, *Red Flag*, and *Reference News*, which I could hardly afford. That way I could hang around her place (she was company clerk) for a few minutes when I came to pick up my periodicals.

Something about her room made all evil thoughts vanish the minute I stepped inside. I didn't dare say more than was absolutely necessary and kept my distance so as not to pollute her with my foul breath. She embraced the purity of moonbeams.

She often went out to slop the hogs; in my eyes, therefore, the decrepit pigsty was as majestic as the Louvre. She wire-brushed one of the sows, and a love for that sow with the sagging belly flooded my heart. Even the stench was ambrosia, for she had breathed that air.

A mysterious curtain fell around everyone she knew and everything she touched. When her colt went lame after Liu Fulai rode it without permission, no one else wanted it. But I did. It may not have been able to pull a wagon, but it had special charms that quickly made it my favorite. I fed it more than the others and couldn't bear to make it work. Even the flies in her room were brushed with a veneer of elegance. I'd have kissed them if I could.

She, on the other hand, treated me not with sympathy but with indifference.

43

HAULING

COAL

COMPANY COMMANDER WANG'S policy was known as the "four littles": "Start a little earlier, return a little later, work a little harder, rest a little less." When he saw someone unemployed, he was like a capitalist watching a machine stand idle and feeling the anguish of diminished earnings. If the mortar wasn't ready, instead of being permitted to sit around waiting for it, the masons were ordered over to the lumberyard to fetch beams. If we were sent up the mountain for rocks, we had to carry a load of fertilizer to a nearby work site on the way. He organized work details so efficiently that no job allowed for any wasted motion or free time.

The busy autumn harvest was no sooner completed than Commander Wang sent First and Second platoons to dig irrigation ditches. Those we had dug in 1970 were now covered by two feet of sand and in some places were level with the ground. He insisted that they be dredged before the cold weather arrived, even though the steppe was sloped there, and everyone knows water can't run up. Even if it could, what fucking good would a few ditches have done for thousands of acres of farmland?

Then, in late autumn, before we'd finished hauling hay, we were sent out like shock troops to fetch coal. The first heavy snowfall of the year hit in early November, and the temperature dove. "Let's get an early start this year," Commander Wang said. "Up and at 'em!" So the four large wagons were out on the snow-covered roads.

The steppes are a blanket of silvery white after a snowfall, revealing no signs of life. Our horses trotted through the snow, keeping plenty of distance between them, their iron shoes sending the white powder flying. The cold wind hitting me in the face as my team negotiated the slopes felt good. It was midafternoon when we reached Company Nine. There were still seventy li to go before we reached the Sixty-third Battalion coal mine.

The sun had set by the time we'd seen to the horses. The other drivers went to spend the night with friends. I had nowhere to go.

Wei Xiaoli's sister was assigned to Company Nine. And when I'd been beaten until I looked like a one-eyed dragon and had to run to save my skin, it was some of the brothers from Company Nine who helped me out. I had a good feeling for this place.

Snowflakes swirled as the horses grazed contentedly in the gentle light from a window in the kitchen quarters; I watched from a distance. What was Xiaoling doing? Did she know I was standing out here in the cold gazing at her window?

I didn't have the nerve to go see her.

The best place to sleep was under my wagon; that way I could handle any situation that arose at night. Like some damned cow coming to steal my horses' hay. So I laid my bedding out under the wagon, wrapped my sheepskin coat around me, and lay down to sleep. The horses, tethered to the rear of the wagon, continued grazing. The powerful front legs of my black horse were only inches from my head, and the wagon wheels served as a windbreak.

Early the next morning we were back on the road. When we reached the mine, we wasted no time loading the coal and starting back. I had decided to go see Xiaoli's sister on the return but didn't want the others to know. So I pushed my team hard, soon opening up quite a distance between us.

But after traveling all morning without reaching Company Nine, I stopped at a yurt, only to discover that I was somewhere near the Baiyinhua Commune. Damn, I'd taken a wrong turn. A wind rose up and dark clouds blotted out the sun as I headed up an incline. Icicles formed around the horses' mouths and frost covered their backs. The weather in that part of the world can change in a minute. Blinded by the swirling snow, I turned my back and let the horses follow the tracks in the snow. If I lost my way again, I thought, or if the horses gave out, I'd be in real trouble, since there were no villages ahead and no inns behind me.

We headed alone into the snowstorm along an unfamiliar road. I was whistling to keep my spirits up and huddling as close as possible to the horses' rumps.

The horses' eyes, noses, and lips were ringed by frost; the whip was superfluous, since the team surged ahead on its own.

At about three that afternoon we pulled up in front of a row of buildings. It was Company Eleven of the Sixty-third Battalion. Shit, another wrong turn. I drove back to the fork in the road and turned left. The horses pulled the heavy load of coal without a murmur. Even after nightfall, when the sky turned pitch-black, they kept up the pace, trotting up the slopes and galloping down the other sides.

At around eight o'clock that night we reached Company Eight. We had been on the road, nonstop, for eleven hours. I entered the company office to arrange for some hay for the horses. Brightly lit and amazingly quiet, the place seemed otherworldly. Director Li, who was on a regimental inspection tour, and four or five soldiers were seated at a table with seven or eight platters of food and plenty of wine in front of them.

"Director Li," I said loudly.

He didn't look up until I'd shouted his name three times. "Oh, what are you doing here?"

I swallowed hard. "I got lost with a load of coal and wound up at Baiyinhua Commune. The next thing I knew I was here."

"You weren't thinking of skedaddling again, were you?"

"No. My horses have been on the go all day, and I need some hay for them."

He looked at me suspiciously, then rested his eyes on the platter of roast chicken. "Where's your wagon?"

"Outside. The horses are famished."

"Sorry," he said in measured tones. "Company Eight's Branch Committee announced that horses would not get any hay until after November fifteenth. Prior to then, no horses are to be fed in the stable."

"Are you telling me they have to go hungry all night?"

"My hands are tied. We must respect decisions of the Branch Committee." He picked up a drumstick, bit off a chunk, and began chewing. A glob of fat quivered on his chin.

"This is Ma Bo of Company Seven," he announced. "His mother is the author of *Song of Youth*." Then he asked matter-of-factly, "How much did she earn from that novel?"

"Don't know. She never told me. Just give me a little hay, Director Li, okay? My horses have been at it all day."

"I said no, and I meant it. How would anything ever get done if I said okay when I didn't mean it?" He bit off another chunk and chewed spiritedly, his lips shiny with grease.

His companions were discussing *Song of Youth*, agreeing that it was a very influential book. "It certainly was," Director Li said authoritatively, "and not just as a novel. They made it into a movie— Technicolor, mind you." They ate, they talked, and they laughed, apparently forgetting all about me. The seductive odor of sautéed liver and quick-fried mutton made me drool. I had to swallow the buildup of saliva. Since I'd be on the road all the next day as well, I couldn't let my horses go hungry tonight.

Director Li turned and looked at me. "Is Xie Chunhua back from Tianjin?"

"Not yet." I forced a smile. "Please, Director Li," I pleaded. "Just a little hay."

"Stop pestering us and find a place to sleep for the night," one of the soldiers said testily. "You can get something to eat at the mess hall after you unhitch your team."

"Is there hay anywhere? What if they find it on their own?"

Director Li glared at me. "It's not our fault you forgot to bring extra hay along for them!"

I turned and walked outside, feeling utterly helpless. The horses stood quietly with drooping heads, but when I approached, they looked up, stretched their necks, and whinnied. Anxiously they sniffed the wagon bed, snorted, and pawed the ground.

I walked over to the stable. Behind the locked gate some horses were grazing. One was Director Li's chestnut (it had once been Daoerji's prized horse). Why were these horses getting special treatment? "No one's horses are to be fed." Bullshit! Strong, well-fed personal mounts were kept in a stable, but workhorses pulled wagons until they were skin and bones, then after a hard day's work were supposed to survive on the wind. It just wasn't fair.

I decided to steal some hay. After all, it wasn't for me. I scaled the wall and crawled over to a small haystack under a layer of snow, where I picked up a pitchfork and began tossing it over. But I'd barely started when some dark figures came charging toward me, and I was encircled by three snarling dogs. I scrambled over the wall and got the hell out of there fast.

Plan A had failed, and my only option was to talk to Director Li again. We met in the doorway. He was roaring drunk by then. "It's late!" he bellowed. "Why aren't you asleep? Don't get any ideas about stealing hay." His boozy breath bowled me over.

I was so tired, I could barely stand, but I could hear my four-legged friends snorting in the cold air outside, calling to me. The sound of drinking games in the company office lasted late into the night. Biting my lip to keep from crying, I eventually drifted off.

At four in the morning, when it was still pitch-black outside, I got up and dumped what little grain remained in my sack into the trough. The horses, crazed with hunger, gobbled it up without raising their heads once. I just looked on sadly. They seemed skinnier than usual, with sweat turned to ice on the sharp ridges of their backs. Tears had frozen into icy beads, frost had gathered around their nostrils, ice covered their hides.

I sneaked back into the stable, where I removed the chestnut horse's halter and tether. I'm sorry, but no one's going to tell me to let my horses go hungry. I wouldn't dare steal other stuff, but anything belonging to Director Li was fair game.

I went back inside to get through the night somehow, awaking at daybreak to go out and see my horses. What I encountered were two black porkers with their front legs propped up on the wagon bed as they grubbed at the grain, their pointy ears twitching excitedly. Picking up a club, I crept up behind them, took aim at one of the rumps, and laid into it. A loud squeal was followed by the hasty departure of the two pigs. The horses reared back in fright and snorted. I guess they had been too kindhearted to use their hooves on the greedy pigs.

Before long a scowling farmworker rushed over. "Who the fuck hit my pigs? One's got a bloody ass. I'll cornhole the bastard! Not even dogs bite asses like that! I'll cut the bastard." He glared at me.

Ignoring him, I adjusted the harnesses so I could be on my way. Just then Director Li sauntered over from the company office, a crystal pipe in his mouth. "You still here? We got a call from the regiment. Little Liu, who drove for the Logistics Section, lost his way last night near Western Ujimqin and froze to death. Get going, there's a cold spell on the way."

"He should have taken an extra gas can," he said with a cough, then spat on the ground, as if even his spittle carried his authority. I drove out of Company Eight, my stomach growling, my hands and feet nearly frozen. The stolen halter and tether were stashed beneath my felt blanket.

Five hungry souls set out on the ten-mile trip to Company Seven in a cold whistling wind. Instead of crossing the bridge I took a shortcut to save a mile or so. But at the river's edge I saw that the ice was probably too thin to support a fully loaded wagon, and it appeared as if I'd have to head back to the bridge, to my chagrin. But every added mile in such weather meant that much more suffering, so I decided to try my luck.

After stopping beside the frozen river to let the horses rest, I checked the harnesses and the rest of the gear. Then I climbed back up, twirled my whip, and yelled for all I was worth.

The team surged forward onto the river and began the dash for the opposite bank. But we hadn't gone ten yards when I heard a loud crash, followed by the fearful sound of cracking ice; then all four horses broke through, sending columns of water high into the air. I whipped madly to keep them moving; since we were on a slight downslope, we managed to slip and slide another ten yards or so. But as soon as we were midriver, and the angle turned upwards, we slowed down. I bellowed like a wild animal and beat the horses mercilessly to keep the momentum going; if we stopped, they wouldn't be able to get us moving again.

Slower and slower, we were about to bog down. I whipped the shaft horse, which lurched forward, only to stumble. It quickly regained its footing and strained to keep moving. But it was too late, the wagon had stopped. By then the three horses up front had reached the bank, but the shaft horse was still mired in the river. I could scarcely keep my eyes open in the gale-force wind. There wasn't another soul around for miles, so my only hope was to lighten the load. It was either that or die there. I began stuffing coal into a burlap bag, the going made difficult by my thick gloves. When the bag was nearly full, I jumped into the river—the icy water nearly made my heart stop—and trudged up the bank to dump the coal by the road.

Then I repeated the process, slowed down by the absence of a shovel, and when the bag was full again, I jumped back into the river and trudged up the bank, blurred by the swirling snow. My hunger returned with a vengeance while I was filling the bag for the third time. All I'd eaten the night before were four small mooncakes. Then I'd set out that morning without any breakfast.

The shaft horse was still standing in the water, shivering. The other three stood stock-still, their heads lowered. In the course of a day and a night their rumps had grown noticeably pointed, their backbones had turned razor-sharp. I could probably take my belt in a notch or two. My leather pants bit my frozen calves every time I moved. I stamped my feet to get the blood flowing again. Just to be on the safe side, I filled one more bag. By then I was covered with coal dust.

All together I carried nine bagfuls of coal up the bank, more than half of my load. Stopping to catch my breath, I cleaned my hands and face with snow and swallowed some to wet my throat.

The horses on the bank were beginning to doze off, too tired to raise their heads. The harness straps were soaking in water.

It's up to you guys. It's do or die.

Back on the bench again, I called out softly to get their attention. Once their heads were raised, I twirled the whip and shouted, "Giddap!" With a sense of desperation, they leaned into the straps and began to pull. I whipped the shaft horse, which pulled as though its life depended on it, maybe because it had been standing in the freezing water so long. Its belly nearly scraped the bottom, its flanks bulged and rippled.

I nearly shouted myself hoarse as I whipped and cursed the horses. The wagon began to move slowly, lurching from side to side, the axles groaning. Giddap! Giddap! *Crack! Crack!* The wagon rolled up onto the bank. The tendons on the horses' legs were taut enough to snap as the animals gasped for breath.

After a short rest, I loaded the coal back onto the wagon, one heavy bagful at a time. The hawkeyed Commander Wang would know at a glance if any was missing. Besides, everyone was waiting anxiously for coal, and it would be my ass if I came back with anything less than a full load. Their warmth depended on me.

I was famished, and I was nearly frozen, unsure if I could even move, and all I could think of was mooncakes. Shit, if they had let me feed my horses the night before, I'd be in camp by now.

One bagful after another, scooping it up by hand, an empty stomach, cinch up my belt. I shook the bag that had held the mooncakes. There were a few crumbs left, which I greedily lapped up. My nose ached from the cold, tears ran down my cheeks.

I'd managed to unload and reload nine large bagfuls of coal with nothing to warm my body or fill my belly. If there's anything good to be said about carrying rocks and driving a wagon, it's that it gives you a good workout, physically and mentally.

Now that we were moving again, I alternated between walking and sitting to protect against frostbite. But that soon wore me out, and I lay in the wagon like a dead man, burying my face in the sheepskin fur to keep my lungs from freezing, and warming the skin with my breath.

The only spot on my body that wasn't frigid was the tiny space beneath my nose. The fur, filthy to be sure, kept me relatively warm against the wind, an enormous white dragon that roared and coiled.

AS SOON AS I reached camp I reported to Commander Wang. "We thought something had happened to you," he declared, obviously relieved. "Everyone heard how little Liu froze to death."

After the coal was unloaded and the wagon unhitched, I fed and watered the horses, then got some anti-inflammation powder and chilblain ointment from the clinic to rub on the chapped, bloody back of the black horse.

At last my kang beckoned to me. After removing my leather pants, which were like ice chimneys, I crawled under my coat. I'd never known such comfort.

When I awoke the following morning the sound of hoofbeats was still pounding in my ears, my bed seemed to be lurching like a wagon, and the cold wind raked my skin like cat's claws. I knew I was sick, since I was shivering under two heavy coats and a lined jacket. My swollen feet ached terribly. Jin Gang had to make two trips to the clinic before he managed to talk Song Chunyan into coming over to look at me. She entered the dark room with trepidation and gave me an injection. I was embarrassed by my smelly, swollen feet. She stared at me with a strange look on her face—a fearful look, it seemed to me—and stayed a good three feet away from me, as if I might spring at her any minute.

Don't be afraid, my little nurse-angel. If you came up and looked carefully, you might find a gentle light hidden deep in these ferocious eyes. I loaded the coal burning in your stove bare-handed in a blizzard, did you know that? Just so you could be warm.

She left some packets of medicine for me, gave Jin Gang some instructions, and walked out with her leather medical kit.

"Driving a wagon is no job fit for humans," Jin Gang mumbled as he sat on the kang. He was leaning against a grain sack, his head buried in his hands. He sighed and began to sing softly:

> *The vast empty steppe.*
> *Such a long way to go,*
> *A man drives his wagon,*
> *Waiting to die on the steppe.*

As I listened to him sing the Russian folk song I swelled with pride. So what if I was curled up in a ball in the freezing air, with snot and tears running down my face? So what if my face was blackened by coal dust until my nostrils looked like dark tunnels? An anonymous wagon master had created the folk song, so let it be sung for a hundred years.

44

SPRING

1975

D EPUTY COMMISSAR LIU, crushed by news of the horrible human cost of the fire, took to his bed and fell ill. He wouldn't eat. "There's nothing wrong with me," he told the doctor, "except that my heart's broken. Those poor kids." Tears bathed his face.

Students from a number of units came to console him.

"Comrades," he choked, "I let the party down. Those poor kids, it's all my fault. While they were at the fire, fighting and dying, I . . . I was home in bed." He was sobbing so hard, they could barely understand him. They wept along with him.

"Comrades, our young troopers are the best in the world. They said Wang Aimin was too sick to go, so she hitched a ride on a Company Seven tractor when no one was looking . . ." The flow of tears escalated. "I, I let them down . . ." He was too choked up to continue.

The girls sobbed softly; the boys' faces were tear-streaked. It was very nearly a religious moment. If, just then, it had been necessary to repeat the tragedy, those youngsters would have answered the call, ready to sacrifice everything if asked to.

Deputy Commissar Liu was a tall, thin man with dark, leathery skin and even features. Genial and approachable, he never lost his temper with his subordinates. Whatever was wrong could be resolved calmly and peacefully.

Congenial cadres were such a rarity in the Forty-first Battalion that he stuck out like a sore thumb. With the girls he was like a strict father, considerate but proper, and when his ailing wife came to visit he was a paragon of husbandly concern: He did the laundry, the cooking, and all the cleaning. He also took her out walking on the steppe for some sun. We couldn't stop talking about him. But after the Lin Biao Incident he turned moody. Was he having trouble adapting to his new surroundings? Or was he bothered by the factionalism among his superiors, who were trying to squeeze him out?

Whatever it was, he and Commissar Kang didn't hit it off from the beginning, and there was constant friction between them. As deputy director of the Military District Public Security Department, Liu had been in charge of investigations of senior commanders and was accustomed to rubbing elbows with important people; he had little use for a minor local commissar like old Kang.

But he was blessed with considerable self-control. Most of the time he treated Commissar Kang with courtesy and deference, for he had a remarkable talent for maintaining a calm exterior even when he was fuming inside. Put in charge of instituting cadre policy, he managed, through diligence and perseverance, to liberate the Mongol cadres, and even though he was unable to find work for them, they were immensely grateful. Any mention of the deputy commissar was met with a thumbs-up and a "Good man!" by the Mongols.

But after the Lin Biao Incident, Kang's attitude toward Liu worsened. He let the students know that Liu had proudly served as one of Lin Biao's bodyguards. No big deal, but Kang milked it for all it was worth, and Liu suffered because of it.

Bothered by migraines, an ulcer, and bronchial asthma, he lived alone behind the regimental auditorium, where he could be seen each morning sweeping the street in front of his quarters. Only the attention and ministrations of a group of girls kept him from being despondent all the time.

One night he was too sick to get out of bed, and when the hospital telephone went unanswered, Little Wu, the telephone operator, personally went for the duty doctor. She then stayed to keep him company. Learning of her desire to go to college, he promised to help, encouraging her to work hard, obey her superiors, and maintain friendly relations with her peers. From then on, she always came to him with her problems and never failed to say good-bye before leaving for a home visit.

On the day of the fire, we learned, Deputy Commissar Liu was the only senior cadre at home. It had been a trying day for him, and he had taken to his bed. Little Wu stayed with him. Late that night he took her hand and said emotionally, "Little Wu, I'm sorry to be so much trouble." She shook her head in awkward embarrassment but didn't pull her hand back. An arm slipped around her waist, and she froze, not knowing what to do. A pair of chapped lips were soon pressing down on hers. "It's all right," he said softly, "don't be afraid."

Growing limp in his arms, she let him have his way with her, as Chairman Mao looked down from the wall. Out there throngs of students were fighting a raging forest fire, while the ailing deputy commissar lay in the arms of a young telephone operator. The next morning he learned of the human tragedy and wept piteously.

Not long afterwards, Little Wu went off to college. By then Liu had overcome his feelings of remorse and had initiated close relations with many of the girls.

These clandestine affairs soon became as central to his life as the sun, fresh air, water, and his medication. If one of them wasn't around, his head ached, his ulcer flared up, and the closeness of his room stifled him. A succession of innocent girls supplied him with the warmth and light he needed to get through the days, so far away from home. An unusual remedy, perhaps, but effective. This, as it turned out, was Deputy Commissar Liu's only defect. In all other respects he was a paragon, but over a period of years, he had affairs with nine different female students.

Commissar Kang ordered an immediate investigation when he got wind of what was going on, but it fizzled out owing to a lack of evidence. In the end it was a guest-house employee who broke the case, quite by accident. The girl this time was a nurse named Ge Xiuzhu, who was on a training assignment from the regimental hospital; she and the deputy commissar were caught together in the divisional guest house, and the news spread like wildfire. It hit the Forty-first Regiment with all the force of the Lin Biao Incident. During the investigation that followed, Liu's so-called "victims" had nothing but kind words for him, but he was relieved of his duties and ordered to concentrate on self-examination.

His physical ailments (migraines, ulcer, asthma) flared up in a frenzy of nausea, vomiting, insomnia, constipation, and coughing. He asked for and received permission to go to Tianjin for treatment. But on the way there he met Nurse Ge, who was on home leave, and their passion was rekindled.

Then in Tianjin's Aquatic Park he was arrested for lewd conduct by the Workers' Militia, who accused him of behaving like a horny teenager. When they learned he was a soldier on active duty, they turned him over to the Tianjin Garrison Command, which in turn notified the leaders of our military division. The news stunned Fifth Division and, typically for affairs of this kind, spread quickly. People began to see Liu in a different light, some even calling him "an old hooligan," "a dirty old man," "a whoremonger." Girls not only avoided him, they even spat in his direction to show their contempt.

Yet he never lost his composure, which was a tribute to his experience and background. He still greeted us affectionately and flirted with the nurses when he went to the hospital, as if nothing had happened.

EVEN BEFORE the excitement surrounding Deputy Commissar Liu had died down, another bombshell hit the Forty-first Regiment: Director Li of the Political Section was accused of raping a student and taking bribes. He was unceremoniously relieved of his duties.

An exciting year, 1975.

Director Li, a coarse, violent man, was famous for graft and a fondness for the ladies. He was one of Deputy Commissar Liu's longtime subordinates, yet curried the favor of Commissar Kang. When he made reports on political work, he paid impassioned lip service to the party tradition of doing things properly, lashing out angrily at people who engaged in illicit practices. Of course, that didn't stop him from arranging the permanent transfer of his relatives from the countryside to the city or from bringing his cousin to town to be treated at the regimental hospital at public expense.

The exposure and criticism of misdeeds by Deputy Commissar Liu and Director Li, two veteran comrades-in-arms, was big news. Companies feverishly reported all late-breaking developments, accompanied by plenty of gloating. If nothing else, the offenders' deeds breathed life into the boring routine of the steppe, particularly for the unmarried wagon drivers, who enjoyed nothing better than a juicy sex scandal. Their ribald comments soon took on an angry edge: An official can plug a dozen girls, but we can't even get one.

Me, I couldn't have been happier. When I heard the news, I loaded my wagon with fertilizer in record time and nearly flew down the road. Just thinking about how I'd been oppressed made me see red. I had envied the girls the special treatment they received at the hands of Deputy Commissar Liu. Pretty girls were always welcome in the offices of the men who ran the show; they were first in line for promotions and got all the cushy assignments. Unlike us boys, who worked our asses off for nothing.

Back in 1970, I had entered some self-critical remarks in my diary and had written to a girl whose family was in trouble. For this, Director Li had called me a dirty-minded hypocrite.

Who was the dirty-minded one now?

If there were a Nobel Prize for being two-faced, it would be awarded jointly to Lin Biao and his military henchmen.

EVIL WINDS WERE blowing on March 16.

I hitched up my team that morning to fetch fertilizer at East River. It was a gray, bitterly cold morning, and after loading up the dried sheep dung, I turned and headed back, my team trotting all the way. I reached my destination at two in the afternoon, and instead of driving into the shed, I just unloaded the wagon by the side of the road. As night fell, the wagon-squad leader tapped at the window. "Ma Bo, the company commander wants to see you."

What now? Was I reported for dumping my load by the side of the road? I walked nervously into Company Headquarters, where Commander Wang was sitting cross-legged on the kang.

"What is it, Company Commander?" I tried to act nonchalant.

"Your case," he said after staring at me for the longest time. "The final disposition is expected any day now."

"They've been saying that for years."

"This time it's true. Corps Command has approved it."

"Honest?"

"I just had a call from the regiment. It came out pretty much the way you had hoped." He smiled.

"Meaning?" I asked unhesitatingly.

"The charge has been changed to serious political errors, and they've rescinded the supervised labor reform. In other words, a slap on the wrist."

At last, the day I'd been dreaming about.

I tried to keep from smiling but failed. I could hardly breathe from what was welling up inside me.

He gave me a friendly look. "How do you feel?"

There was so much I wanted to say; how could I convey to him what I felt at that moment? In order to satisfy his curiosity I replied simply, "Happy, very happy."

"I hate to splash cold water on your excitement, but have you ever wondered how old Shen was able to nail you so easily?"

"He had the power."

"Your standoffish attitude had a lot to do with it. Except for wrestling, you refused to have anything to do with anyone. You've got a tough exterior, and you whipped Wang Lianfu pretty good, but deep down you're weak. Why? Because you're all alone, because you've got no one. Standing with the masses would have given you the strength to resist. Am I right or not?"

I nodded.

"Standing on your own two feet is one thing, standing alone is quite another."

He was making sense, but I was too happy, too excited to worry about it right then. A couple of people strolled into the office just then, so I slipped out with a hurried nod to the company commander. My feet nearly flew once I was outside. I was choked with emotion. Lifting my head to the night sky, I let out a howl.

Once home, I felt as if I were about to burst. I sent a bucket flying with one kick; the next kick spread the pile of cowchips like a blooming flower, its petals ricocheting noisily off the chimney. I jumped onto the kang, where I somersaulted, kicked the air, laughed madly, and howled like a banshee. A knock at the door. I ignored it. I kissed the frost on the wall, I kissed the grain sacks, I kissed the pile of cowchips. I danced.

"Open up, Ma Bo, open up!" Jin Gang shouted impatiently.

I composed myself, wiping the insane expression from my face and the spittle from the corners of my mouth before opening the door. "Congratulations." He was smiling broadly.

"As soon as it's formalized," I said nonchalantly, "I'm on my way back to Beijing."

"Seeing Deputy Commissar Liu and Director Li get what they deserved was a real shot in the arm. Your success is another," he said.

Lacking the fixings for a proper celebration, we sat cross-legged on the kang, Mongol-style, and talked late into the night, smoking cheap cigarettes and drinking plain boiled water.

A denunciation session was called on April 1, 1975. Even Commissar Kang showed up. Company Commander Wang opened the session by announcing the Regimental Party Committee's decision on Old Gigolo, who had misappropriated six hundred catties of animal feed, had corrupted students by pretending to be a matchmaker, and was guilty of promiscuity: He was labeled a bad element.

Following the announcement, each squad weighed in with its denunciations against him as he stood up front scowling, taking the abuse silently with no sign of contrition. Company Commander Wang closed the meeting with an announcement from Corps Command:

To: Party Committee, Fifth Division

The division verdict on the active counterrevolutionary Ma Bo and the results of his appeal have been received. After careful deliberation, the Corps Command Party Committee orders the verdict changed to serious political errors and the rescinding of supervised labor reform.

signed/Political Section
Inner Mongolian Production Corps

I wasn't completely off the hook, but I was satisfied.

"Ma Bo, come up and say something."

The silence was nearly deafening as a hundred pairs of eyes settled on me. My heart was thumping nervously, but I managed to calmly deliver my prepared comments: "The Corps Command Party Committee disposition of my case reaffirms the party's concern for students who have answered the call to go up to the mountains and down to the countryside. I am eternally grateful. Today is the first day of my new political life, and I will cherish it always. I humbly dedicate my life to serving the people."

I had finally shed the label of counterrevolutionary. No longer would I have to claw my way through wind and snow from one authority to the next or cower among the animals to keep out of sight. Now I could sit with everyone else as an equal.

45

CHAOTIC

THOUGHTS

Some of the drivers were having a bull session next door, cigarettes dangling from their mouths.

"All that hell-raising by Ma Bo looks like it paid off."

"He's a real pisser."

"I could never take having my belly rubbed that hard."

"He gets that from his old lady."

"A mother's no substitute for physical strength. That's what I envy about him, that rock-hard body of his."

Respect always comes to someone who's willing to struggle long and hard to reach a goal. I lay in the dank hut, breathing in the familiar odors of halters, wrestling clothes, and tattered leather pants. As darkness fell, rats came out for their nightly rounds, bolder than usual, assuming that the room was empty. They ran squealing to the grain sacks to scrounge corn.

My thoughts were chaotic. Having gotten used to going a month or more without seeing another human being, all those smiling faces at one time, all that encouragement, and all those friendly feelings threw me off stride. I mulled things over as objectively as possible.

I'd reached my goal, not because I was a "real pisser," but because

I'd been spurred on by the people around me: Xu Zuo, Liu Yinghong, Jin Gang, Li Xiaohua, Dumbbell, even Lei Xia. I had to earn their respect. No matter how tough the going got, no matter what I had to put up with, I would never crawl or give them cause to laugh at me. One person among them spoke only an occasional word to me, yet her image and her voice, even her smell, were a constant encouragement. I was determined that she never see me as a mangy, whipped dog.

After my troubles began, I accused the people around me of betrayal. But even then, human kindness occasionally filtered through the layer of arrogance and reached a man who disdained tenderness, who had always thrived on cruelty and violence.

And there was my mother, without whose help I'd never have seen this day. The words of the lowly carry no weight. One letter from her did the trick, while five of mine were completely ignored.

In 1967 a spate of posters criticizing Yang Mo went up in Wangfujing and around the Tiananmen viewing platform; rumors flew. But instead of trying to comfort you, Mother, I came with fellow students to ransack your home. I loathed that book of yours, with its tender sentiments. I wanted to break with you completely and throw myself into revolutionary struggle. I even smashed your carved, inlaid wardrobe and stole money for the War to Resist U.S. Aggression and Aid Vietnam.

The spirit of blood and steel was a flood tide; compassion served only the weak. To keep from being discovered when I left home, I tied up my sisters and stuffed their mouths with dirty socks despite their tearful protests. Then I scribbled slogans on the walls, the door, the floor, even the desk:

YANG MO MUST BOW HER HEAD AND ADMIT HER CRIMES!
THOROUGHLY CRITICIZE THE POISONOUS WEED *Song of Youth!*
DOWN WITH THE STINKING NOVELIST YANG MO!
LONG LIVE THE RED GUARDS!

I was spurred on by the action of trampling my own mother, bursting with self-righteous pride as one of Chairman Mao's loyal followers.

I showed my revolutionary mettle by attacking the woman who gave me life; I proved I was on the path to honor and glory by attacking my own mother; I satisfied a need for cruelty by attacking my own mother. I don't know if a wolf cub will bite its mother when she falls into a hunter's grasp, but with the Cultural Revolution as my justification, I greedily plunged a knife into my own mother's breast!

I left home, to return only on the warrior's shield.

Then my troubles began and I became an outcast. The three thousand members of the regiment kept me at arm's length, but the mother I had wanted to destroy, the woman I had robbed and abused, quietly went from place to place on my behalf, begging where necessary, even writing to Premier Zhou himself. Only a mother has a heart big enough to repay evil with good.

I began to understand this better when Xu Zuo appeared in June, having talked *his* mother into allowing him to return. In addition to some good food, he was weighted down with a satchel of books. At first we assumed he had come back to take care of the paperwork to get transferred. So we were amazed when the company commander put him in charge of the farming squad; we were sure he'd lost his mind. A team of farmworkers had been organized to harvest rocks on the mountain, and even though we advised Xu not to go, telling him that anyone who had just recovered from a liver infection was crazy to take on hard work like that, he insisted on going. He said it was peaceful there, a good place to study.

The company commander, concerned that the farmworkers would goof off if they weren't supervised, had approved his request.

We sat up talking the night before we left.

"Ma Bo, when you were in trouble, people avoided you not just because you were a counterrevolutionary, but because you were so spiteful. You denied the existence of love in the name of revolution, even labeling your mother's novel a representation of bourgeois tenderness. You enjoy cruelty, you worship it. You're mean, violent, and indifferent. That's why no one stood up for you. Am I making sense?"

"Yes," I acknowledged truthfully.

"Like the way you think Jin Gang's beneath you, even though you refuse to try to understand him. Why do you think he's so gutless? Why is he so fickle? Haven't you ever wondered? People who have room in their hearts only for themselves never try to understand others. Not even your own mother. You should be ashamed of yourself."

He really gave me hell, and I held my tongue.

Early the next morning he climbed onto my wagon with his satchel. We chatted for a while before he turned his attention to his books. It's easy to lose touch with reality from too many books and turn into a pedant with weird ideas. Killing Ingush, fighting with me, and debating Director Li were, in part at least, the actions of a pedant. All kinds of strange people share this earth. Among the students there weren't many like Xu Zuo, but there he was.

46

HER

As I was returning my wagon one afternoon I spotted some people firing assault rifles and ran over to see what was going on. Commander Wang, Wei Xiaoli, and several others were using a haystack for target practice. The regiment had ordered all companies to turn in their weapons, and they were using up the remaining ammunition before complying with the order. I looked on enviously, wishing I could join them. I hadn't fired a gun once in the seven years I'd been here, but I was too embarrassed to say anything.

After firing off two quick shots, Xiaoli turned excitedly to Commander Wang. "Let Ma Bo try!"

He smiled and handed me the rifle. "Be careful, don't shoot anybody."

Pow pow pow! I fired three shots into the wilderness, the bullets whistling through the air. The crack of the rifle was nearly deafening—me, holding a deadly weapon!

I returned to my room to savor the day's pleasant memories, particularly her look and behavior. They were encouraging signs.

Every encounter with her over a six-year period had been carefully noted in my diary, and whenever I was in one of those moods, just reading the entries perked me up:

JANUARY 16, 1972

Saw Wei Xiaoli this morning at the post office. She seemed surprised. After sizing me up, she walked to the adjoining window, a couple of feet from me. She asked for Company Seven's mail, as if doing it for my benefit.

SEPTEMBER 7, 1972

Saw Wei Xiaoli tonight at the road bend near the entrance to Company HQ. Her eyes widened when she saw me, and her lips parted slightly. A second later she lowered her head and walked on. Wore a strange expression.

SEPTEMBER 17, 1973

Went to her dorm to get some poster paper. "Did the company commander give his okay?" She was smiling. When I said yes, she opened the storeroom door, jumped onto the kang, peeled ten sheets off a roll, and handed them to me. She was still smiling, barely. Why had she jumped up there instead of taking her time?

AUGUST 5, 1974

About five this afternoon drove my wagon over to the western wall to water the horse. She was walking ahead of me. I called out gently so my inside horse could go around her, but she didn't turn to look until she reached the road bend.

NOVEMBER 13, 1974

After work I noticed that the wooden yoke had rubbed the shaft horse's back raw. The cushion had ripped and lost its contents somewhere on the road. I asked Song Chunyan in the clinic if they had any pillows stuffed with grain husks, since the company didn't. She shook her head but said she'd ask Wei Xiaoli. A few minutes later she emerged with a basin half filled with husks. She told me Wei Xiaoli had ripped open her own pillow and dumped out the husks without hesitation.

MARCH 20, 1975

Went to her dorm tonight to get a letter for home leave. In the dark hallway she was three yards from me when she held out the letter, then walked up to me with it.

JULY 3, 1975

Getting water this afternoon when she walked up. I tried to pour my bucket of water into hers, but she pulled it back and wouldn't let me. She had a gentle look on her face but stood firm.

Maybe she had feelings for me, who knows? Why else would she have made it possible for me to shoot? Or why had she given me the husks from her pillow? Or why had she walked all that way just to hand me a letter? Of course I had to admit that in general she was pretty aloof toward me. Was that because I was so mean-looking? So ugly? I often tried out different expressions in a mirror that might make me look better. If someone could have altered my wolfish eyes, pointy head, and thick lips, I'd have let them cut and drill all they wanted. I began wearing glasses so my eyes would look gentler, and a hat to cover my pointy head, even indoors. There wasn't much I could do about my thick lips, except lick them a lot to keep them moist.

Maybe I was too old (she was five years younger). Stubbornly and patiently I plucked the stubble on my chin every day, but it just grew right back. I even massaged my face to keep it looking young. Every time I washed my face I scrubbed each cheek fifty times. But time is unforgiving, and I was beginning to look like old Jiang when he was up on the mountain. I hated that mirror.

How to get her to like me? Show her I was strong as a horse? Try to be a better wrestler? Become a squad leader like Jin Gang? In the wake of the forest fire at the Sixty-third Regiment, I often thought how wonderful it would be if her face had been scarred by the flames; that would have made everything different. But she had come away unscathed.

She was so noble in my eyes that I could view her only from afar. Yet my longing grew stronger every day, fanning the flames of desire inside a twenty-eight-year-old body.

I went to ask the company commander's advice. "She won't stay here forever," he said sympathetically. "Her mother's trying to arrange a transfer home."

"I don't plan to stay here forever, either."

"She'll probably be accepted into college this year."

I didn't say anything.

"Ma Bo, be practical. As a party member, she has her position to consider." In other words, I carried a political tail around with me and was unworthy of her.

I knew I'd have to outflank Wei Xiaoli instead of mounting a frontal assault. I had to get on good terms with her friends and improve my reputation in the company. Most important of all was getting relieved of duties as a driver, because even the local girls avoided you as soon as they heard you were a driver. They called us "horse-ass nibblers."

For her sake I had to transform myself from a "horse-ass nibbler" to a horseman. So when the company accountant, who had an easy job that required frequent contact with her, was sent to the hospital in Ulanhad after being thrown by his horse, I broached the subject to the company commander. "I know how you feel," he said, "but give it time. I can't remove someone who was injured on the job. You understand, don't you?"

Maybe I should find a way to make his injuries permanent, I thought wickedly; then the job would be mine.

She seemed to be oblivious to the flame blazing in her presence. At twenty-three she was in the flower of her youth. She dressed simply: In the summer she wore a green army shirt and blue cotton trousers; in the winter she wore a lined army cap, with no scarf or mask over her face, which made her look like one of the men from the rear. No one had ever seen her in fancy clothes or leather shoes.

Maybe she considered sex sinful and romance bourgeois. Trying to figure her out was harder than guessing whether there was life on Mars. Jealously guarding her private thoughts, she avoided letting others know where she stood on sensitive issues and clammed up whenever my name was mentioned.

I sometimes wondered if she might know a lot more than we gave her credit for. As regimental branch secretary, Jin Gang had more contact with her than most, and I was forever trying to pry information out of him.

"What makes you so thickheaded?" he asked. "Marriage is the furthest thing from her mind. She just wants to get out of here."

"Me too."

"She's an ordinary girl, average-looking, with completely orthodox thoughts. You two couldn't be more different."

"I'm not talking about looks, and I don't want a girl who's like me. How much fun would it be to spend time with somebody who loves to fight and is a notorious slob?"

"Don't forget she took a safe stance where your problem was concerned, like everybody else. And she wouldn't have helped you write your posters, like Xu Zuo did."

"Just knowing she was there helped. People in trouble need a spiritual boost. I read somewhere about a man who spent years in the Bastille alone in a dark, damp cell. Then one day he found a blade of grass and was ecstatic, for from then on, whenever he was lonely, he consoled himself by looking at his companion, the blade of grass. But one day, after he'd been there over a decade, the jailer spotted the blade of grass and uprooted it. The old prisoner cried and wailed until he went mad.

Well, I had my own blade of grass while I was a target of the dictatorship of the proletariat; she was it. Whenever I wasn't sure I could go on living, seeing her made everything okay. When I felt empty and despondent, just thinking about her face and her mysterious movements put me in a better mood. When I was up on the mountain I nearly froze during the day, but at night I'd dream of her, and it was like a bonfire that drove the cold away. How can you expect me to be anything but devoted to her?"

If WEI XIAOLI was an illusory spirit off in the distance somewhere, her sister was my earthbound contact. I wrote her the day after my rehabilitation was formalized to share the good news. In late August I received a reply:

29 July 1975

Dear Ma Bo,

Your letter was waiting for me on my return.

I heard you'd been rehabilitated before I left on home leave, but didn't know the details. I'm very happy for you. Since you're no longer a counterrevolutionary, you can start a new life. What are your plans?

I can tell from your letter that you're an emotional person, especially during times of pain and stress. I felt sorry for you back then, but I'm afraid you placed too much importance in that. Maybe I didn't understand you because I'd never been in that situation. I hope the lessons you've gained from this experience will help you make important contributions to society.

This is only a hurried response to your letter. Come visit Company Nine anytime, and we can have a nice talk. I'm in the kitchen squad. This place depresses me, but that's not surprising, since I'm not a very strong person.

Sincerely,
Wei Xiaoling

Her letter arrived during the busy autumn harvest season, and although I wanted to go see her, I couldn't get away. Company Commander Wang watched us like a hawk to make sure we hauled at least two full loads a day; any less and we got yelled at.

I wished it would rain so I could go over to Company Nine. But the sun shone in a cloudless sky day after day, turning the grassland as dry as a bone.

47

EVERYONE

IS CHANGING

ONE DAY IN August I was sent to Regimental Headquarters with a wagonload of wool. Lei Xia, in a brand-new blue uniform, was coming out of the office, deep in thought. When he heard the creaking of my wagon he looked up, then lowered his head again without any discernible expression.

Director Li was walking up the road toward me. Since being relieved of his duties, he looked sick all the time, his face gaunt, his back bent as he shuffled along. Even in the oppressive heat he had a green padded jacket thrown over his shoulders. No longer interested in the female students, he smiled at everyone. Lei Xia greeted him politely, and they began talking. I'd heard that he was on temporary assignment to the Regimental Political Section; the Lei Xia who had written a protest letter to the PI was a changed man.

Back when Director Li was off on an assignment or doing grassroots work, Lei Xia would rush over to help the director's wife sweep the floor, carry water, clean out the stove, build a chicken coop, and take care of the kids. Even on home leave, this tough young man who hadn't batted an eye when I'd slapped him that time didn't forget to write Director Li to report on his thoughts. It was always "Uncle Li" this and "Auntie Tong" that.

He was a magician at networking, at uniting certain cliques, at kissing up to the leaders, and at finding cracks in the web of authority. Director Li, once his mortal enemy, was now his closest ally. That took some doing with a man who had once called him an "out-and-out reactionary."

In 1974, when Director Li went to Beijing on medical leave, Lei Xia managed to get him into a hospital. A rented car was waiting for him when he emerged from Beijing Station, and he stayed in Lei Xia's home for over a month, where he was treated like royalty. That brought the director around. Even with his questionable background, Lei Xia was admitted into the Youth League and assigned to the Political Section. I hear he made it into college, and that his future looks bright.

He was a man who would kick his best friend when he was down or grind himself into a puddle of dog piss if that's what it took to get what he wanted. Like a chameleon, he changed into whatever color the situation demanded. Repulsed by the sight of him, I cracked my whip and sped off down the road.

"Ma Bo!" someone yelled. Quickly reining in the horses, I looked to see who it was: Liu Yi of Company Three.

"How's it going? Haven't seen you around. I hear you've been rehabilitated."

He smiled and nodded. His weathered face was more leathery than ever, and he could have hidden pencils in the furrows on his brow. His lips were chapped and splitting.

"Yeah, but my wife remarried and left me with three kids." His eyes reddened.

"You'll find someone else," I consoled him. "A woman like that isn't worth getting upset over."

He smiled grimly and nodded.

"Where you off to?" I asked.

"I hurt my back and can't work. I came to get permission to go to

Hohhot to have it looked at." His eyes were so gloomy, I didn't know what to say.

"What happened to that old herdsman in your company?" he asked softly.

"Gonggele? He was reclassified as an impoverished herdsman, but the poor bastard hardly had his label removed before he up and died. It was crazy. He had only eighteen sheep, and they classified him as a herdowner."

"Oh." A pained expression spread across his face.

Gonggele, an insignificant human being, as ordinary as clay and as common as a cowchip, was gone. The cause of death was listed as respiratory failure, but I knew that my fists had hastened the end. In 1966 he was baffled at being labeled a herdowner, and in 1975 he was baffled at being rehabilitated. He was guileless as a donkey and just as docile. Not a word of protest when we beat him and ransacked his home. He was dirty, skinny, and swarthy. Like a lowly ant, he ate, he crawled into his hole, and he died, and no one took any notice. Eternal silence.

A layer of mud—he never bathed—was his constant companion all those years. Then, less than a month after he died, his wife married a man in Company Nine and took her four kids with her.

Now the face that had smiled even when being pounded lay rotting in the ground out there someplace.

Liu Yi scowled. "What good came of making a useless old man like that suffer? Get away from here while you can, Ma Bo. You're still young. Unlike me, you've got your whole life ahead of you."

That made me so sad, I wanted to cry. Time and a bitter life had taken their toll on him. The skin on his face was pitted and gouged; his eyes had the kind yet tragic look of a dying cow. He had been rehabilitated, but who would give him back his wife?

The encounter with Liu Yi cast a pall over my heart: My future didn't seem bright. I could never recapture my youth; a string of serious political errors was recorded in my dossier; and the girl I loved would have nothing to do with me.

———

EXPERIENCE SHOWED THAT settling injustices with my fists hadn't worked, so it was time to take my mother's lead and let my pen do my talking. "Face" had been important to me ever since childhood. In my senior year of middle school I had applied for admission into the Youth League by cutting my finger and signing in blood. My father had beaten the hell out of me when I got home, so infuriating me that I'd written to Premier Zhou accusing him of child abuse. Then I'd angrily ripped up a photo of him and my mother.

But that beating paled in comparison to the humiliation I suffered on the steppes. Director Li and Staff Officer Zhao had used their authority to turn me into a contemptible figure who was forced to get down on his knees and beg; there is no greater humiliation than that.

All this had to be written down. I knew I lacked a rigorous theoretical stance, was burdened with no profound philosophical views, and was woefully ignorant of contemporary aesthetics; but as long as I could reveal even a tiny slice of the society in which I had lived, and shed some light on the "up to the mountains, down to the countryside" movement, my efforts would not be wasted.

When Jin Gang found out what I was doing he said, "Why write about your sufferings? Most people couldn't care less. They've got their own problems. It'll never see the light of day, even if you do finish it. I know you want to be the voice of the downtrodden, but what good will it do if you can't get it published? Haven't you learned your lesson yet? Why make things hard on yourself?"

"I have to write it. I'll go crazy if I don't."

48

THE FINAL
STRATEGY

TALK SPREAD THAT the regiment would soon be disbanded and returned to local control. Commissar Kang tried to squelch what he called "a pack of malicious lies spread by enemies of class struggle," but cadres who had read the directives and attended the meetings knew the truth: It would be dismantled by the end of the year.

Once again the students pondered their fate.

During that period, recruitment for 1975 college admissions got under way. The competition was murderous. Thirteen members of the company signed up, including Jin Gang, Wei Xiaoli, and Li Xiaohua. Xu Zuo refused to go along with what he called a fad.

Jin Gang promoted his own case any way he could. He handed out his meal tickets like they were water, until by the end of the month he had to borrow just to get something to eat. Realizing that the regimental leadership would be reassigned elsewhere, he knew the importance of striking while the iron was hot. His heart sank when he learned that Commander Wang had chosen this critical moment to go on home leave. But Wang had his own worries.

Hardest hit by the news of the dismantling were regimental and company cadres, who ran around trying to open up avenues for the days to follow. Commander Wang had taken the unprecedented step of going on home leave on the eve of the autumn harvest, our busiest season, solely to grease the skids for his future assignment. Poor Jin Gang was like an ant on a hot skillet as he waited impatiently for Commander Wang's return.

The company rank and file held an election for college assignments: Wei Xiaoli received the top nomination, followed closely by Li Xiaohua. Jin Gang came in first among voters in the maintenance squad, farmworker squad, wagon team, and First Platoon, but got only three female votes. His offenses against so many of them had doomed his chances. Having fallen from grace, he tried to prove his mettle by finding fault with everyone else, particularly the girls in Second Platoon, reserving his harshest attacks for those who were out of favor with Commander Wang. He won the respect of his superiors at the cost of alienating his peers.

In September the vote was authenticated and the results announced. Three people were selected: Wei Xiaoli, Li Xiaohua, and Li Guoqiang. Jin Gang was furious. "It's my own fucking fault for not going to see Director Li! Who knew he'd still be running the show after being relieved of his duties? Lei Xia was right after all." Lei Xia had accompanied Director Li to Beijing after the spring planting and was now a student at Jilin University.

Once the search for college students was completed, an air of lethargy settled over the company. Hardly anyone showed up for meetings, and the pace of work slowed dramatically.

Commander Wang returned in September; when he saw the grain stacked in the compound, he launched a general mobilization. He was the company's soul: With his return, loafing was replaced by good-natured competition, as we threw ourselves into our work. No one wanted to be the butt of Wang's taunts, since he was a farmer himself. Sacks of wheat were lugged into the silos as shadows moved across the square late into the night.

On one cold autumn night I spotted Wei Xiaoli carrying a sack so heavy that her legs nearly buckled. Li Xiaohua, Song Chunyan, and the others were also carrying their loads silently, limping along under the weight. An occasional thump emerged from the silo, followed by a feminine sigh of relief. I wonder if there's another country anywhere in the world where the daughters of laborers, office workers, professors, government ministers, and provincial party secretaries work shoulder to shoulder far from home, carrying impossibly heavy sacks of grain.

WHEN I LEARNED that Wei Xiaoli would be going to the Dalian Language Institute, I lay despondently on my kang. I had worked unstintingly to get ahead, filling my wagon to overflowing every trip and doing all the loading and unloading myself, just to make sure I got a share of the praise. But I had wasted my time. Being a driver and being separated from her were my fate. Losing the fantasy of winning Xiaoli's love terrified me. Murky though it was, at least I could hold on to the illusion of love and keep a thread of hope alive.

"If you want something, first you must give it up." Keeping a woman at arm's length, giving her the cold shoulder, makes a man that much more desirable. So I feigned disinterest, saying only what was necessary when I picked up my periodicals and leaving as soon as I paid, even if we were alone. That was the way to stir up her emotions. If she looked at me in the canteen, I averted my eyes; that, too, was the way to stir up her emotions. If we were on the same tractor heading to Regimental Headquarters, I stood as far away from her as possible.

Now she was leaving. But before losing her, I would let her know what it would feel like to lose me.

The place called Three Buildings was five miles from Company Headquarters. I volunteered to pick up a load of hay there and deliver it to the East River stable. The company commander assigned Dumbbell and Liu Fulai to accompany me. We would be responsible for our own food and lodging.

Before setting out, I asked Wei Xiaoli to take my name off the mess roster (she had assumed the duties of mess officer). "And take care of my newspapers," I said. "Don't lose them." She nodded casually. I knew she'd be gone in two weeks. I turned, strode purposefully to the door, and slammed it shut behind me. Not a sound from inside. I felt so disgraced; my face was burning. You'll never see me again, slut!

We arrived at Three Buildings, where it was just us, the horizon, and the grassy steppe. It rained every day, so we took it easy. Dumbbell and Liu Fulai played cards and got drunk. I slept in a separate hut, but even with the door closed, their raucous sounds seeped in through the cracks.

I lay on the kang, wrapped in my sheepskin coat, lost in my thoughts, unable to get my mind off Xiaoli. Jin Gang said I was infatuated, not in love. Maybe so, but my feelings energized me. When she was around, even smiles from carpenter Liu's flirtatious wife had no effect on me. When she was around, I could lug two heavy sacks on my back without feeling the weight. Wherever she walked the air was fresh; wherever she sat it was warm; whatever she touched emitted a delicate fragrance.

After a few days, when the rain didn't let up, Dumbbell and Liu Fulai rode back to the company on the pretext of rounding up stray horses. Now I was all alone.

Had Wei Xiaoli left already? Would our paths cross again? I couldn't stop thinking about her. Even if she was gone, she would never forget the counterrevolutionary who had once written to her, never. Let her suffer.

The constant rain wore me out. I couldn't get her off my mind. What had I accomplished with all my schemes? Had they left a mark on her heart? Had they won her over?

Ten days passed, and my patience ran out. I decided to go back and see what was happening. That night the sky opened up, but by morning it had turned into a light drizzle that covered the grassland with a layer of mist. Dark clouds rolled up from the south. Lightning split the sky. Another downpour wasn't far off.

After changing my clothes and saddling the horse, I rode off. The rain had washed the steppe clean and green, and there were puddles all around. But the horse charged right through them, the spray soaking my pant legs. As we headed southeast, his thick black tail flew in the wind; his powerful muscles rippled.

Then the rain came again, covering the land and blotting out the sky. Cold water soaked my hair and ran down my face, chest, abdomen, legs. Still, I felt only joy, excitement, and sweetness. She can't have left already. A man was galloping through the rain toward her.

The sky cleared as I drew up to Company Headquarters. After dismounting, I wrung the water out of my clothes and stood on the crest of a hill to dry off in the wind, soon lost in my thoughts again. Is she still here? Should I go see her? If I did, all those days of avoiding her would have been wasted. Of course, I had to pick up my newspapers. Or should I ask someone to do that for me? But that would only make me look more repulsive than ever, as if I'd done something wrong. No, I'd better go. I'd do what I came to do and leave without saying much.

I checked my hand mirror to get the look just right. It seemed okay, so I remounted and rode casually up to headquarters. The horse was lathered by the time we reached the door. I knocked crisply. A girl answered: Wei Xiaoli. She looked surprised.

"Did my newspapers come?"

"No."

I turned, my heart pounding, then climbed back on my horse and dug my heels into his sides. He trotted proudly toward First Platoon. She hadn't even smiled. Are you aware, Miss Wei, that I came five miles through the rain just to see you?

I regretted my decision to return. If I'd held out a few more days, maybe she'd have greeted me with more enthusiasm. Then I learned from Jin Gang that the rain had delayed the girls' departure three days. Which meant that even as she prepared to leave, saying good-bye to me had not been in her plans. Why hadn't her face been scorched in the fire, too?

BUT STILL I wasn't finished. A young woman who had quickened my pulse for seven years was about to leave my life forever. How could I let her go without talking to her one final time? On her last night, I hid in the shadows behind the women's dorm and looked up at her room like a cat on the prowl. Giggles floated out through the window.

Don't those girls ever stop gabbing? Why don't they leave? I'll never get a chance to talk to her tomorrow, so it has to be tonight.

Eight o'clock, eight-thirty, nine, nine-thirty. On and on it goes. I'm not going to lose my last chance to talk to her, am I? I set my jaw and waited. Whenever someone walked by, I pretended I was coming from the toilet, then rushed back to my hiding place. Finally, after ten, the girls left, and I tiptoed up to her door, knocking lightly with a shaky hand.

"Come in."

She froze when she saw me, hardly able to believe her eyes.

"Since you're leaving I wanted to . . ." I swallowed hard when I saw the cold look on her face. I was going to say "chat," but changed it to "say something to you."

She sat down nonchalantly and stared at the chimney.

"Everyone's had a turn at humbling me in the name of the dictatorship of the proletariat, but I didn't deserve it." There was a scowl on my face and a sharp edge to my voice. Her eyes were still fixed on the chimney. "They were scurrilous rumors."

Silence.

"Clubs, handcuffs, fists and feet, denunciation meetings, backbreaking labor, I endured it all, but none of it changed me. I'm the same as always."

More silence. The room began to swell with it.

"What's wrong? Can't you see I'm talking to you?"

Without taking her eyes from the chimney, she said softly, "Can't this wait till tomorrow? It's getting late."

That was it, over and done with! She showed no interest in anything I had to say. I had played my trump card and lost. Sad and embarrassed, I slipped out like a thief, closing the door behind me. The light in her room wasn't shut off until very late. I know, because I stood in the darkness below grumbling to myself. "Slut, no-good slut!"

The next day was September 26, 1975. Xu Zuo came down from the mountain to take some pictures. He smiled when he saw me. "Sleep well last night?" he greeted me.

"Like a baby."

"Come on, use your head."

"Don't worry."

I walked into Wei Xiaoli's room. Her kang was piled high with note-books, hankies, shoes, mugs, and clothes her friends had given her, plus some yoghurt from the Mongols. Pieces of candy and melon seeds covered the top of her desk.

I couldn't take my eyes off her. For the first time in seven years I was free to look at her as long as I wanted and in broad daylight. Her hair, her eyes, her cheeks, her neck. I took it all in greedily. She was wearing a brand-new uniform, green as a fresh head of cabbage and just as simple. She had an oval face, a nose like a tiny shallot, high cheekbones, and a short neck, all glistening with the lustre of youth. Her breasts jutted out pertly, and she was smiling, displaying white, even teeth. Her eyes, beneath single-fold lids, radiated with the promise of a new life.

Some of the boys were there to see the girls off. "You damned well better not forget us after you start college," they said. "We expect you to write."

"I wonder if you'll admit to ever having known us once you enter the cadre ranks."

"Take heed, whoever forgets her comrades-in-arms is the daughter of a whore!"

The girls kept up a constant chatter, telling each other what to do and not to do. It had the feel of a deathbed farewell.

"Don't worry, I won't forget. Up till now all I ever thought about was leaving, but suddenly I hate the idea," Li Xiaohua said through her tears. Things had turned out pretty well for her, now that she was off to college; if she'd remained on the steppe much longer, she'd have gone stark-raving mad, for her pretty face had brought her nothing but trouble. This decent girl was taking with her the reputation of "soldiers' whore." Leave-taking has a way of wiping clean the emotional slate. Enmities, hostilities, jealousies, and scorn are canceled.

Students from all over China were suddenly struck by the beauty and permanence of the tiny bit of friendship they had shared during seven years together on the steppes, in good times and bad. In the heart of winter, after a hard day's work you returned to discover that your bed-ridden roommate had gone to the mess hall to pick up your food, which sizzled on the stove. When you were sick someone hitched up a wagon to take you across the steppe to the regimental clinic. People returned from home visits loaded down with pastries, candies, and peanuts to pass out to less fortunate friends. If you forgot toilet paper, one of the students unhesitatingly tore a clean page out of his diary for you.

Conflicts were unavoidable among people with such diverse back-grounds, experiences, personalities, and interests. But seven years of living together—sleeping in the same yurts, eating from the same pots, drinking from the same wells, using the same washboards—had erased differences in customs, emotional displays, language, and habits, until you could no longer tell what was yours and what was mine.

The company commander had neither given the order to stop working nor encouraged people to see their friends off—it was all quite spontaneous. Even some of the more feudal-minded boys, who hardly ever spoke to girls, came to say good-bye to Wei Xiaoli and Li Xiaohua as a tractor chugged up, spewing dark clouds from its smokestack. Nearly everyone rushed up to help the departees load their luggage.

"See you later, Ma Bo," Xu Zuo said as he climbed into the driver's seat. "After I drop them off, I'm heading back up the mountain." I was too busy watching Wei Xiaoli to worry about him. She had climbed aboard, her face radiant. I watched her every move, mesmerized.

"Oh!" she blurted to Li Xiaohua. "I left my book bag in the room."

"Go get it, hurry. There's still time."

She jumped down and ran back to her room, which was now deserted. I followed her, like a stalking panther. After picking up her bag, she turned and found herself face to face with me. Her eyes widened in amazement. The blood rushed to my head.

"Xiaoli, since you're leaving, I . . . I have something to say to you." I took a deep breath, as everything I meant to say vanished without a trace. Trying to talk to her was the hardest thing I'd ever done. "Oh, it's nothing, I said it all last night. I guess that's it, then. So long." I don't know how I got those last words out.

Her look of amazement gave way to a smile, a warm, gentle smile that flooded the room with its light. It was meant for me, for me and no one else!

The sound of the tractor revving up outside was nearly ear-splitting. A signal for her to hurry. I looked at her one more time, then steeled myself and said softly, "Time to go."

Not knowing how to respond, she nodded and blushed deeply, then turned and ran out the door.

On my way out I scooped up one of her cast-off melon seeds from the desktop and stuffed it into my pocket.

She grabbed the railing and hoisted herself up by stepping on the tire of the tractor, which roared again, spewed another cloud of black smoke, and began to inch forward. Even with the gas pedal all the way to the floor, producing noise that was deafening, the tractor moved at a snail's pace.

We all waved, as though on command. The tractor wrenched sobs from the girls left behind, the decibel count rising as the sobs turned to full-fledged wails. I waved as she lowered her head to wipe her tear-filled eyes with the back of her hand. That was when Li Xiaohua lost it: Her head sagged onto Wei Xiaoli, and her shoulders began to heave.

As the radiant autumn sun climbed into the clear sky, forty or more young women gave themselves over to their emotions. Some lay on the ground and wept, others leaned against the wall, and still others stomped their feet and thumped their chests in torment. It was a loud, persistent, alarming noise; even Liu Fulai, always the clown, was un-characteristically subdued.

The tractor, heartless in its unconcern, moved farther and farther into the southwest, eventually vanishing into the horizon. Still, the girls cried: tears for friendship, tears for themselves, tears for their fate. What else could they do? Other girls were heading off to college, or had been reassigned, or were going home on sick leave, or had departed for jobs elsewhere. But where were they going to wind up? Were they supposed to become apprentices or find husbands, now that they were already in their thirties? Who would want to look at a face so far removed from its youth? How about mating with one of the locals, like some farm animal? Someone to cook and bear kids for, someone who needed a seamstress? These thoughts were so painful that crying seemed the only answer.

Fate had played a cruel trick on those girls.

Finally, everyone drifted off, leaving the Company Headquarters area deserted. No more sounds of crying, or of food service in the mess hall, or of card-playing. Each room was quieter than the next. It was like the stillness of death.

I returned to the wagon-team hut, where Dumbbell was lying face down on the kang, sobbing. I felt like crying too. Finally, unable to stand it any longer, I went to the clinic to pick up a sedative and visit with Song Chunyan, Wei Xiaoli's best friend. I don't know why, but the moment I saw her, tears welled up in my eyes and were on their way out, just as Liu Fulai walked in. Pride won out over emotions— barely—as I forced back the tears.

It was after six o'clock when I strolled out into the night and gazed off to the west, where a few threads of light held on tenaciously. A tiny flock of wild geese was heading south, an occasional honk breaking the silence as they passed overhead.

Was my angel gone forever? Impossible. There was always her sister, my link, the one I would never abandon. Fidgety and distracted, I decided to take her up on her invitation to go visit. I hastily saddled the black horse, which snorted loudly, reared its powerful head, then galloped out onto the dark steppe. Sorry to make you work tonight, old friend.

Faster, faster! I whipped him on. The wind whistled past us as we crossed Company Seven pastureland, and when we entered the barren territory of Company Three, the horse was transformed into a black dragon that arched and coiled through the night sky.

I pulled up to the Company Nine kitchen-squad dorm at around nine o'clock. After tethering the horse, I went to the mess hall. I could still feel the wind in my face and the ground rising to meet me as I walked unsteadily up to the door and banged on it.

"Who's there?"

"It's me."

The door was opened by a frightened, chubby girl whose hair was a mess.

"Is Wei Xiaoling in?"

"She left for Regimental Headquarters two days ago."

I looked past her into the room. Three trunks wrapped with burlap bags and tied with hemp cords rested on an empty bunk. Blue cloth tags on the cords fluttered from blasts of wind coming in through the door.

"When will she be back?" What was going on here?

"She got permission to leave. But she might still be at the regiment."

The news hit me like a haymaker. Trying hard to compose myself, I glared at the girl before turning to leave. It was nearly ten o'clock.

She saw me out the door. "What's the rush?" she asked with a smile. "Xiaoling is probably scheduled to leave with the kids going off to college."

The horse was all lathered, but I didn't have time to worry about him now. I leapt into the saddle and took off for Regimental Headquarters. The road, packed hard by the wheels of trucks and wagons, rose to meet us, and the hills retreated slowly into the distance. As the animal's panting grew more labored, his gait slowed. I whipped him mercilessly, not content to move at a canter when a gallop was required.

The night was deepening. The horse's hooves were pounding. My brain was clouded, my seat was rubbed raw, my pant legs were soaked by horse sweat. I was fucking crazy, crazier than I'd ever been, and loving it. The crazed are pure and innocent, unafraid, and powerful. Madness is a magnificent force for creating miracles.

It was midnight by the time I reached Regimental Headquarters. The plodding of my horse's hooves was the only sound on the deserted street. When my head cleared, I realized I had no idea how to find her, and even if I did, she would be sound asleep.

The horse was so exhausted, he couldn't raise his drooping head. I reined him in as I passed the regimental guest house. Maybe Xiaoli herself is sleeping on the other side of that hazy window, I thought to myself. She'll never know that someone, more an apparition than a human being, had turned his eyes toward her as she slept on this particular night.

Eight hours of riding, over thirty miles, until my powerful mount was frothing at the mouth, his legs covered with mud, lathered from head to tail, and surely skinnier than when we had started out. It took us until two that morning to drag ourselves back to the wagon team.

I was worn out, sleepy, and sore from the long, futile ride. All I had to show for my seven-year pursuit of an angel was the inky darkness of night. I wrapped my hand tightly around the melon-seed husk, a sacred memento.

49

THE GRASS
IS GONE

THE LIFE WENT out of Company Seven. Her quarters lost their redolence, the sow with the sagging belly became hideous, even the sky was a duller blue. I continued taking my wagon out each day, but so list-lessly that I didn't notice when the rigging got tangled around the horses' legs. My nights were devoted to writing about my experiences in Inner Mongolia. I wanted to put every bit of it in there.

Three weeks later I received a letter from Taiyuan. Could it be from her? As I tore open the envelope, my hand shook with nervous excite-ment. I was like a man standing in the dock awaiting the verdict, heart pounding madly.

October 20, 1975

Dear Ma Bo:

I've been transferred to my home in the provincial capital. I can't find the words to describe my feelings during those last few days there. I was beaten down.

Our status plummeted after my father's tragic death. I know I never suffered like you did, but those six years in the border region took a terrible toll on me. I wasn't even a member of the Youth League when I left.

My father's good name has been restored now, but that won't bring him back. Even coming home hasn't helped much. I think I've forgotten how to laugh. Those six years are a murky image that won't go away. I know I'll never forget the steppe.

I don't know what I have to look forward to. I guess we have to make our way through life as best we can. Everything we relied upon is gone. Even the sad image of my father will disappear soon enough. In August Deng Xiaoping ordered the restoration of my father's good name, and my transfer home was approved by the Provincial Party Committee in conjunction with party policy. But my boyfriend is still out there on the steppe.

I sympathize with you where your feelings for Xiaoli are concerned, but there's nothing I can do. She says it's too early to think about marriage. I told her to treat you better, but she won't listen. Don't let it get you down. They say first love never works out anyway, since it's so beautiful and life is so ugly. Besides, you two are totally different. She hates brute force, so even if you got together, you could never be happy.

There's an air of tragic romanticism in all your frustrating experiences. I don't think anyone should have to know such a hard life, but I respect your will to keep struggling. I hope you take advantage of the lessons you've learned to make real contributions to society. I've always known you're not someone to let your life slip idly by.

Wishing you the best,
Wei Xiaoling

I read the letter at least a dozen times, wanting to absorb every drop of information it held. It was getting dark outside. I closed my eyes and lay motionless. As night fell it began to rain. Even the heavens were weeping for me. Freezing rain fell the next day, a perpetual moan.

Autumn grass, withered and yellow,
Autumn nights, dark and bleak,
Autumn winds, softly sobbing,
Autumn rains, cascading tears . . .

I lay quietly under my sheepskin coat, blotting out the light by burying my face in the thick wool. My little blade of grass was gone. I lay in bed the whole day, neither eating nor drinking. I sought solitude, darkness, the embrace of my coat, and no interruptions. Life was bitter— bitter and meaningless.

The next day was the same. A pair of rats chased each other around my bed and across my body. I could have scared them off by merely shrugging my shoulders, but didn't feel like it.

Xu Zuo returned the next day, and the moment I laid eyes on him, I began to weep. I was calm enough, but tears slid unchecked down my cheeks.

"You haven't eaten for two days?"

I didn't say anything.

"I thought you were a bigger man than that."

"Shakespeare wrote that ninety percent of the people are slaves to their emotions."

"That may be," he said, "but not willing slaves like you."

"She was the sole blade of grass in my tortured life."

"Whatever happened to equality? A carrying pole needs a basket on both ends. Why did you chase her when you saw she was ignoring you? You should be ashamed of yourself."

I glared at him. "True love *means* being ashamed of yourself! Just because she doesn't love me doesn't mean I can't love her. In case you're interested, she smiled at me before she left."

"You see, that's your problem. You think Wei Xiaoli has the hots for you."

"No, I don't."

"Okay, then tell me what's so great about her?"

"I don't know."

"I think you're in love with love," he said maliciously. "You don't care who it is, so long as you can go off half-cocked and fall in love."

"True love is always going off half-cocked. You aren't supposed to be able to say why you love somebody."

"Bullshit! You call yourself a man, but I say you're a disgusting fucking wimp."

His words cut like a knife. Throwing off the coat covering my face, I sat up and thundered, "You goddamned queer, you've got a prick but no balls! You don't know the first thing about love, and you don't give a shit about me!"

"Who says so? There are all kinds of wimps, but I've never seen one like you. You're pitiful!"

"So what? Get out and leave me alone!"

He stormed out of the room.

THE WORST PASSED after a few days, and I returned to the land of the living, throwing myself into my writing as never before, since it alone gave me strength and healed my wounds. I cut myself off from the outside world. Except for the time spent working, eating in the mess hall, and going to the toilet, I wrote. No visiting, no bull sessions; I didn't even wash my clothes.

Everything coalesced into a single point of light at the tip of my pen. She had returned the twenty pages I wrote her. Now I was going to write fifty times twenty pages. Let her return *them*. Let her try to run away from *these!* Skeins of tangled emotion spilled onto the pages. The kang became my desk, an upturned bucket my chair. I wrote until I was light-headed and breathless; then I wrote some more. I didn't have to worry about the creative process. I just wrote what happened, letting the story tell itself.

50

THE CORPS
IS DISBANDED

In November 1975, Directive 95 from the State Council and Central Military Commission ordered the disbanding of the Production Corps and the transfer of all its property. The farmer-herdsman regiment thus became a state-run farm and ranch. All active-duty cadres were transferred out.

Trying to take advantage of the confusion of turning over the property, I asked Jin Gang if he would purge my dossier of evidence of my serious political errors. As Xiaoli's replacement, he had a key to the file cabinet where the dossiers were kept. After a contemplative pause, he said, "If anybody found out, it'd be my ass."

"Only you and I would know, so what's the problem?"

"It's still dangerous. We'll have to wait for the right moment." He rolled his foxlike eyes, awaiting my reaction.

The right moment? He had access to the key, so the moment was always right. His position would be eliminated in two days, and where the fuck would that leave me then? Keeping a tight rein on my disappointment, I said in the friendliest voice possible, "What's the big deal? It's only a lousy piece of paper."

The next evening he came to see me, closed the door behind him, and said softly, "I did it, but don't you dare tell anyone."

I took the sheet of paper from him, then put a match to it. The misguided disposition of my case turned to ashes without so much as a crackle.

"Ma Bo, never ever breathe a word of this to anyone. I mean it. Even if we wind up on different ends of the earth."

Another group of students was preparing to depart in conjunction with the disbanding of the corps. The girls whose faces had been scarred by the fire, who never appeared in public without gauze face masks, were allowed to return home. Meanwhile, there was a frenzy of cadre nominations, promotions, and firings. Compassion was the order of the day; maybe guilty consciences were getting the better of certain people. Whatever the reasons, the cadres bent over backwards to satisfy all reasonable requests from the common folk. But that didn't keep the herdsmen from vilifying them.

The first order of business for the new commander of Company Seven was to announce that reclamation activities had destroyed the ecology of the steppes, with a loss of water and topsoil, virtually turning them into a desert. So, in accordance with directives from the Agricultural Bureau of the Local League, Company Seven was to be converted from a farmer-herdsman unit into a stock-raising unit exclusively. Maintenance squads would be reassigned to Company Three. All agricultural activity was to cease in accordance with the new policy.

With that order, the reclamation of twenty thousand acres of barren land over a six-year period was invalidated. We simply abandoned the forty grain silos, each of which had required twenty thousand adobe blocks, a total of eight hundred thousand. The thirty seed warehouses were converted to animal enclosures where cattle, donkeys, and pigs could shit, sleep, drink, and scratch themselves.

With that order, the sweat from laying thirty-five thousand square yards of concrete was wasted. The ground beneath the concrete square, which was the size of a soccer field, had been prepared with a rock foundation a foot thick—hundreds of wagonloads of rocks lugged down the mountain, day and night; now the glistening concrete floor was the repository of cowshit, the cracks home to clumps of tall weeds. In town it would have made a great skating rink. Too bad the only skaters here were a few donkeys and cows.

Over and done with. For eight years we had labored for this. And it was worse, for we had wreaked unprecedented havoc on the grasslands, working like fucking beasts of burden, only to commit unpardonable crimes against the land.

All that back-breaking labor to smash rocks that were spread across the steppes; hundreds of thousands of adobe blocks left to crumble in the elements; lumber from countless trees harvested under a blazing sun plundered and gone.

A huge international joke. The depletion of resources was staggering; the waste of manpower, mind-boggling; the financial losses, incalculable.

Everyone stopped working. Why not? Leaving was all we cared about, one way or another, even if it meant slipping a coin in front of your chest during an X ray. A few even tried carving official-looking seals out of carrots. One by one the students left, and as our number dwindled, those of us who remained behind grew increasingly anxious. The exciting, tense, fulfilling days in corps units were gone forever. The paper over the glassless windows in now-empty rooms rustled and snapped in the cold late-night winds. The grounds were littered with worn-out shoes and socks and empty paper cartons abandoned by departing students.

Off to the north, grain silos we'd built without the luxury of lumber, after earnestly studying the progressive experiences of the Thirty-first Regiment, collapsed in the wind and rain, the ruins burying rocks that had served as their foundations.

To the south, irrigation ditches we had gouged out of the rock-hard earth in the winter of 1970 with explosives and burning road apples, "learning from Dazhai," were clogged with yellow sand. During the previous autumn, Company Commander Wang had ordered us to dredge them, but that had not altered their fate.

To the west, weeds stood knee-high in private experimental gardens parceled out by Company Commander Wang. The produce in the ground had long since been eaten by roving stock animals.

And to the east, vast stretches of reclaimed wasteland were covered by artemisia taller than a man. The cattle and horses wouldn't touch it.

The corps ended its days amid destruction and desolation.

The once-beautiful steppe, with its blanket of downy green, looked as if it had been ravaged by wild dogs.

LIU FULAI, who inveighed against company women for being so ugly, got cozy with a nurse at Regimental Headquarters. He also had his way with several of the others. They called him a thug, but he just tossed his long hair and growled, "They're all a bunch of fucking thugs, from the PI all the way up to the corps leaders. If they're not scam artists, they're womanizers. And the higher the rank, the bigger the thug. We're forbidden from laying our hands on local women, so they can take the cream of the crop."

As for Dumbbell, when he wasn't scrounging food somewhere, he was busy trying to find someone to marry him. The locals, men and women alike, looked down on bachelors. In their eyes, anyone who couldn't find a wife was worthless. So he spent much of his time primping: changing his clothes, polishing his shoes, dyeing his hair, squeezing his zits. He rubbed so much scented lotion all over himself, you could smell him coming a mile off, like a musk ox in heat.

Then there was Jin Gang, who not only failed to get into college but offended so many people along the way that he was universally seen as a ruthless person. Knowing that his days of glory were over once the new regime was in place, he holed up in his room in the throes of a major depression. Cold reality had shattered his hopes and his modest ambitions. Everything wearied him now, everything but getting drunk and being a glutton. Even sleeping with his new girlfriend couldn't rouse him. Naturally he took advantage of the situation, but inattentively and cavalierly. When they did it, he usually forgot to lock the door or left the curtain open, and they were caught more than once. He didn't care what other people said.

One after another his bubbles burst—entering the party, going to college, returning to Beijing. Since his dreams were shattered, he concentrated on working in the kitchen, where he sat at the table shucking beans, sometimes all morning long, or plucking pork bristles with a pair of tweezers, often from noon till bedtime. He wore a gloomy expression during the day, hardly ever speaking. But his smile reappeared when the bottle came out, and you couldn't shut him up.

His obsession with pork was astonishing. If he heard it was being sold at one of the other companies, he borrowed a horse and was off, even if it was miles away. And if you walked in on him while he was cooking some of it, he made sure you knew that it was more important to him than you were. He would chat reluctantly and inattentively, his eyes seldom straying from the pot on the stove.

As for me, as soon as the workday was over, I returned to my little room to write, oblivious to my surroundings.

Write, write, write.

The nib of my pen seemed to spew flames and thick clouds of smoke, for beneath those ugly, scribbled characters lay my heart and soul, which I desperately wanted her to see.

51

THE PI

IS PROMOTED

PILES OF BOOKS, newspapers, and old issues of *Red Flag* were stacked in the corner of my sod hut; a thin layer of murky ice adorned the surface of the washbasin, which had once been filled with cowchips; a half-eaten bun on the stovetop was covered with ash. I sat on the water bucket and leaned over the kang to write, a dozen or so sheets of manuscript strewn across the comforter. This was my battlefield.

Write, write! Pour out my loves, my hates, and my shames. I wanted the world to know.

Write, write! Every night, without fail, and during every break of every day. So little time to create a bombshell to hurl at all those enemies of the people. Taking care of Wang Lianfu had only been a warm-up. I was setting my sights on those at the top, determined that history judge them for what they were.

Write, write! Keep carving this marker in the wilderness.

In early December I went to Western Ujimqin to arrange for a transfer, hoping to catch a ride back on a truck from the radar station; my family had lined up a job for me in Shanxi. The company commander said no, the truck was overloaded. But I begged and cajoled until I wheedled permission out of him.

The truck was piled high with furniture reputed to belong to a high-ranking cadre. At around dusk we got stuck in a frozen lake, and the poor driver couldn't get us moving again. Since the light was fading, we had to unload the truck. Off it came: huge wooden chests, large rugs, bundles of lumber, sacks of flour, sheaves of animal skins. I'd never seen so much stuff. The girls complained bitterly: "How can somebody who arrives with only a bedroll accumulate enough stuff to fill a five-ton truck?"

I picked up a cabinet tied with cords and heaved it to the ground. *Crash!* The door flew open. Served him right. A knife fell out. I picked it up and studied it in the moonlight. It was suspiciously similar to the one I'd confiscated from the herdsman back in '69, the one the PI had accused me of holding back. Upon closer inspection, I noticed that the top of the cabinet was carved with Mongol markings, and suddenly everything came clear. Old Shen had appropriated the stuff we had taken in our house searches.

Crash! Bang! I began heaving things off the truck as if they were spent lightbulbs. The others followed suit. *Bang!* A large wooden chest broke apart, and all sorts of junk rolled out into the snow. The greedy bastard had saved up all the fountain-pen caps, soap dishes, vacuum-bottle shells, tattered comforter covers, and split shoes we had discarded. It didn't take much for his eyes to light up. Even an old bridle for a camel thrown away in the wilds by a herdsman, so moth-eaten that you couldn't make shoe inserts out of it, wound up in his chest. A pitiful specimen of a man.

Two large chests remained on the truck when the driver tried to get the truck unstuck, but no matter how he raced the engine, the wheels just spun on the ice. No good, we'd have to unload those last two chests, which were twice the size of coffins. They were so bulky, four young men couldn't budge them. As he wiped his sweaty brow, the driver said, "How do you expect to lift those? They needed a crane to load them."

"What the hell's in them?"

"Grain. No one will ever accuse your bosses of having too many scruples. I've carted belongings for lots of them, and every one takes this much. Even if I'm fully loaded, they insist on piling more stuff on. What am I supposed to do?"

Late that night a truck arrived to give us a tow. We tossed Political Instructor Shen's junk back up onto the truck, like so many stones, which added to the breakage.

While waiting for the tow truck I thought back to the summer of 1973, when the students covered the grain silos with their quilts, always ready to sacrifice. When we ransacked the herdsmen's homes I was the only one who ever took anything, and only one lousy knife. Nothing of value ever stuck to our fingers. Liu Yinghong would rather sleep under a threadbare commune blanket than a borrowed sheepskin coat. So what happened? It all wound up as the personal property of the PI and his cronies. No wonder Old Gigolo complained, "This gang of 'Communists' did things even the old landlords wouldn't do!"

Political Instructor Shen, a man who had tirelessly led us in our studies of the works of Chairman Mao and patiently taught us to create a revolutionary outlook and serve the people with all our hearts— strange how someone like that could whore around and get his sticky fingers on anything he wanted while remaining unyielding in his political principles.

The next day I went to see Section Chief Lei, who was home dandling one of his children and seemed genuinely pleased to see me.

"How are you doing, Ma Bo?" He shook my hand warmly, offered me a cigarette, and poured me some tea.

I said I needed help getting transferred out. I was worried that my papers might get stuck at the relocation office, which left me no option but to try a "back door."

"No problem. Give me your papers."

I told him about Shen's truckload of junk.

He didn't bat an eye. "He's been promoted and transferred to the Second Independent Division in Inner Mongolia as number two man in a regimental logistics department."

"What? They must be fucking blind to assign someone like that to run a logistics department!"

"It's always the grassroots cadres who take advantage of their material contacts."

"What happened to Deputy Commissar Liu and Chairman Li from our regiment?"

He answered calmly, "Some problems are harder to resolve than others. Li flatly denied the charges, and the evidence was inconclusive. So our hands were tied. Liu is on party probation for a year. After that he'll be sent to a military farm in Shanxi as commissar."

We talked a while longer, and the way he played with the child the whole time left a deep impression on me. He didn't need guns or handcuffs to frighten people; his humanity was the only weapon he needed.

"What about my diary and letters, Director Lei? I'll get them back, won't I?"

He smiled broadly. "They're still at the Security Section. Let them stay there. They're very problematic."

5 2

A TOAST

At noon on the first of April we chipped in to buy some wine and canned food. Dumbbell, caught up in the emotions of the moment, got his hands on some pork and five eggs, which Jin Gang whipped into a pot of his renowned stewed pork; we set a table for four in the dilapidated wagon-team hut.

"I've got news for you guys," Dumbbell said. "Political Instructor Shen decided he wanted his chickens to lay more eggs, so he started burning a lightbulb in the chicken coop twenty-four hours a day. The old guy's got a head for modern technology."

"Don't sell old Shen short. He got stacks of lumber without spending a cent, then used it to make himself some furniture. And that's just the tip of the iceberg. So what happened? He got promoted."

Xu Zuo looked at me. "How about our friendly public-security officer, Zhao, who always bragged about how clean his hands were? Remember how mad he got when the subject of graft or corruption came up? Well, he was probably Injgan Sum's 'prince of graft.' He shipped out nine huge crates of loot. He and his family arrived as paupers and wound up with a three-room, tile-roofed house. He got fat here, then when he left he bellowed, 'You're all jealous. There wasn't a decent human being in all of Injgan Sum, me included!' Can you believe that kind of talk from a military man?"

"He was a master at kissing Director Li's ass."

"Okay, enough already. There's wine to be drunk," Dumbbell said.

"They ought to shoot those ass-kissers," Xu Zuo insisted through clenched teeth. Jin Gang kept his head lowered and his mouth shut, his stock still not improved.

Since we had no glasses, we poured the wine into enamel mugs, rice bowls, even a kettle lid, then raised the liquor in a solemn toast: "To our generation. Bottoms up!"

We drank.

"To comrades who gave their lives in the fire! Bottoms up!"

We drank.

"To our half-assed production corps!"

"To Ma Bo, who came back from the brink!"

"To Dumbbell in his quest for the ideal wife."

Our borrowed table was covered with cans of salted walnuts, lunch meat, braised pork, preserved fish. We slugged the wine down like water as we ate, the sounds of four busy mouths reverberating through the freezing sod hut.

"A song," Xu Zuo suggested. "Let's liven things up."

"Jin Gang, you start."

He wiped his greasy mouth, cleared his throat, and began:

> Good-bye to my home, good-bye to Mama,
> I've come to the Inner Mongolian steppes,
> Where loneliness is my sole companion.
> No meat, no greens, no oil,
> Skinny as a rail, I lug stones on my back.

> I go out dressed in stars and return wearing the moon,
> I rearrange the earth,

It is my sacred duty.
No back door to enter, no gifts to hand out,
Just coolie labor, and no chance of going home.

"Drink up, guys," Dumbbell blubbered. "Don't let it get you down."

We wanted to cry, we wanted to scream: Long live our generation, long live the students. Fuck!

Jin Gang, seemingly unaffected, sang on:

My song greets the golden sun,
My oars break the waves.
The young navigator keeps the eternal lamp burning
With the sparks of his youth.

Wei Xiaoli had sung that once. Hearing it now released a torrent of tears. She's lost to me forever. My only mementos are the green patches she sewed onto my pants back in 1970 and the husk of a single melon seed.

No, the girl I love is alive and breathing, a Wei Xiaoli who will never perish. She is sacred, a goddess. I'll cherish my love for her forever and always.

A real man doesn't sip his wine, so I polished off a bowlful of the dark red liquid without coming up for air. Jin Gang, who had a reputation as a pretty good drinker, couldn't match that.

Xu Zuo refilled my bowl. "Drink up, Ma Bo. What do you have against getting drunk? The herdsmen say that a man stops thinking about himself when he drinks, and concentrates on the bonds of friendship."

I happily drained a second bowlful of sweet, dark wine.

"Say, Ma Bo, I hear you ran into Lei Xia at a restaurant in Western Ujimqin Banner," Dumbbell said as he shoved a piece of pork into his mouth.

"Yeah. He asked me to slug him, but I wouldn't do it, so the drunken bastard hit himself over the head with a bottle."

"Finally you did the right thing, Ma Bo," Jin Gang said. "Fists are for kids. You should put all that behind you."

"Why would I want to slug him? Back when we were wrestling, I could toss him around like a head of cabbage."

"I'll say this one more time, Ma Bo," Xu Zuo said. "Stop bragging about how tough you are, because brute strength won't take you very far in this world. Sooner or later everybody gets old and soft. I'm not trying to make you feel bad, but how do you think you drove Wei Xiaoli away? If she had seen you go after Gonggele that time, with murder in your eyes, I'll bet she wouldn't have smiled at you before she left. That's no bullshit."

"Drink up," I said, not wanting to talk about it.

"Hold on, I'm not finished. The Inner Mongolian Production Corps claimed to have one hundred thousand students and six mechanized divisions with thousands of trucks and tractors. We cultivated thousands of acres of barren land and smashed millions of rocks. So what good did all that strength do anybody? How long will it take for the steppes to return to what they are meant to be? The losses, counted in years, will never be completely recouped. It's the same with people. Take my word for it, a clear head is worth ten strong legs."

"Keep drinking, and quit lecturing me. I've thought about what you're saying, but this is neither the time nor the place to discuss it. Here, let's drink to the future of our bookworm."

Xu Zuo drained his glass, his pale face beginning to turn red, and quickly refilled it. "Let's not forget to toast Jin Gang's early admission into the party and the beginning of his meteoric rise."

Jin Gang glared at him. "You're drunk. Don't make fun of me."

"Who's making fun of you? And stop scowling all the time."

"Ma Bo, you won't forget the border region and your hoe-wielding brothers after you leave, will you?"

"Why the fuck would I do that? Of course not." That pissed me off.

The company had three buildings when we arrived; now the people were housed in nearly two hundred. There wasn't a single tree on the steppe when we arrived; now there was a line of them, all green and shiny, behind the company area. The herdsmen never ate green vegetables before we arrived; now the company could boast a fifty-acre truck farm, with turnips, squash, potatoes, and scallions. Those were the changes we wrought.

Underpaid, poorly dressed Production Corps troopers were fed coarse, gritty millet and endured bitter cold and back-breaking labor that exacted a heavy toll on their bodies. They risked life and limb to fight a forest fire that left them scarred and crippled or dead. They made adobe blocks until they couldn't lift their rice bowls at night. They crawled over rocks and tumbled down rock-strewn paths, so cold that their tears froze on their cheeks and their brittle tendons nearly snapped. Contributions? You can count on it.

How could I forget those students, with their dirty hands and muddy feet, the electrical cords that held up their pants, the legs of worn trousers wrapped around their necks as scarves? Me? Forget those sallow-faced bandits? Never!

A ringing in my ears drowned out all other noises. I reached out for my bowl of wine with a trembling hand and gazed at the ripples in the dark red liquid that had the sweet fragrance of fresh grass and the kick of a wild bronco.

I tipped my head back and drank it down.

Dumbbell, by now pretty drunk, raised his glass and sang a song we'd first heard upon our arrival:

> *Sure I miss my dad,*
> *Sure I miss my mom,*
> *Sure I miss my home,*
> *But they won't let me leave.*
> *What am I to do?*

Memories flooded my mind.

Some people adapted easily to life in Inner Mongolia, while for others it was a constant struggle. A small number actually thrived out there, moving effortlessly up the ladder. Me, I had to crawl every inch of the way, squeezing through the cracks amid boulders like a crippled dog.

Eight years. How many "eight years" are there in the prime of a man's life?

I don't cry as a rule, but this time the tears really flowed. I was joined by Xu Zuo, also overcome with emotion.

"Drink up, you guys," Dumbbell said sympathetically. "Don't get carried away by your emotions."

How could we avoid it? If ever there was a time to let it all out, this was it.

The "Empress Dowager's" gloomy face materialized in front of me. Blood rushed to my tear-streaked face. "How could you have been such a fool, Chairman Mao, to marry someone like that? Your people are suffering terribly!" I'd never have said this aloud if not for the wine.

Jin Gang's face was ashen. He was grasping his hair with one hand and stuffing a piece of meat into his mouth with the other. He didn't bat an eye at my reactionary outburst. He was too busy eating. Dumbbell and I were amazed to see how much food and wine a scrawny guy like that could put away. In order to lighten the general mood, he jumped up, ran back to the dorm, and returned with another bottle of wine and a pack of Peony cigarettes.

My belly felt as if it would pop. So did my head. Everything in the room, from halters to grain sacks, floated and spun in the air.

What a rotten shame! We fought like animals. For what? To be chosen for college, to get an easier job, to hear a word of praise.

A clever yet naïve Qi Shuzhen traded her body for party membership; Lei Xia, once so loyal, turned to snitching on his buddies in order to survive; and there were others who would drive a tractor, guard grain silos, work a stove, or anything else that came along, just to land a job in the health clinic.

What had turned decent young people into animals like that? We were dupes of class struggle, made to howl at the moon like a pack of dogs.

China, you cowered beneath the skirts of a witch.

We wept silent tears over the incalculable waste created by the Production Corps and the meaningless years of zealous labor. We wept for our nation and for our scars.

We were drunk, yet we kept drinking, as if each swig meant one less wolf out on the steppes or one more sack of grain for the nation.

The blood red wine was everywhere: the table, the rug, the floor, the air. A red mist, red waves of light, red silhouettes, red everywhere, red red red, emitting a strong fermented odor.

Tons of fresh red blood surged toward me, engulfing me. Rivers of fresh red blood flowed to the mountains, flowed through the ravines, covered the fields, inundated the steppes. Where had it come from? Where was it going? The blood of youth, was it worth nothing in the end?

On my slow trip to oblivion I sensed dark figures moving through the waves of blood. The forest fire raged in front of me, turning the sky a deep red. Liu Yinghong's smiling face appeared in the midst of the conflagration, only to be consumed by flames. Sixty-nine sweat-soaked students charged the wall of flames, shouting, cursing, screaming. One by one they fell and were burned to cinders.

53

FAREWELL TO
THE STEPPES

THE TRANSPORTATION COMPANY phoned to say the bus would not be leaving the next day as scheduled, so we climbed onto the kang fully dressed and slept like tightly packed logs.

The next day our new boss sent Xu Zuo up the mountain. The nationwide "Learn from Dazhai" conference had been concluded, and the Agricultural Section of the Autonomous Region ordered a wintertime "Learn from Dazhai" movement, thereby transforming a slack period into a peak farming season. Our boss was worried that the gang of farmworkers on the mountain would stand around if Xu Zuo wasn't there to watch them.

"Ma Bo, I won't be able to give you a sendoff after all," he said, now that he was needed up on the mountain. "They won't take no for an answer."

"Why knock yourself out while everyone else takes it easy?"

He nodded and said sadly, "When I see all those rocks we carried down the mountain lying buried in the ground, and the houses we built all crumbling and falling apart, and the irrigation ditches we dug clogged with sand, it makes me sick. An officer gives an order and the soldiers work till they drop. I wonder how many other countries have seen their riches squandered by the incompetence of the people in charge? I've learned my lesson. If I do nothing from now on, I'll still earn my thirty-two fifty a month. I'm going to immerse myself in a bunch of good books up there."

He and Jin Gang were bundled up in felt boots, tightly cinched sheepskin coats, fur caps, and gloves, like mountain climbers about to assault a peak. We shook hands good-bye, then Xu Zuo climbed onto the wagon and, in a muffled voice, gave the command, "We're off to learn from Dazhai!" Jin Gang grumbled, "The more we learn, the worse off everyone is. But what the hell, the steppe doesn't belong to me."

As the wagon rolled onto the road, they nodded and smiled, then faced forward and buried their necks in their collars. Everything on the quiet steppe was frozen and white as pure jade.

As soon as the wagon was out of sight, I returned to my room to continue writing, and kept at it for two solid days like a man possessed.

Dumbbell tried to get me to put my things together, but how much time could it take to pack a suitcase, a few books, two sets of wrestling gear, and a small bag? All I had to do was tie up my bedroll, and I was ready to go.

He also tried to get me to take a bath so I wouldn't catch hell when I walked in the door at home. But I didn't want to wash off the smell of the steppe; where I went it went.

I was in bed by nightfall. The room was freezing. Up again the next morning, I wrapped my coat around my legs after a quick washup, took out a clean sheet of paper, and started writing again. My mood was calm, I was focused, and my pen never faltered.

After lunch I was at it again, bursting with emotion. Write. Write! So what if the emotions are unclean or ugly! Let the wind carry them where it will. Write. Write! So what if it isn't "literature"? The experience of millions must be told.

My last night on the steppe, I walked alone to the western edge of Company Headquarters to gaze out at the grass and at the stones we had carried down the mountain. The wall stretched as far as the eye could see. My youth was buried forever in the stones of that wall, some even stained with my blood. I ran my hand over them.

Because of those stones we went hungry, we froze, we sweated, and we bled; we carried them on our backs, up against our bellies, and on our shoulders. We wore out a pair of shoes and a pair of leather pants every winter. The skin on our hands, on our backs, on our arms, even on our bellies was rubbed raw. Those stones exacted a terrible human toll. The song of youth for our generation.

We grew old and ugly out there. Our hair turned white, our faces turned wrinkled and coarse. Those stones wore away the most precious years of our lives. Stained by our blood and our sweat, they were then abandoned to the untamed land, exposed to the elements until the blowing sand buried them forever.

Would our work disappear with the passage of time? No, that must not happen! I declare here and now that a generation of young people who left for the mountains and the countryside in 1968 to toil on the nation's farms and pasturelands, all the way to the farthest border regions, left an indelible mark on the history of mankind.

Red Guards, who soared to the heights early in the Cultural Revolution, only to later endure every conceivable hardship and suffer every imaginable indignity, were forced to make the agonizing transition from people who bruised their knuckles on the bodies of others to people whose hands grew callused from manual labor. No longer were they fanatics who yelled "To rebel is right!" while beating their victims and raiding their homes.

The vast, silent steppe, how bleak and hideous you became: your glossy skin gouged by coarse, blistery sand; your broad chest crushed by thudding hoes; your lovely face pocked and scarred by rat holes, stove pits, wagon-wheel ruts, electric poles, firebreaks.

Huolin Gol, forgive us our ignorance, our fanaticism, and our cruelty. There's consolation in the knowledge that we too suffered and that we made horrible sacrifices, even the ultimate sacrifice for some. Tens of thousands of lovely flowers bloomed and died here, silent and unnoticed.

Huolin Gol, thoughts of you will remain with me all my days. Granted, you are desolate and barren, but your vast reaches once played host to a youthful army the likes of which has never been seen before.

I paced the ground beside the stone wall, entertaining wild thoughts. The sun sank below the horizon, and the sky grew black, leaving behind a sliver of red, a stain of blood hanging over the land.

I AWOKE EARLY the next morning to the sounds of Dumbbell's snores.

Old Jiang walked in, hat in hand. His eyes darted around the room as he made small talk, a sure sign that he hoped I'd give him the junk I wasn't taking with me. Grinning from ear to ear, he became the proud owner of a crushed bucket, a broken whip handle, and a rusty stoveplate.

When he saw my luggage, he asked incredulously, "Is that all you're taking?"

I nodded.

He said nothing, but I could tell by the way he squinted and screwed up his face that he thought I was a class-A fool for not carrying off everything I could lay my hands on, after spending all those years in Inner Mongolia. While corps cadres filled trucks with their loot, I was leaving Inner Mongolia with little more than my bedroll, and I was proud of it.

The company was quiet, since most people were still in bed. Old Jiang grabbed the lead horse's bridle and turned the wagon around, then climbed into the driver's seat and cracked his whip.

We rolled past the wagon-team compound, with its mottled mud walls, past the rammed-earth wall of the stable, past the brickyard, with its crisscrossing ditches, past all those lonely, cheerless places. I thought sadly back to the day when Wei Xiaoli and the others had left. A wagon driver leaving the steppe and a college student leaving the steppe are two entirely different matters. When we reached the transportation company, and it was time to say good-bye to old Jiang, I asked him to take good care of my horses and not overwork them. They were getting on in years and had once saved my life.

He nonchalantly agreed, and I had the sudden urge to give him everything, including the clothes on my back, if it would make him treat my horses well. I took a scarf and some leather gloves out of my bag. He accepted them gratefully. "Don't worry," he said, "I'll be good to them. Who ever heard of a driver mistreating his own horses?"

I buried my face in the big black horse's bristly mane, breathing in that familiar smell.

THE ENGINE ROARED to life and the truck sped across the steppe; I calmly watched Injgan Sum slip into the distance, a montage of images drifting in and out of my head: Gonggele, who covered his head with a burlap bag and braved a downpour to get me medical attention. Yang Shufen, who once handed me two steamed buns and is still scrubbing pots and pans in that poorly lighted kitchen. And you, Jin Gang, who criticized me behind my back, changing colors as often as a chameleon. When the chips were down you removed that stain from my dossier.

Farewell, all you people who came to my aid during those hard times. I'll never forget you, never!

I was jolted around by the speeding truck as I said silent good-byes to the cold, the snow, the swarming flies, the rats, the cowchips, even the collapsed walls lining the road.

When we reached the highway, the regiment buildings had vanished from sight. I stuck my head out the window again, this time taking off my cap to let the wind cool my feverish head.

Let "her" take one last bite out of me.

The same bone-chilling winds that had welcomed me eight years earlier were giving me a final cruel reminder of Injgan Sum. My head was numb from the cold, my nose ached, and that was just the way I wanted it. Those biting winds held the fullness and fragrance of her body.

From 1968 to 1976, eight long years, I endured unrelenting criticism and suffered miserably. Yet I loved the steppe, and I hated to leave her. I wondered if there was anything of worth I could leave behind. Reaching into my bag, I took out some wrestling gear, ripped and stained with my blood and sweat, held it by its wide green belt, and flung it into the snow by the side of the road, where it landed without a sound.

From 1968 to 1976, eight long years.

I clasped my bag tightly. A heavy package wrapped in oil paper crackled when I squeezed it.

I took one final look at Injgan Sum. The mountains in the distance had grown so tiny, they were barely visible on the horizon, looking like a row of ragtag students standing tall where the sky met the earth.